Public Diplomacy

Contemporary Political Communication

Public Diplomacy

Foundations for Global Engagement
in the Digital Age

NICHOLAS J. CULL

polity

First published in 2019 by Polity Press

Polity Press
65 Bridge Street
Cambridge CB2 1UR, UK

Polity Press
101 Station Landing
Suite 300
Medford, MA 02155, USA

ISBN-13: 978-0-7456-9119-0
ISBN-13: 978-0-7456-9120-6(pb)

A catalogue record for this book is available from the British Library.

Library of Congress Cataloging-in-Publication Data

Names: Cull, Nicholas John, author.
Title: Public diplomacy : foundations for global engagement in the digital
   age / Nicholas Cull.
Description: Cambridge, UK ; Medford, MA, USA : Polity Press, 2019. |
   Includes bibliographical references and index.
Identifiers: LCCN 2018032458 (print) | LCCN 2018045664 (ebook) | ISBN
   9780745691237 (ebook) | ISBN 9780745691190 | ISBN 9780745691206 (pb)
Subjects: LCSH: Diplomacy--Technological innovations. | Public relations and
   politics--Technological innovations. | Communication in
   politics--Technological innovations.
Classification: LCC JZ1305 (ebook) | LCC JZ1305 .C85 2019 (print) | DDC
   327.2--dc23
LC record available at https://lccn.loc.gov/2018032458

Typeset in 11 on 13pt Adobe Garamond Pro by
Servis Filmsetting Ltd, Stockport, Cheshire
Printed and bound in the UK by CPI Group (UK) Ltd, Croydon

For further information on Polity, visit our website: politybooks.com

For Eytan Gilboa

Contents

List of Figures

Preface and Acknowledgments

This is a book about what Bruce Gregory of George Washington University has called "the public aspects of diplomacy." It is written to provide a single foundational text for diplomat students and student diplomats. This book is not only about the emergence of new approaches to global public opinion; it was born because of them. At the turn of the millennium, I was Professor of American Studies at the University of Leicester in the United Kingdom. I had been writing and researching about the history of British and American propaganda for some years but had little opportunity to integrate that work into my teaching. I worked from time to time with the British Council but my role was to apply a multidisciplinary approach to the study of British identity. I got to talk about British science fiction television in Turkey and "Englishness" in Finland. The advent of the Blair government, with its focus on issues of international image, opened new avenues. My British Council contact – Nick Wadham Smith – was seconded to a new in-house think tank within the Council called Counterpoint, with a mandate to examine the future of British cultural relations. Nick and his boss Martin Rose invited me to give a keynote talk to the Council's board and I found myself commenting explicitly on the contemporary implications of my historical research to an audience of British cultural figures. That was the first time I presented what became my five-element breakdown of public diplomacy. More seminars followed. The terrorist attacks of 9/11 accelerated this work. Suddenly, government and scholarly interest in public diplomacy kicked into high gear on both sides of the Atlantic. It was only to be expected that an academic institution would spot a gap in the market. The University of Southern California moved first. In 2003, working with the School of International Relations, the USC Annenberg School for Communication, as it was then known, launched its Center on Public Diplomacy. The next step was to offer a master's degree in public diplomacy, and I was hired to direct it.

I arrived at USC in September 2005 but, before the master's degree in public diplomacy had truly got underway, I was persuaded to take part in a further project from which these essays derive. The distinguished Israeli scholar Eytan Gilboa was attached to the Center on Public Diplomacy as a visiting fellow for my first year and proposed that he and I organize a summer institute in advanced public diplomacy for diplomats. The institute ran in the last two weeks of 2006 and the chapters in this book have evolved from lectures delivered at that time. In the intervening years, my research and teaching have happily converged. My first attempt to set these ideas in print came in 2007 when the UK Foreign and Commonwealth Office commissioned me to write a short primer on public diplomacy for their own use. That work reached its final form as the booklet *Public Diplomacy: Lessons from the Past* (2008). This book is an expansion and updating of that work. In the years since, I've had wonderful opportunities to deliver and develop this material in classes for foreign ministries and diplomatic academies around the world, including those of Canada, Chile, India, Mexico, Netherlands, South Africa, South Korea, and Switzerland. Some audiences deserve special mention. For some years, I've served as a guest lecturer at the US Department of State's Foreign Service Institute in Arlington, Virginia. Chapters 1 and 3 will be familiar to FSI students. I am also honored to have taught this material as a guest lecturer at Beijing Foreign Studies University's Center on Public Diplomacy as a guest of Professor Zhou Xinyu and for the Masters of Cultural Diplomacy of Catholica University of Milan as a guest of Professor Federica Olivares. This book was also shaped by the Spring Institute in Internet Diplomacy which I organized in March 2016, so thanks are due to Fadi Chehadi, then CEO of the Internet Corporation on Assigned Names and Numbers (ICANN), and his colleague Nora Abusita for making that happen. My motive for writing this was to pull together the lectures and material developed for reports into a fuller synthesis.

Any writing and research process requires support from family, friends, and colleagues. In writing this book, I am grateful to the directors of the USC Center on Public Diplomacy for keeping the Summer Institute going: Jay Wang, Philip Seib, Geoffrey Wiseman, and most especially Joshua Fouts, who gave Eytan and I the go-ahead for the original iteration and thoroughly spoiled us for his successors. The forays into psychology were inspired by the work of the third man in the original Summer Institute lineup, my USC Annenberg colleague Kelton Rhoads. Soumi Chattergee of UCLA has helped to clarify some of the finer points of what was new territory for me. I appreciate the rest of the public diplomacy team at USC, especially Bob Banks, Doug Becker, Pam Starr, and Conrad Turner, and my interlocutors around campus, especially Mina Chow, David Craig, Jerry Giaquinta, Garry Wexler, and the incomparable Robert Scheer. Colleagues beyond USC whose work has been influential on me or who have provided help include Amelia Arsenault, Martha Bayles, Caitlin Byrne, Ali Fisher, Kathy Fitzpatrick, Vasily Gatov, Jessica Gienow-Hecht, Robert Govers, Bruce Gregory, Craig Hayden, Charlotte Lerg, Jonathan McClory,

Jan Melissen, Ben Nimmo, James Pamment, Peter Pomerantsev, Sean Powers, Monroe Price, J. P. Singh, Nancy Snow, Cesar Villanueva Rivas, Rhonda Zaharna, and the late Benjamin Barber. James Pamment deserves a double mention for reading the whole work in draft and making it better by frankly pointing out its limits. I am grateful to friends who have allowed me to try this material on their students especially Barry Sanders at UCLA, Derek Shearer at Occidental College, and Senem Cevik at UC Irvine, and, further afield, Odette Tomescu-Hatto and Ronald Hatto at Sciences Po, Paris. Dalia Kaye and Sohaela Ameri at the RAND Center for Middle East Public Policy were kind enough to invite me to try out my conclusion on their colleagues. The influence of Joseph Nye and Simon Anholt is present throughout. I've valued the opportunity to discuss US elements with the small band of practitioner/scholars Matthew Armstrong, Dick Arndt, Don Bishop, John Brown, Katherine A. Brown, Bill Rugh, and Mike Schneider. Adam Clayton Powell III and his colleagues at the Public Diplomacy Council have been a terrific home crowd for a number of relevant presentations and panel discussions in DC. The mentions of Canada show the influence of Evan Potter, Daryl Copeland, and Sarah E. K. Smith. I have learned much from friends in the UK foreign policy community and have been privileged to chew over some of these issues with distinguished retirees Ian Cliff and Martin Rose. A book like this also needs many conversations with serving diplomats of many nations over the years. I'll spare blushes. You know who you are!

An eclectic work requires advice from unusual quarters. My old friend and airline pilot Paul Ambrose provided an example for the chapter on listening. Another old friend, Arnar Gudmundsson of Reykjavik provided advice on bird calls for the same chapter. I appreciate the help of the distinguished church historian Thomas McCoog, SJ, of Fordham University with the material relating to the Jesuit Order, the originators of the term "propaganda," and of the great German artist Gunter Demnig on the international use of his *stolperstein*. Catalan scholar Marc Argemí Ballbè helped with Spanish folk sayings. This work has been shaped by input from students at USC and further afield. Anna Loup has been a terrific assistant. Neftalie Williams has demonstrated the power of sport diplomacy. Saltanat Kerimbayeva opened the door to Kazakhstan. Caitlin Schindler, whose Leeds University PhD I co-supervised, picked up my own phrase "foreign public engagement" as a useful alternative to public diplomacy and encouraged me to do the same. I have also benefited from being examiner on the excellent PhDs written by Alice Srugies and Molly Bettie.

I have appreciated the support of Polity Press, especially Ellen MacDonald-Kramer and Mary Savigar, and the attentive editor Gail Ferguson.

The wonderful cover design by Jason Anscomb inspired by the Council of Europe's European Day of Languages. This book was supposed to have been ready by the middle of 2016 but was overtaken by events and my diversion to practical projects in the public diplomacy field. Glad we got there in the end!

Friends in Redondo have been part of the story. So many happy working days have begun with Joel Futerer's summons to breakfast at Classic Burger on Torrance Boulevard and I appreciate the company of Brian Kastner, Peter Kurbikoff, and Bob Reid, the co-recipients of those electronic invites. My three young sons, Alex, Magnus, and Olly, have provided a welcome distraction from the screen and gave this project meaning. They are the embodiments of the future that the best public diplomacy is working to create. My youngest son was recently challenged by a fellow eight-year-old in an exchange that is relevant to this book:

> *Girl*: Your dad's job is bogus. Public Diplomacy is not a real thing.
> *Olly*: It certainly is. It has stopped a bunch of wars.
> *Girl*: OK. Name them.
> *Olly*: Easy. They were all called World War III.

If lawmakers around the world had Olly's confidence, public diplomacy work would have fewer worries. My wife Karen Ford Cull has provided both emotional and intellectual support and encouragement. Finally, given the origins of so much of this work in the CPD Summer Institute, I cannot but dedicate this to my colleague and friend Eytan Gilboa with thanks and in anticipation of joint projects yet to come.

Nicholas J. Cull, Redondo Beach, California, May 2018

List of Abbreviations

ANC	African National Congress
BBC	British Broadcasting Corporation
CIA	Central Intelligence Agency
CBI	Country Brand Index
CFPNI	Children's Friendship Project for Northern Ireland
CVE	countering violent extremism
ERASMUS	European Community Action Scheme for the Mobility of University Students
EU	European Union
EUNIC	European Union National Institutes of Culture
FBIS	Foreign Broadcast Information Service
FCO	Foreign and Commonwealth Office
FIFA	Fédération Internationale de Football Association
INF	intermediate nuclear forces
IRI	Office of Research and Intelligence
IVLP	International Visitor Leader Program
LAPD	Los Angeles Police Department
NATO	North Atlantic Treaty Organization
NBI	Nation Brand Index
NGO	nongovernmental organization
OSCE	Organization for Security and Co-operation in Europe
PEGIDA	Patriotic Europeans Against the Islamisation of the West
PEPFAR	President's Emergency Fund for AIDS Relief
RFE/RL	Radio Free Europe/Radio Liberty
RIAS	Radio in the American Sector
RT	Russia Today
UNESCO	United National Economic Scientific and Cultural Organization
UNICEF	United Nations International Children's Emergency Fund
USAID	United States Agency for International Development
USIA	United States Information Agency
VOA	Voice of America
VoIP	Voice over Internet Protocol
YALI	Young African Leaders Initiative

1 Diplomacy through Foreign Public Engagement: Core Terminology and History

The small town of Muscatine, Iowa, USA is not one of the world's great crossroads. With a population of 20,000, its only claim to fame was being the "Watermelon Capital of the World." On the afternoon of February 12, 2012, however, the town was crowded. There were local well-wishers, international students in from Iowa City, police, camera crews, and protestors too. Spectators waved flags of the United States and the People's Republic of China, and some carried homemade signs with slogans like "Iowa ❤ China." At the appointed hour, the motorcade arrived. The guest of honor – Xi Jinping, then still China's vice-president – made his way to a modest clapboarded home at 2911 Bonnie Drive. As cameras flashed, he greeted a row of civic dignitaries and an elderly couple – Eleanor and Thomas Dvorchak – who had flown in from Florida just for the meeting. This was not Mr Xi's first visit to Muscatine nor his first meeting with the Dvorchaks. More than thirty years previously, in 1985, they had welcomed him to their home when he was part of a touring delegation of Chinese officials seeking to learn about life in the United States. China's future president slept a couple of nights in their son's old room surrounded by American football-themed wallpaper and *Star Wars* action figures. Returning in 2012, Xi Jinping spoke warmly of his happy memories of Muscatine, the Dvorchaks, and the positive view of ordinary American people that he had formed.[1]

The original event in 1985 and its commemoration in 2012 only happened because people in power in Beijing and in Washington, DC understood that international relations are not solely a matter of government-to-government contact. Sometimes the best way to conduct foreign policy is for a government to engage a foreign public or, indeed, for foreign publics to engage one another directly. These kinds of activity are known in the United States as public diplomacy. For some observers, public diplomacy is simply a variety of propaganda; however, practitioners and scholars have learned to see the two as distinct. Propaganda is about dictating your message to an audience and persuading them you are right. Public diplomacy is about listening to the other side and working to develop a relationship of mutual understanding.

↳ defs: propaganda v p.d.

1

Terminology

There is no universally agreed vocabulary for the business of conducting foreign policy by engaging global publics. Israelis speak of "explaining" (*hasbará*); the current French term is "influence diplomacy" (*diplomatie d'influence*) and the British Foreign and Commonwealth Office use the term "strategic communication." Japanese officials tend to call the whole process "cultural exchange," even if it includes neither culture nor much of any two-way exchange process. Chinese officials speak of *xuānchuán*, a compound word uniting the concepts of "declare" and "pass on/teach" which was adopted by the country's communists as their translation for the western term "propaganda." Canada at one point referred to its entire approach to the public as "advocacy." Many smaller countries conceive of the whole process through the lens of "nation branding" or other commercial practices, such as international public relations or tourism promotion. All these terms are partial and some actively misleading. The preferred American term – "public diplomacy" – may be the least-worst term in common use.

The take-up of the term "public diplomacy" owes more to the coincidence of the need to explain the post-Cold War role of publics in foreign affairs with US preeminence than its theoretical perfection or otherwise. It has, however, achieved sufficient currency in the West to have been adopted within many bureaucracies beyond the United States, not only as the title for sections of foreign ministries and professional specializations but also by academics. As Eytan Gilboa has pointed out, while many scholars have examined public diplomacy, there is no overarching theory, but rather contributions from multiple disciplines. History, international relations, and communication have been especially significant, and scholars of psychology and public relations have been part of the discourse as well.[2] The term "public diplomacy" accordingly has found its way into the titles of articles, books, journals, academic organizations, professorial titles, and even one or two master's degree programs.[3]

None of these terms comes without baggage; each carries within it a metaphor which consciously or unconsciously shapes the work and often represents its goal or claim to legitimacy. "Strategic communication" evokes the military realm and seems well chosen to please those who hold the purse strings and who understand the world in security terms above all else. "Cultural exchange" speaks of benign artistically focused conversations: ballet tours and biennales of art. "Diplomacy of influence" suggests an ability to manipulate an audience, summoning perhaps the mental picture of an extravagantly mustachioed stage hypnotist flourishing his hands to extend his *magnétisme animal.* "Nation branding" conjures up the realm of the urban creative professional with slick sales pitch, sample logos, and an open-plan office. "Public diplomacy" also paints its own picture. It courts an image of a seasoned foreign affairs professional – the diplomat – communicating for the ends of the state. The term "public diplomacy" is influential not only because of the ability of the United States to export its ways of thinking; there is also a special value in a term for foreign public engagement which locates the practice in the realm of civilian international relations. The world of diplomacy is better than the business world of state public relations, let alone the covert and manipulative realm which English speakers understand from the term "propaganda." The term "public diplomacy" is helpful insomuch as it places the engagement process as a form of diplomacy, which is to say, one of the ways in which an international actor seeks to manage the international environment.[4]

The components of foreign public engagement

While the term "public diplomacy" is fairly new, wise rulers have always known the importance of public opinion and the value of avoiding the counterproductive currents that attend acts of violence, even for winners. Two-and-half millennia ago, a Greek thinker named Bias led the small democracy of Priene in Ionia on the coast of what is now Turkey. He had a reputation as a skilled advocate and in time would be famed as the wisest of the Seven Sages of Greece. His advice to fellows was unequivocal: "gain your point by persuasion, not by force." [5] Making the same point through fable, Bias's contemporary Aesop told the story of the bet between the North Wind and the sun over who could remove a certain traveler's cloak. The North Wind blew and merely caused the traveler to draw his clothing closer, but a few minutes of sunshine soon saw him remove his cloak. Warmth had won. Part of the story is the understanding of the dynamics that Joseph Nye dubbed soft power: that wise policies, attractive culture, and admirable character bring foreign policy benefits. In ancient China, Confucius spoke of wise emperors "attracting by virtue," noting "it is for this reason that, when distant subjects are not submissive, one cultivates one's moral quality in order to attract them." A reputation for wisdom bolstered the rule of Roman Emperor Marcus Aurelius in the second century and of the Frankish Emperor Charlemagne in eighth-century Europe. The thirteenth-century Islamic leader Saladin was admired even by his enemies: feared in war but trusted in peace. Kings of France from the 1500s onward proclaimed themselves *roi très chrétien* (very Christian king) and understood that such a reputation helped them do business everywhere in the world, including with nonbelievers. But there was more at work than just appreciating the value of persuasion and developing a reputation for admirable policy. Historically, there are five distinct ways in which international actors have engaged foreign publics: listening; advocacy; cultural diplomacy; exchange diplomacy; and news/international broadcasting.

Listening

The foundational form of foreign policy through public engagement is listening. Listening is an actor's attempt to manage the international environment by collecting and analyzing data about international publics and using that data to redirect its policy or its communication accordingly. In its most basic form this covers an event whereby an international actor seeks out a foreign audience and engages them by listening rather than by speaking. While systematic assessments of foreign opinion are modern, estimating a neighbor's morale has long been a goal of statecraft, most especially in time of war. Writing some half-millennium before the Common Era, the Chinese sage Sun Tzu observed: "What is called 'foreknowledge' cannot be elicited from spirits or from gods, or by analogy with past events, nor from calculations. It must be obtained from men who know the enemy situation."[6] In our own time, listening is conducted through all manner of contact with publics including opinion research, open-source media study, and many, many conversations between diplomats and members of the public.

Advocacy

Advocacy is an actor's attempt to manage the international environment by presenting a particular policy, idea, or the actor's general interests to a foreign public. Ancient examples include Xerxes of Persia, who, according to Herodotus, used envoys to successfully appeal to people of Argos for their neutrality during the empire's invasion of Greece in 480 BCE. The Persians stressed kinship between the Argives and Persians through shared descent from the hero Perseus.[7] In modern times, advocacy includes the set-piece communication campaigns (including the social media), embassy press relations, and informational work. The obvious relevance of advocacy to policy has made it an especial priority for the masters of foreign policy and it has often been given a privileged position at the center of any overall engagement structure.

Cultural diplomacy

Cultural diplomacy may be defined as an actor's attempt to manage the international environment through facilitating the export of an element of that actor's life, belief or art. Ancient examples include the Greek construction of the great library at Alexandria in the third century BCE or the Byzantine emperors Michael III and Basil I, who sponsored Orthodox Christian evangelism across the Slavic lands in the 860s, understanding that the work of missionaries like St Cyril and St Methodius carried with it imperial influence. The investment created an extensive Orthodox cultural zone which allowed Byzantium to punch above its weight for several centuries and which still exerts a pull on the peoples whose common writing system is named for St Cyril: Cyrillic.[8] Modern examples of cultural diplomacy have included the world tours of the Bolshoi ballet sponsored by the Soviet government during the Cold War or the US government's analogous sponsorship of visits from jazz musicians, or the work of Britain's agency for cultural relations with foreign publics: the British Council.

Exchange diplomacy

Exchange diplomacy is an actor's attempt to manage the international environment by sending its citizens overseas and reciprocally accepting citizens from overseas for a period of study and/or acculturation. Here the classic ancient examples are the child exchanges practiced for centuries by the Celts and other archaic peoples which seem to have played a key role in diffusing cultural practices and stability within their cultural regions.[9] Today, exchanges are a major tool of international engagement and a particular priority of the United States, which supports exchange beyond most other elements of public diplomacy.

International broadcasting

While advocacy is based on extending an argument, there is a parallel tradition of engaging a foreign public not by arguing but by presenting (or claiming to present) an objective picture of the world at large. In the

* each w/ e.g.s

twentieth century, this was done through the international broadcasting of news but the pre-electronic era had its equivalents. The Holy Roman Emperor Frederick II (1194–1250) regularly wrote and distributed letters to neighboring courts. These letters related world events, such as the Sixth Crusade, his wish for what would now be termed a "Middle East peace process," and his ongoing quarrel with the Pope, who preferred victory to peace.[10] The advent of electronic media has made it possible for an international actor to transmit news across frontiers instantly. While from its outset advocacy, culture, and exchange elements were a part of international broadcasting, it was the news content that made the medium special. International news broadcasting was part of the Allied victory in World War II, the waging of the Cold War, and the management of the transition to a global society. Whether transmitted via radio, television, or as content for a handheld device, news is a vital part of public diplomacy.

Divergences and interrelationships

These five elements may share a common objective but they are separated by important differences. Consider first the direction in which the information is flowing: in listening, the information flows from the public to the actor; in advocacy, from the actor to the public; in cultural work, the flow is from the sources of the actor's culture and the public; in exchanges, it is a two-way flow between selected individuals or wider publics. In international broadcasting, the characteristic flow is between a news bureaucracy and the public.

Second, consider the source of credibility for each element: The credibility of listening comes from the perceived responsiveness of the listener to what is heard. The credibility of advocacy is based on the proximity of the advocate to the actor's policy. The credibility of cultural diplomacy is based on cultural factors – the authenticity or representativeness of a cultural form or practice shown. The credibility of exchange is based on a perception of mutuality. The credibility of international broadcasting is based on its compliance with the professional standards of journalism.

Third, consider the timescale in which these activities are expected to work. Listening is part of a continuous process. Advocacy has a short cycle, timed to immediate policy objectives. Cultural diplomacy has a medium-term horizon, while exchange diplomacy looks to the longer term. International broadcasting works over a long time frame but is also expected to respond to a crisis. These disparate qualities mean that elements are ill-suited to being housed too closely together and may even be mutually antithetical.

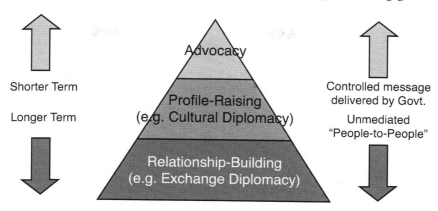

Figure 1.1 The Canadian public diplomacy pyramid. Author, after Foreign Affairs Canada, 2005.

The task-specific logic and centrifugal pressures on each element of engagement are sufficiently strong that many countries use specialist agencies for most or even all of these functions. They look to open-source intelligence and think tanks for listening; communication units within the foreign ministry for advocacy; freestanding cultural agencies for culture; exchange agencies for exchange; and an independent broadcasting organization like the BBC World Service or Deutsche Welle for broadcasting. The US term "public diplomacy" could have been simply an umbrella set over these activities but became something more: an argument for a centralized approach.[11] Practitioners should be aware that a unitary term does not necessarily require a unitary bureaucracy to deliver it.

Bureaucracies around the world have attempted to conceptualize the interrelationships between these elements of engagement. For some, the key has been to assert their need for a fire wall. Britain's British Council and Germany's Goethe Institute insist on independence from the policy makers. The Council even rejects the term "cultural diplomacy" in favor of the words "cultural relations" to stress its distance from an immediate policy agenda and the one-way communication dynamic that it implies. Similarly, western international broadcasters demand full editorial independence. The differences were helpfully sketched in 2005 by a team from the Canadian foreign ministry who devised what they termed the "Public Diplomacy Pyramid."

The pyramid locates advocacy at the summit as a short-term activity, closely controlled by the government. In the middle is profile-raising work, which corresponds to most cultural diplomacy, taking place in the medium term and with a moderate level of government oversight. The base of the pyramid is provided by relationship building: the kind of work typified by exchange diplomacy which requires a long timescale and over which the international actor can exercise little control. Most exchanges ultimately become a process of turning the people loose and hoping for the best. The "public diplomacy pyramid" is in some ways aspirational. While it would be nice to conceptualize exchanges as the broad and well-resourced foundation of the whole structure of global engagement, it is often not the case. Ironically, one of the most outrageous cases of divergence from this model was that of Canada itself under Prime Minister Stephen Harper who focused only on advocacy with detrimental results for Canada's image.[12]

Propaganda

It is impossible to understand the role of public engagement in foreign policy without paying attention to the history of propaganda. Comparing the two is rather like comparing a crystal clear mountain stream to a vast and churning ocean. Both are water, and hence from one perspective, the same thing, yet their natures are profoundly different. One – public diplomacy – is pure and life sustaining, the other – propaganda – is powerful, untameable, and should not be drunk. One is hard to find, the other is ubiquitous. Yet the two are joined. As the river rolls to the sea, so public diplomacy always tumbles downhill toward propaganda. The study of propaganda is an essential element in understanding the context of public diplomacy, and practitioners of public diplomacy must have a clear sense of what propaganda is in order to avoid slipping into it.

The history of propaganda in foreign policy

phases

Propaganda is not a moment in the history of international relations. It is an element in the structure of international relations.[13] It began with war. Humans have always understood that cultural factors can act as a force multiplier in combat. From the earliest times, warriors have enhanced their appearance with war paint and sought to boost their own confidence and blunt that of the enemy with drums and trumpets and stories of their heroism or ruthlessness. Tricks are part of the story. Bias of Priene – the Greek sage who claimed that it was better to win by argument than force – was perfectly prepared to resort to deception when required. When the Lydian king Alyattes besieged Priene – busy amassing the fortune that would make his son Croesus a byword for wealth – Bias arranged for two specially fattened mules to be released into the enemy camp. Amazed that the city had sufficient reserves to keep its livestock so well, Alyattes sued for peace. When his ambassador arrived in the city, Bias ordered that he be shown sacks of grain (in reality sand with a layer of grain on the top) and, to complete the ruse of self-confidence, when Alyattes demanded that Bias come quickly to his camp to conclude the terms of the Lydian departure, the thinker sent the defiant message "go eat onions" and left the king to stew until he was ready to conclude their business.[14] Four centuries before the Common Era, the Indian sage Kautilya placed great emphasis on psychological warfare. His manual on statecraft, *Arthashastra*, includes long passages with suggestions for what might be termed "messing with the heads" of the enemy and one's own military too, including the employment of bards and soothsayers to depress the enemy and build up the home team:

> Soothsayers and court bards should describe heaven as the goal for the brave and hell for the timid; and also extol the caste, corporation, family, deeds, and character of his men. The followers of the priest should proclaim the auspicious aspects of the witchcraft performed. Spies, carpenters and astrologers should also declare the success of their own operations and the failure of those of the enemy.[15]

As ancient states took shape, rulers learned to use the symbols of their state and of themselves to enhance their ability to project power. No one did this better than Alexander the Great, whose authorized portrait – chiseled into busts, laid into mosaic, and stamped on coins from Greece to the Hindu Kush – was carefully crafted and circulated to enhance his reach. As portrayed, he was a man but his shaggy hair communicated the power of a lion and his raised chin and eyes fixed beyond the horizon made a visual claim to his being a god. Man/lion/god, he was not lightly to be defied. As the centuries rolled by, the techniques of enhancement became more sophisticated but the overall objective remained much the same. Image was an essential element of power.[16]

The next major phase in the evolution of propaganda came as Europe lurched into its first communications revolution and its concurrent era of religious competition: the Reformation. As the Roman Catholic Church struggled to hold its ground in Europe and win new souls abroad, a former soldier saw the way forward. Ignatius of Loyola, a warrior-turned-priest from Spain's Basque country, understood that the same kind of systematization that an effective commander brought to a military campaign could be applied to the task of communicating religion. In 1539, he drew up a plan to create a new holy order which he named "the Society of Jesus," or the Jesuits. Its foundational document – the Formula of the Institute – defined its purpose as for the "defense and propagation of the faith" (*propaganda fide* in Latin) and "for the progress of souls in Christian life and doctrine by means of public preaching, lectures, and any other ministration . . ." Pope Paul III approved the document in September 1540.[17] As the Jesuits deployed a range of techniques for communicating their faith – including recovering classical approaches to rhetoric – the words *propaganda fide* began their journey into the church's vocabulary and the lexicon of the world.[18]

In the 1570s, Pope Gregory XIII, best known for his calendar reform, founded a string of colleges and schools including a committee of three cardinals, known as the Cardinals' Commission for Propagation of the Faith, to coordinate missionary activity. The full institutionalization of the term and the process of propaganda came in 1622 when Pope Gregory XV founded a substantial bureaucracy known as the Sacred Congregation for Propagation of the Faith in Rome as a permanent institutional home for the counter-reformation process. He also made Ignatius a saint. With a generation of Jesuits trained in its arts and its own palazzo in the middle of Rome at one end of the Piazza di Spagna (just turn left at the bottom of the Spanish Steps), the term "propaganda" was here to stay. The term entered wider usage and, for Northern European Protestant writers, thanks to its Catholic origins "propaganda" soon had the taint of totalitarian excess.[19]

The religious changes in Europe prompted the next phase. As Protestant states threw off their old allegiances and embraced revolution, they also began the task of explaining their new systems of government to their neighbors across Europe whose trade they needed and whose friendship and understanding they valued. Campaigns included that undertaken by Prince William the Silent of the United Provinces of the Netherlands to justify his nation's revolt against Spain. In 1580, William himself sent a defiant *Apologie* to Philip II explaining his actions in terms of universal principles of liberty and denouncing Spanish atrocities at home and abroad. The document, actually written by William's chaplain, was published in French, Dutch, English, German, and Latin and clearly sought an audience far beyond the Spanish court, which in any case refused to recognize the independence of the Netherlands until 1648.[20] In a similar vein, following the overthrow and execution of England's Charles I in 1649, the Commonwealth government of Oliver Cromwell took care to explain this and other actions overseas. Cromwell appointed the poet John Milton as Latin secretary to the Council of State (or "Secretary of Foreign Tongues"). Milton's Latin arguments on behalf of Cromwell's government were widely read in Europe.[21] Perhaps the most successful international outreach by a revolutionary government came in 1776 when revolutionaries in Britain's

American colonies issued their Declaration of Independence to "let the facts be submitted to a candid world."[22]

The democratization that flowed from the new political ideas and systems brought ordinary people into the foreign policy process. Governments began tracking and even reaching out to foreign electorates. In 1793, the French Revolutionary diplomat "Citizen" Edmond Charles Genêt outraged the neutral United States by organizing Jacobin clubs to promote the revolutionary cause.[23] Countries launching propaganda campaigns in the nineteenth century included both Mexico and the Ottoman Empire. Mexican presidents Benito Juárez and Porfirio Díaz both worked to win US opinion; envoys included the pioneer of Mexican diplomacy Matías Romero. Around the same time, the Ottoman Sultan Abdül Hamid II tried various gambits to improve the image of his empire. As Selim Deringel has related, his strategies included the positive (presenting photographic collections to major western libraries) and the negative (applying diplomatic pressure to try to change overly exotic representations of his country in popular culture). Dutch skits set in harems were a particular irritant. When all else failed, his agents simply bribed western journalists to give the empire a good press.[24]

The final element in the emergence of propaganda as a dimension of foreign policy was the coming of an era of total war driven by the convergence of democratization and the industrialization of the military. The combatant powers needed to secure their own population's service in armies, navies, and munitions plants to draw neutrals to their side and to break their enemy's "will to resist." World War I saw the tactics in full flood. The Italians pioneered the airdropping of leaflets. The French private sector blended religion and patriotism. The British demonized the enemy as the perpetrators of horrific atrocities before switching to a more idealistic approach, promising – in concert with the US president Woodrow Wilson – a better world for ally and enemy alike.[25]

By the mid-twentieth century, all these drivers of propaganda were in play in the person of Joseph Stalin and the foreign policy of the Soviet Union. Stalin's regime understood the psychological factor in war initiating a complex mix of gambits including disinformation campaigns to misdirect and confuse the enemy. They understood image, seeking to export Stalin's cult of personality. It worked to propagate its communist ideology in much the same way as a religion and to explain its revolution as vigorously as any previous regime. Democratization presented opportunities. Its early post-war victories came through elections in Poland and Czechoslovakia. Italy came perilously close to falling to communism in an election in 1948. The decolonization process promised to open new territory for communism. The logic of total war, with its emphasis on the role of ordinary people, remained. The world had never seen a country or a campaign like it. It pushed the United States to respond.

The emergence of US public diplomacy

Although American actors and institutions had for many years worked to spread their country's ideas around the world, as of 1945 the US government had tended to see its sponsorship of information work as a tool only for crises. This led to a kind of "hokey cokey/hokey pokey" dance in which the country variously put its "whole self" into foreign public engagement during the Revolutionary War, Civil War, World Wars I and II, but then hurried to pull its "whole self" out of such activity when the danger passed. By 1948, the scale of the Cold War challenge convinced a majority on Capitol Hill that once again the time had come to act. They moved to provide funding for a range of outreach activities both overt and covert. The country's early efforts were an alphabet soup of programs. Congress variously reinvigorated pre-war work like the educational exchanges with Latin America; extended the life of wartime operations like Voice of America (VOA) radio or the embassy-based United States Information Service posts; and adapted post-war initiatives like the re-education work in Germany and Japan or communication aspects of the Marshall Plan in Western Europe. The result was administrative chaos. Seeking a coherent response, in 1953 President Dwight D. Eisenhower pulled most of the existing overt programs together and created a single integrated United States Information Agency (USIA).[26] Initially, this new agency was happy enough to refer to its work as information or exchange, but a decade into its existence the United States Information Agency needed a new banner term under which to campaign for funding. The answer was the term "public diplomacy."

The term "public diplomacy" was the creature, if not quite the creation, of an ex-diplomat turned dean of the Fletcher School of Law and Diplomacy at Tufts University, Edmund Gullion. Gullion's initial object in devising a term was to create a democratic equivalent to the word "propaganda." He explained in 1967: "I would have liked to call it 'propaganda.' It seemed the nearest thing in the pure interpretation of the word to what we were doing. But 'propaganda' has always had a pejorative connotation in this country. To describe the whole range of communications, information and propaganda, we hit upon 'public diplomacy.'"[27] The USIA was happy to embrace the term. The term was like a map which showed a beleaguered country's right to retain a wayward province (read Voice of America) and extend control over a sliver of a neighbor's territory (read the State Department's cultural program). It promised to be one term to rule them all. The term "public diplomacy" also played to the professional aspirations of the Agency's staff. Now they could be diplomats rather than a variety of public relations men and women. Within a year or so of its arrival, they went from being second-class citizens – quite literally as members of the Foreign Service Reserve – to full Foreign Service Officers with enhanced pension rights and promotion prospects that extended all the way up to the rank of ambassador. Whatever the impact of public diplomacy overseas, the term made an immense contribution to its practitioners' battles for recognition at home.[28]

Public diplomacy versus propaganda

Despite the origins of the term as a euphemism, it was not long before practitioners began looking on public diplomacy as something qualitatively different from propaganda. They worked to make public diplomacy a different kind of practice. This was not wholly surprising. As the historian Frank Ninkovich has documented, the State Department's pre-war foray into public engagement was driven by a vision of mutual knowledge between peoples, not a crude extension of power.[29] The two-way vision was repressed in World War II and struggled to return in the Cold War. The United Kingdom saw a similar rebellion as the British Council rejected the term propaganda in favor of its own benign language of cultural relations.[30]

It is possible to tease public diplomacy and propaganda apart and contrast the two:

- public diplomacy is based on truth but propaganda selects truth;
- public diplomacy is often two-way but propaganda is seldom two-way;
- public diplomacy listens to learn but propaganda listens to target;
- public diplomacy can change the sending/initiating society too but propaganda is intended only to change the target society;
- public diplomacy is flexible in its approach but propaganda has a tight agenda;
- public diplomacy tends to be respectful of others but propaganda assumes that others are ignorant or wrong;
- public diplomacy is open-ended but propaganda is closed;
- public diplomacy is ethical but propaganda's ethics cannot be taken for granted;

Ironically, while the acceptance of the principles of an ideal public diplomacy within the US practitioner community is widespread, the political leadership in Congress and at the helm of the Department of State plainly still expect a practice much closer to propaganda. Public diplomats learn early to keep notions of conducting global engagement for its own sake to themselves and to speak a language of threats, counter-campaigns, and unilateral influence when presenting their work to their political masters. Evidence of this is hard to come by, but there are clear pointers in the survey Kathy Fitzpatrick, then of Quinnipiac University, conducted among veterans of the USIA in 2008. She found that on average they rated "defeating communism" as eleventh in their assessment of priorities in Cold War public diplomacy and "defeating terrorism" as seventh in their assessment of contemporary priorities. The prime goal was "to create understanding and support for the United States and its policies." They also gave high priority "to establish and maintain good relationships with people abroad" and "to demonstrate respect for other cultures and values."[31]

One of the clearest indications that US outreach to the world during the Cold War was understood as propaganda by Congress was their loss of interest in the subject when the Cold War came to an end. In the years following the collapse of the Soviet Union, budgets plummeted and programs were cut. In the end, in 1999 the United States Information Agency was merged into the Department of State, and America's capacity to engage the global public reached a low point.[32] Ironically at the precise moment US public diplomacy foundered, the concept was riding high elsewhere in the world. The rise of the network society inspired many international actors to upgrade their international engagement. The surge of interest not merely in outreach of governments-to-people but of people-to-people links led scholars like Rhonda Zaharna, Ali Fisher, and Amelia Arsenault to explore the importance of a public diplomacy built on relationships, and others, such as Jan Melissen and James Pamment, to examine the new public diplomacy.[33]

The terrain of the new public diplomacy

Surveying the world today, there are multiple factors that set it apart from that of the previous generation. The old world was dominated by the bipolar fault line of the Cold War which had such overarching importance as to overshadow and color all other stories such as decolonization, regional integration, and so forth. Today, there are many stories competing for public attention and many sources for those stories, not simply a handful of governments and their associated centralized media machines. A generation ago, international relations was largely a monopoly of the nation-state. Today, international action and communication rests not only with nation-states but with a bewildering array of actors including international organizations, regional groupings, nongovernmental organizations (both genuine and fake), corporations, subnational governments like provinces, and networks of individuals who wish to be connected to one another because of shared ideas.[34] In fact, by 2015 a non-state network –ISIS/Daesh – had established itself in US government rhetoric as the principal threat to its national security. All players on the international stage have a story and seek to advance their interests by telling it.

The new world has its new mechanisms of communication. The communication satellite and the World Wide Web together brought a simultaneous speeding up and diffusion of communication. In ancient times, the biblical notion of "all flesh" seeing an event "together" was the ultimate miracle.[35] Today it is routine. The trick is not to create the hardware for such a convergence of attention but to imagine something compelling enough to attract it. The direction of communication has changed. In the old world, messages flowed from the top down, emanating from a limited number of bureaucracies and media institutions. In the new world, messages are passed horizontally across networks of peers. We live, as the sociologist Manuel Castells has put, it in a "network society."[36]

The new world is characterized by an erosion of many barriers and boundaries. The forces of economic and cultural globalization have created markets, corporations, and conversations which transcend any one location. This has had profound implications for government communicators. It is no longer possible to have one story for a home audience and one for foreign listeners. Today, words spoken in Kansas are heard in Kandahar. This change has caught out politicians who have spoken hastily without thought for a foreign audience, as when President George W. Bush proposed a "crusade" against terrorists following the attacks of 9/11.[37] It has also altered the nature of many nations' approach to international communication. Where a generation ago a diplomat abroad might have had freedom to engage as they saw fit, today they can find themselves tightly constrained by regulations and requirements to maintain "message discipline." Words are spoken by diplomats in Kandahar because of concerns over how voters in Kansas might react.[38] More than this, it seems that major initiatives in national promotion are driven not by a desire to engage foreigners but by a need to underline the legitimacy of actors for a domestic audience. The driving force behind the Beijing Olympics of 2008 or the Shanghai Expo of 2010 was not simply to win the admiration of foreigners but was a more complex move on the part of the Chinese government to be seen to give the Chinese people the gift of the admiration of the world.[39]

Other eroding boundaries include those between commercial

communication and government. It is now commonplace for governments to speak about the brand of a place or nation and to employ branding strategies. It is also commonplace to see different kinds of international actors working together – governmental, nongovernmental, local, international, and even commercial – to resolve an international issue.

Soft power

The qualities needed for success in the modern environment have shifted. Rather than being able to trust to the traditional leverage of military and economic power, international actors need to consider their ability to lead by other means. Consider the experience of Alejandro Philion. In 2005, Alejandro Philion was a young diplomat from Mexico with a tough job to do. Posted to a United Nations team in West Africa, he had been tasked to travel into the camp of a notorious warlord and attempt to persuade him to stop fighting and join peace talks. Initially, events unfolded as he expected: the slow 4x4 drive through the camp; the men in fatigues and dark glasses cradling the ubiquitous AK-47s; the suspicious scowl of their commander as he strode toward their first meeting. The young diplomat extended his hand and introduced himself: "Alejandro . . ." "Alejandro?" the warlord interrupted. "Like the boyfriend of Rubí?" In an instant, it dawned on Philion that the warlord was referring to a character in the smash-hit Mexican telenovela *Rubí* from the previous year: the handsome doctor embroiled in a love triangle by the devious *femme fatale* of the title. "Yes," he replied, "just like the boyfriend of Rubi." The outsider, 10,000 kilometers from home, was suddenly familiar and welcome. In the space of a few minutes, the warlord had agreed to take part in the talks.[40] Philion had been able to accomplish something not because his country had applied economic leverage or military force but simply because the warlord thought his culture was attractive. This is what Joseph Nye has termed "soft power": the quality of attractiveness flowing from an actor's culture or behavior which makes it easier (or by its absence harder) to build partnerships, advance agendas, and work in the international space.[41]

While the concept of soft power is used widely – it is a favorite term of recent Chinese leaders[42] – it is not necessarily used consistently or accurately. Nye initially coined the term as a way of explaining why the economic strength of Japan did not translate into the relative decline of the United States, but some US-based analysts insisted on conflating soft power with wealth. In the famous picture of the child attempting to move the donkey with a carrot and a stick, soft power is certainly not the stick, but neither is it the carrot. Both are material resources which the child is deploying to motivate behavior. Soft power would come into play if the child had a reputation for being kind to donkeys or could tell the donkey a story about how donkeys on his farm felt like Arabian stallions. Of course, it is impossible to motivate a donkey that way, but one might ask why – given the human capacity to imagine multiple futures and understand the world through narratives – we look to models of motivation designed for livestock? The great insight of soft power was to find a way to help nation-states to understand this.

Soft power helps make sense of a number of dynamics in contemporary international politics. It helps explain the value of actors like Pope Francis or Malala Yousafzai who have moral influence but no ability to compel attention or compliance. It fits with a world whose transparency makes it increasingly difficult to deploy hard power without a backlash against the actor and a surge of sympathy for the victim. Soft power has been a surprise resource for some. Thailand was astonished to find that it had an edge over its regional competitors because people admire Thai cuisine. The state actively promoted that admiration by encouraging excellence in Thai restaurants and sending Thai chefs out to teach guest classes at the world's culinary schools.[43]

Soft power does not work solely in positives. There is such a thing as negative soft power: negative policies and behaviors can reduce an actor's ability to lead on the international stage: cultures of discrimination and inequality; ugly words from bigoted leaders; and withdrawal from alliances can all repel as surely as noble ideals can attract. The situation is made more complex by the lack of universals in ethical perception. Values are not static across time nor place. New priorities emerge by which international actors are judged, such as the current priority given to the issue of sustainability as a source of morality. Moreover, values shift from place to place. A priority for one country may not appeal to another, and an agenda which is offensive to one group may reflect moral strength to other audiences. One response in the United States – which in the post-9/11 period faced a complex array of both hard and soft power problems – was to imagine a blend of force, economic leverage, development, and soft power outreach. They called it smart power.[44] Smart power was a gift on Capitol Hill. Senators who had been self-consciously trying to avoid the public endorsement of something "soft" were happy to endorse something called "smart."

Soft power is not the same thing as public diplomacy; rather, public diplomacy is a set of approaches which an international actor can use to leverage or even increase its soft power. Important scholarly projects around soft power have included the process that Daya Kishan Thussu calls "de-Americanizing soft power": charting the global appeal of other actors including India, China, Turkey, Venezuela, and Russia.[45]

Meet the new superpower

While many of the elements of this world of soft power and public diplomacy have existed for centuries, their current centrality is new. In fact, for some observers the accumulation of trends amounts to a fundamental shift in the international system, leaving representatives of nation-states uncertain how to respond. Speaking at the UN Climate Change Conference in Cancun in December 2010, the British analyst Simon Anholt went so far as to note: "There is only one superpower on the planet. That superpower is public opinion."[46] Any actor working in the international space needs to pay attention to this new superpower and seek out ways to engage and marshal it. In the years since Anholt's speech, it has become clear that the direction of the new superpower cannot be taken for granted. Many national governments have had success in redirecting their public's attention to identities limited by national scope, often founded on accounts of victimhood. Some actors have found that publics can be distracted with disinformation and fake news, allowing the deft exercise of hard power in the confusion. The superpower is still to play for.

Faced with this kind of challenge, it is tempting to focus on new technology and assume that in the era of social media the past has no relevance. It can be overwhelming to realize that the world's biggest retailer has no physical shops, the world's biggest taxi firm owns no cars, and the biggest social media site has more citizens than the most populous country. But the past has lessons to teach that can empower us in the present and help us to shape the future. In the era of social media, as in the era of the quill pen or the printed broadside, the best foreign public engagement is of limited use against bad policy, but equally the best policy in the world is of limited value if the world knows nothing of it. Foreign policy alone can't save the world but – whether it is called *diplomatie d'influence*, soft power work, or public diplomacy – foreign public engagement is an excellent place to look for answers, and a book on the subject is an excellent place to begin the search.

This book

This book will provide, in turn, an overview of each of the five foundational elements of public diplomacy in its classic form – listening, advocacy, cultural diplomacy, exchange diplomacy, and international broadcasting. It will then extend its analysis to consider the two major elements to emerge from the new public diplomacy: nation branding and partnership. The text seeks to cross disciplinary boundaries and incorporate insights from international relations and diplomatic studies, communication, media and area studies, and even from behavioral psychology. However, my home discipline of history will never be far from the surface. I draw particularly on the three cases of public diplomacy that I know best – Britain in World War II, the United States in the Cold War, and the international campaign around apartheid – which are revisited throughout the text. I also track the process that James Pamment has called "the re-imagining of British diplomacy in the light of the digital revolution,"[47] some portions of which I saw at close quarters. Yet public diplomacy is not an Anglo-American monopoly and I have also attempted to incorporate examples from a range of countries and different types of international actor. I hope the gaps in my analysis will inspire others to fill in more detail and broaden the conversation for their own home discipline and region. This is a book *for* the age of social media but not necessarily *about* the age of social media. Digital approaches and the developing impact of social media will not be dealt with in isolation but rather woven into each chapter. I feel that it is misleading to separate the use of social media into its own area as if it were a set of distinct magic tricks which can transform an actor's international profile. The reality is that one needs to understand the whole evolution of the field to see both the true capabilities and limits of the emerging platforms and technologies. My conclusion will draw threads from the whole book together to consider how global public engagement might address the crisis of our time in which – in Peter Pomeranzev's chilling phrase – information has been weaponized.[48]

2   Listening: The Foundational Skill

By the end of the 1990s, Switzerland had an image problem. From the revelation that Swiss banks had protected Nazi gold to the country's isolated position as a non-member of the European Union, Swiss prestige and influence was in serious decline. In 2001, the Swiss Federal Department for Foreign Affairs responded by creating a new unit to promote a better image for Switzerland though partnership with other key sectors of Swiss government and society, to be known as Presence Switzerland (PRS) – *Présence Suisse* in French and *Präsenz Schweiz* in German – under the leadership of a rising star in the Swiss foreign service, Ambassador Johannes Matyassy. From the outset, Matyassy emphasized the need for research. PRS immediately launched seven rolling image surveys in key target countries to provide a dashboard of problems and progress. Methods included polling and media analysis. The data shaped output and helped to evaluate its effectiveness. The surveys soon pointed to glaring discrepancies in the image of Switzerland. Matyassy and his colleagues were amazed to find that the best known and most valued aspects of Swiss life at home – direct democracy, modernity, and a humanitarian commitment – were often the least known and least understood overseas. There were local problems too. A 2002 survey of comparative attitude among publics, business managers, and politicians in key European countries found a curious spike in the British political sample. Only 30 percent of British politicians reported a positive attitude toward Switzerland when the European average was 65 percent. PRS investigated and found that Britain's political elite associated Switzerland with conservatism, and that this wasn't a cute Swiss cultural conservatism of embroidered blouses and mountain horns but a heavy-duty identification of Switzerland with the British Conservative Party then in opposition to the government of Tony Blair. A further investigation found that during the Thatcher and Major eras, the Swiss embassy had sponsored events for British Conservative groups and continued to do so well into the era of the New Labour government. No one had thought to change tack. The embassy duly switched its event sponsorship from Conservative to Labour-affiliated groups. The polls duly fell into line with the attitude toward Switzerland in other areas. In time PRS could claim credit for many things, including a string of excellent world expo pavilions and one of the best managed national images of any nation-state. It all began with focusing on one thing: listening.[1]

In an era of technological miracles in which a tweet can flash simultaneously across millions of handheld screens and a single thought jump thereby to a million minds, it is tempting to assume that global public engagement begins with hardware. This is not the case. Neither is the key to public diplomacy simply crafting a powerful message. Advocacy has its place, but it cannot lead the process. The foundation of sound public diplomacy must always be listening. The first duty of a public diplomat is to listen. In this chapter, I will unpack the process of listening as a mechanism of engaging a foreign public. I will consider examples of successful listening in public diplomacy and also examples of it going wrong. Much of the chapter will consider exactly what makes it so hard to listen – the social and cognitive barriers to effective listening – which public diplomats must learn to anticipate in themselves. Finally, I will consider what an effective approach might look like.

The listening deficit

It is remarkable, given the value which is placed on being a "good listener" in interpersonal relationships, how little attention has been paid to the process in the formal study of international relations or political science more broadly. The British political scientist Andrew Dobson took an important step to redress this neglect in his 2014 book *Listening for Democracy: Recognition, Representation, Reconciliation.* Dobson sees the neglect of listening as a kind of original sin in western political thought: a corollary to Aristotle's emphasis on speech. For Dobson, listening is an essential, conscious, and deliberate activity which goes beyond the more superficial act of simply hearing. He argues that through listening rulers know their people and subjects can understand their rulers; Dobson goes so far as to argue that listening can act as a "solvent of power," overcoming its negative effects. Through mutual listening, groups separated by asymmetries of power can build or rebuild trust. While his argument is developed with reference to domestic politics, it illuminates the challenge facing global public engagement.[2]

Definitions

Listening in public diplomacy may be defined as engaging a foreign public by gathering and analyzing information from that public and feeding what is learned into the policymaking process. Its more limited form is going through the process of collecting data but using what is learned only to adjust the message-making process. Listening is an active form of actor to foreign public engagement. Like the proverbial firewood which warms you twice – once when you cut it and once when you burn it – listening in public diplomacy has double value. It is of most value when it leads to a responsive and effective policy and/or approach to a foreign public. It also helps when it is seen to be done. Publics like to be listened to. A reputation for listening is a soft power asset, but publicizing listening has its risks if what is publicly learned is equally publicly ignored.

Who listens?

The listening elements of public diplomacy bureaucracy are varied. The front line historically has been officers in the field who are exposed to publics on a day-to-day basis through conversation and contact with local media and who report on their findings. Behind them stand the analysts with region-specific knowledge at the ministry of foreign affairs or headquarters, who track the incoming material and often have their own regional sources, perhaps based on diplomats or on contact with the diaspora of the country in question. Public diplomacy actors commission conventional market research on attitudes among publics of interest, and the largest actors have in-house survey and research capacity. Listening overlaps with the covert realm of intelligence gathering. Historically, covert intelligence has entered into the public diplomacy listening process both through open-source research work, such as the monitoring of international radio broadcasting, and through covert surveillance and signals intelligence work. The drawbacks and hidden costs of covert listening can be significant. Other elements in listening might include attention to the output of research in the nongovernmental academic sector which can track political developments at more length and greater detail than is possible in a bureaucratic setting.

Precedents for listening in public diplomacy

As with other forms of public diplomacy, it is possible to find historical examples of good practice. When Sun Tzu urged his reader to "know your enemy," he was stressing the need to engage with the interlocutor who actually exists and not a mental projection of the adversary drawn from one's imagining.[3] The same applies to public diplomacy. Even if it has been neglected in formal political theory, listening has long been part of the popular culture associated with leadership. It shows up in folk tales through the archetype of the king in disguise, the idealized monarch who passes undetected through the masses of his own or his neighbor's territory in order to better understand his business. Examples from European history alone include Denmark's Magnus the Good, Hungary's Mathias the Just, Poland's Casimir III, or Sweden's Charles XI *Gråkappan* whose nickname comes from the gray cape he wore as his disguise. England's Alfred the Great reputedly infiltrated the ranks of the Danish invaders disguised as a minstrel to better understand their mentality and morale. Perhaps the ultimate version of a wise ruler-in-disguise story is the religious doctrine of the incognito god walking on earth – Odin, Krishna, Jesus Christ – divinities who understand the human condition from the inside. In our own time, Jordan's King Abdullah is reported to use disguise to check on the conditions of his people and the fairness of his government.[4] The wildly successful reality TV show format launched in the United Kingdom in 2009 under the title *Undercover Boss* transposes the disguised king into the modern corporate leader, disguised among his or her employees.[5] The acclaimed 2017 motion picture portrait of Winston Churchill in May 1940 – *Darkest Hour* – includes an invented scene in which the prime minister mingles with ordinary people during a ride on the London Underground. The fantasies and longings we project onto leadership have remained remarkably consistent across the millennia.

From earliest times, morale has been a focus for intelligence collection. Sun Tzu spoke of "the art of studying moods,"[6] but listening is more than a key to battlefield conquest; it is an essential habit of governance. The great Tang dynasty Emperor Taizong noted, "The emperor, living in the palace, is blocked from direct access to information. For fear that faults might be left untold or defects unattended, he must set up various devices to elicit loyal suggestions and listen attentively to sincere advice . . ."[7] Listening can be a skill of the oppressed or endangered. Those living under tyranny become adept at interpreting tiny changes in rhetoric or image as a way to understand what they may be facing next. Listening can also be balm. One could debate whether it was the act of confessing or the fact that a priest listened which gave the Christian church's sacrament of confession its power, and the same could be asked of the process of speaking and being listened to in therapy.

During the Counter-Reformation, as Catholic religious communication became formalized in practices of propaganda, practitioners learned to build feedback into the process, charting the ebb and flow of the spirit of the faithful. As soon as the print media became a forum for political activity, their analysis became a concern for diplomats seeking to understand that country. The first properly published volume of the American diplomatic archives – dubbed *Foreign Relations of the United States* and, in a remarkable display of democratic openness, published in the midst of the Civil War – included numerous estimations of foreign opinion as gauged by the country's ambassadors of the era.[8]

In the twentieth century, the tools of social science, including polls, were added to the diplomatic toolbox. Such pioneers as George Gallup and Elmo Roper acted as advisors to the public diplomacy agencies of their era. Gallup was considered so valuable to the United States Information Agency in the 1950s that he was allocated one of the agency's special slots in the government's deep shelter so that he could survive a nuclear war, though exactly who he was expected to poll in the incandescent aftermath of Armageddon is unclear from the archival record. Public diplomacy also incorporated research practices associated with public relations and advertising. Practitioners who led the early days of US public diplomacy included the great William Benton, founder of the New York advertising agency Benton and Bowles and pioneer of research-based advertising behind the rise of such brands as Maxwell House coffee.[9]

The twenty-first century has greatly expanded the speed and scope of listening. Actors acquired a host of analytic tools and real-time blog monitoring software, and the potential for data mining in public diplomacy is only just beginning to be understood. Listening has a special role in social media platforms because of their inherent transparency, enabling actors to track ideas and messages and build their knowledge of a target population.[10] But the transparency works both ways. A Twitter profile discloses exactly how many other users a Twitter user is following and who they are. One of the major problems in the first generation of US diplomatic Twitter accounts was that they were focused on attracting followers and transmitting only and were plainly not interested in using the medium for listening to foreign publics. Many accounts were following either no one or no one foreign, which did not reflect well on the user.

While listening may be a missing dimension in much of the international digital media, it has emerged as an important component of some of the most innovative political practices of our time. Dobson flags the importance of listening in the South African Truth and Reconciliation Committees, the emphasis on listening in the Occupy movement, and the way in which the Rio+20 climate conference opted for keynote listeners – who gathered their impressions of proceedings and reported back to attendees as a whole – rather than plenary speakers bringing preformed ideas in from outside.[11]

Great listeners in public diplomacy

The history of public diplomacy is full of examples of excellent listening. America's first public diplomat – Benjamin Franklin – was sent to Paris in part because of his dazzling rhetorical skills, but what most impressed the French was his willingness to listen.[12] Examine any great public diplomacy campaign and you will find great listeners. In the case of the British campaign to draw the United States away from neutrality and into World War II, the listening component included a massive operation to collect editorial material from across the country at a specially established British Press Service in New York. Among those who contributed to the work was the Oxford University philosophy professor Isaiah Berlin, who from 1941 on and for most of the war wove material collected from his own conversations in Washington with material gathered by the British Press Service in New York to create a compelling weekly picture of American political life. In time, even the Roosevelt White House became an eager recipient of his analyses. Britain also connected to pollsters and established a nuanced understanding of the regional, generational, ethnic and even gender dynamics of American isolationism. Britain understood that women were one of the most skeptical groups when it came to the suggestion that the United States might join the British in a war against Hitler. Countermeasures included such specifically gendered outreach initiatives as the development of a radio soap opera about life in London under the German blitz called *Frontline Family*.[13]

Research was a key element in the work of the United States Information Agency, the public diplomacy agency created by President Eisenhower in 1953. The agency inherited a small group of public opinion analysts from the Department of State's Office of Intelligence Research which became the core of an Office of Research and Intelligence (IRI), founded in 1954. IRI was initially led by Henry Loomis (who rose to become Voice of America director), and its staff included a mercurial polling expert named Leo Crespi. Crespi had served in the occupation of Germany and remained a mainstay of USIA research work until his retirement in the 1980s. The unit both studied major trends in opinion around the world and evaluated agency tools and programs.[14] Some of its most startling findings became news in their own right. The USIA found ample evidence that, following the launch of *Sputnik* in 1957, it was the USSR which seemed to be winning the Cold War for most of the world. During the presidential election of 1960, the USIA IRI reports showing the prestige which had accumulated to the Soviet Union at America's expense were leaked to the Kennedy campaign, and their findings became part of the famous television debate between JFK and Richard Nixon. The profound concern for international opinion was more than a stump posture for President Kennedy. Once in office, he remained a keen consumer of USIA polls and of the digests of world editorials sent in by public diplomats in the field, and he integrated what he learned into his policy and self-presentation.[15]

Evaluation

One final aspect of listening within the field of public diplomacy is the evaluation of public diplomacy work. It could be seen as listening *to* public diplomacy. Evaluation uses many of the same methods as more general listening activities, including polls, focus groups, and media content analysis. However, it is limited in its outlook, focusing only on the effectiveness of existing public diplomacy operations. In the current era of diminishing budgets and evermore demanding legislatures, evaluation has become a major preoccupation of most public diplomacy bureaucracies. The activity can be as prone to the same cognitive traps as any other listening project, and has a few others of its own. One major problem is that a bureaucracy that fails to appropriately consider its approach to evaluation may find itself overvaluing the forms of public diplomacy which deliver changes that are detectable in the short term and neglecting those which can't easily be managed. There is a danger that such analysis might give exactly the wrong answer and prompt resources to flow toward easy-to-measure advocacy campaigns and away from activities like leader exchanges which, although slow to bear fruit, have been shown to deliver long-lasting impact through the later careers of participants. Evaluators would do well to remember the dictum beloved of Einstein that not everything that can be measured is significant and that not everything significant can be measured.[16]

Historically, public diplomacy presented itself internally though an emphasis on output rather than outcome. USIA reports were full of statistics giving the number of people who saw this film, heard that radio program, or attended the other exhibition in Minsk or Magnitogorsk. Kennedy-era agency director Edward R. Murrow was aware of the need for qualitative indicators of success but pushed back against the expectations of Congress for data, arguing, "No computer clicks, no cash register rings when a man changes his mind or opts for freedom."[17] Times have changed. Social media have made it possible to deploy a host of real-time listening tools to track responses to a piece of public diplomacy from retweets for messages on

Twitter to detailed real-time analytics of the responses to a speech, both positive or negative.

Today, a wise public diplomacy bureaucracy includes evaluation in the original design of a piece of public diplomacy and determines clear benchmarks and key performance indicators that the campaign will be measured against. An extension of this involves setting aside a portion of the budget specifically for evaluation. Public diplomacy is regularly measured not only against mission specific goals but also as to whether it contributes to centrally determined agendas. In the early 1970s, all USIA programs were examined with an eye to their contribution to the fight against communism. The evaluation matrix currently employed in the United Kingdom requires that all activity include within its assessment its contribution to women's empowerment.[18]

Failures of listening

Despite these cases of careful listening and effective evaluation it is even easier to find examples of failure to listen or failure to listen properly. The history of US foreign policy is full of such instances. Listening fails if an unguarded listener is being manipulated by his interlocutor, and hears what he wants to hear. The George W. Bush administration listened to the Iraqi exile leader Ahmed Chalabi. Secretary of State Colin Powell and others apparently considered his account of Iraqi public opinion and its openness to "regime change" to be reliable. In retrospect, Chalabi was plainly telling the administration exactly what it wanted to hear.

Listening fails when it is not tied into policy. The USIA's tracking of international opinion around the Vietnam War had no value when President Johnson refused to be guided by it. Moreover, he became so concerned by the political damage that could come from publication of polls on international hostility to US policy that he ordered them to be cancelled.[19] Listening fails when it is applied to the wrong thing. A case in point is the State Department's Shared Values campaign of 2002. It was the brainchild of Undersecretary of State for Public Diplomacy Charlotte Beers whose background in advertising taught her that no campaign could succeed without proper research. But while her staffers certainly pre-tested the multimedia campaign she launched to show the Muslim world that Americans shared their most cherished values of faith and family and that Arab-Americans lived in prosperity amid tolerance, they failed to listen to what the core question in the minds of the audience might be. Their campaign answered a question that no one was asking. Muslim hostility to the United States was based not on an erroneous idea that Arab-Americans had a hard time in Dearborn, Michigan, but a fairly accurate idea of US policy in the Middle East.[20]

The exposure of listening can be a problem. The US image in Europe was hurt by the revelations in material leaked by Edward Snowden in 2013 of the scale of National Security Agency surveillance of internet traffic. Listening is of limited value when it is just a process of changing the superficial surface of communication to appease public opinion and is not linked to a deep consideration of a situation. Listening fails when it is merely an affectation to allow the speaker a pause to "reload" before resuming a tirade. Needless to say, the most frustrating behavior of all is simply not listening.

One of the most famous cases of a US public diplomat not listening has been somewhat overstated. In 2005, deep in the dark days for the US international image that marked the start of George W. Bush's second term, the president appointed his long-term aide and communication advisor, Karen Hughes, to serve in the role of Undersecretary of State for Public Diplomacy and Public Affairs. Hughes immediately announced that she would undertake a "listening tour" of the Middle East. She invited the US media to join her and set off on her merry way. Unfortunately, the press was not impressed by her performance, noting that her default mode was electioneering and deriding her for telling an audience of well-to-do Saudi women that she longed to see them able to drive cars. Some women in her audience assured her that they'd rather keep their chauffeurs. Yet, despite the poor optics, she really was listening – just on behalf of an audience of one. After her return, she gave the president a detailed account of the currents of Arab opinion, emphasizing the centrality of the Israel–Palestine issue and the importance of the United States being seen to be working to improve the lot of the Palestinians. The plan to revise US policy was unfortunately preempted by the success of Hamas in the Gaza elections of January 2006 and a subsequent rise in tensions.[21]

Poor listening is not just an American political trait. It is an occupational hazard of politics that leaders read too much into their arrival at the summit and even those who have been good listeners in the past have come to overestimate their own judgment. The political media are part of the problem. A change of course is generally depicted as a sign of weakness. Some politicians – in public at least – make their refusal to listen into a virtue. Britain's Margaret Thatcher boasted about not listening to criticism of her economic policies, declaring in October 1980: "To those waiting with bated breath for that favourite media catchphrase, the 'U-turn', I have only one thing to say: you turn if you want to. The lady's *not* for turning."[22]

The problem is not in the politicians or the self-confident policy makers, but in the underlying hardware of human perception. The fault is in ourselves.

The challenge to effective listening: cognitive and social biases

It is hard to listen. Wise communicators have always known the limits of human perception. Bias of Priene remarked that "naive men are easily fooled" and generations of hucksters and scam artists have made livings off that fact. The problems are compounded when one is attempting to understand something or someone foreign, which is necessarily the case in public diplomacy. This is not an empty lament. Social science researchers have long since demonstrated that rationality in human perception frequently breaks down. The distortions are known as cognitive and social biases. There are many explanations for the presence of cognitive and social biases in human psychology. The world is a complicated place and if every situation was analyzed on its merits as if encountered for the first time, the analyst would likely be left behind. For reasons of convenience, humans had to develop a set of shortcuts or more properly *heuristics* to speed decision making and make the business of life – from hunting a woolly mammoth to buying a smartphone – as efficient as possible.[23]

Since classical times rhetoricians have segmented their thinking about a message into "who, what, when, where, why, in what way, by what means."[24] The same framework can be applied to cognitive and social biases and exactly how elements within these categories distort our ability to listen.

Cognitive/social bias: who we listen to

The most obvious bias is *prejudice*. Listeners filter information through a mesh of stereotypes and beliefs and give preference to information which affirms preexisting notions and opinions.[25] This can play out in the levels of credibility given to particular sources. Important information can be missed when a source is regarded as not credible. It is a feature of the failure to initially believe many of the biggest stories of the past century. On April 17, 1968, Radio Hanoi broke the news that a month previously 500 South Vietnamese civilians had been murdered in cold blood at a village called My Lai. The US army dismissed the report, pointing out that the Hanoi report blamed units of the 82nd Airborne Division, who were nowhere near at the time. The event, of course, was all too real. The perpetrators were from the 23rd (American) Infantry. The news only broke in the western media thanks to the investigation of reporter Seymour Hersh in November 1969, some months after the secret trial of the officer commanding that day had commenced.[26]

There are biases associated with a listener's psychological state. Optimistic people seek out good news whereas individuals and societies with a predilection for the darker side prefer information that confirms a pessimistic worldview. A sense of this led the early twentieth-century Danish film industry to routinely film two endings for their films: a happy ending where everyone lived, which they exported to the West; and a sad ending where everyone died, which they exported to the Russian Empire.[27]

There are social biases associated with a listener's identity. Humans extend greater credibility to people with whom they share (or believe that they share) an affinity. Nationality, gender, social class, or group membership can all come into play.[28] Today, the *affinity bias* is understood as a major obstacle to diversity in employment, but it is an ancient vulnerability. Old-time confidence tricksters knew it paid to keep a stock of lodge pins in their suitcases so they could rapidly decorate their lapels and become a fellow Freemason, Odd Fellow, Knight of Columbus, or similar as needed to lull their "mark" into a false sense of security. The failure of British officials to detect the Cambridge spies of the immediate post-war period seems to have flowed from an inability to consider that someone who went to the same school or whose mother knew your mother could really be working for Stalin. Trust of professional status, social standing, and shared religion all seemed to have helped Wall Street's wizard of lies, Bernie Madoff, attract investors and avoid suspicion. Such susceptibilities plague us all. It is also evident that listeners favor information from people who have admirable qualities even though unrelated to the subject on which they are speaking, hence the world of the celebrity spokesperson. This is known as the *halo effect*.[29] The international community is not immune to such things. From time to time, particular world leaders have extra traction simply because they are young and nice looking. Canadian Prime Minister Justin Trudeau has benefited from this.

Cognitive/social biases: what we listen to

Listeners filter events based not only on who is speaking but on what is said. An otherwise credible messenger will be considered incredible if the content of their message is too extreme. Policy makers are notoriously overreliant on past events as a guide to future possibilities. There is a bias against first occurrence which is a part of the failure of experts to successfully warn against such catastrophes as the flooding of New Orleans during Hurricane Katrina in 2005 and may account for the discounting by some of warnings over carbon-caused climate change.[30] The historian Deborah Lipstadt identifies this kind of failure of imagination in the US media's inability to accept news of the Holocaust which to them was, as her title puts it, *Beyond Belief*.[31] Even when bad things have happened before, there seems to be a bias against believing that they can happen again: known as the *ostrich bias* or *normalcy bias*, this seems to be especially easy to find among people who coincidentally have a vested interest in continued confidence, such as certain Wall Street investment bankers.[32]

Cognitive/social bias: when we listen

The bias to existing thoughts is not simply an extension of prejudice or content. A listener's response to a piece of information can be greatly shaped by as simple a cause as having heard a different piece of information first. This is called the *confirmation bias*. The confirmation bias means that people prefer and are more likely to believe information that confirms any pre-held idea. A parallel problem is the *exposure effect*. Familiarity with an idea promotes its acceptance irrespective of its inherent veracity. In a similar vein, listeners give greater emphasis to pieces of information which they can recall most easily (a process sometimes called the *availability heuristic*) or which is repeated most often in the media (a process known as the *availability cascade*). A listener can be influenced by such potentially spurious factors as whether the piece of information was embedded in a rhyming couplet, which is exactly why these have been so ubiquitous in commercial advertising.[33]

Once established and held over time, an idea can be very hard to shift. There is the *endowment effect* which leads people to prefer the possessions they already have – because they are theirs and they have an aversion to losing them – not merely above available objects of equivalence but also of those with several degrees of superior quality.[34] What works for objects also works for ideas. A listener's preference for one of their own flawed ideas can extend for a long time, and attempts to accelerate the process by counter-argument seem to strengthen attachment rather than destroy it, presumably because their aversion to loss increased by a perceived endangerment.

There are a number of other distortions that come from early introduction of data. The *priming effect* suggests that an incidentally mentioned word or concept can predispose the perception of an occurrence or question in a particular way.[35] A diplomat who has read two reports of a full-blown revolution will be predisposed to look at evidence of unrest in an unrelated location as a manifestation of the same. Moreover, a single piece of information when introduced first will influence subsequent discussion and estimates. This is known as the *anchoring effect* and is especially evident in negotiation.[36]

Cognitive/social bias: where/why we listen

The context in which information is acquired – the where and why of listening – can have an important impact on perception. One bias of especial concern to listening in a foreign policy process is the overhearing or *eavesdrop bias* which curiously, although treated as obvious in everyday life, has proved difficult to reproduce in a controlled environment.[37] Humans are so mistrustful of one another that they give greater credibility to messages which are not targeted at them directly but rather are overheard, more especially when the information heard is favorable to them. Old-time con artists knew the best way of hooking a mark into a fake investment was to allow him to overhear a conversation between the "grifter" and a confederate.[38] Perhaps scarcity has predisposed humans to suspect that a direct message might be a misdirection to protect a resource. Whatever its root, the bias seems to have inspired a whole genre of television advertisements which play out as conversations between people who might either be perceived as peers (two housewives) or authority figures (two doctors) by potential customers, and whose conversation communicates the merits of a household product, medication, or other item in such a way that the information flies under the listener's skepticism and is mentally "filed" under "useful overhearings" rather than "potentially tendentious nonsense." In politics, the dynamic plays out in the sometimes inordinate attention devoted to "open-mic gaffes" as revealing a candidate's true nature.[39] The correlation in foreign policy is that governments plainly tend to give disproportionate weight to secret intelligence material at the expense of material in open sources which anyone could find. An obvious example of this is the US preference for secret evidence of Iraqi weapons of mass destruction over open-source evidence that such programs had been abandoned.[40]

Cognitive/social bias: ways/means of listening

To further bar the way to accurate perception, there are biases relating to the ways in which information is received. Listeners become used to particular sources which may not necessarily reflect new realities. Classic cases include the failure of a number of embassies in Iran to realize that the revolution of 1979 was about to happen. They had been reading the secular newspapers, whereas Ayatollah Khomeini and his comrades had been building a base through hand-to-hand distribution of sermons on tape cassettes.[41] Similarly, few foreign missions in Washington, DC had a media diet that prepared them for the result of the 2016 presidential election. Furthermore, listening is active, and part of listening is examining and/or testing one's perception to ensure accuracy. Unfortunately, once a hypothesis is established in the mind of the listener, there is a tendency for it not to be tested properly. This is the *congruence bias*, by which a listener prefers information that fits with existing ideas and explanations of events or trends and is disinclined to consider or test alternative explanations that do not fit.[42] This kind of bias helps explain how intelligence analysts in the Cold War US government could continue to apply a one-size-fits-all "communist revolutionary" frame to so many Third World popular movements and fail to probe for country-specific explanations. Such issues are compounded by various distortions associated with the social context in which the information is collated. Collective wisdom, "groupthink," and other varieties of conformity have historically hampered much public diplomacy listening and have led to the underestimation of innumerable popular upswings, including the Arab Spring of 2011.

Bias blindness

Perhaps the most dangerous bias which threatens listening in public diplomacy or any other field is the so-called *bias blind spot*.[43] West Africans are reported as saying, "We do not see others as they are, but as we are."[44] Most people, however, won't acknowledge this. Human beings seem hardwired to be unable to perceive their own biases and prejudices even as they are quick to identify them in others. Ironically, it seems that the worse one's own experience of bias has been, the less likely one is to be aware of one's bias against others. Hence, many of the worst listeners in history had formative stories which emphasized their own victimhood. The rhetoric of the Afrikaner minority government in apartheid South Africa and of Adolf Hitler during his rise to power in Germany are only two of the more obvious cases. The former emphasized the atrocities that the community suffered at the hands of Britain in the Anglo-Boer wars; the latter repeatedly emphasized the injustices of the peace "dictated" to Germany at the end of the Great War. Some bad listeners have managed without a story of suffering. During the British rule of India, British imperialists learned Indian languages, studied Indian traditions, and recorded Indian folk ways, yet seem to have understood very little given that their quest was based on an assumption of Indian inferiority and British superiority. A case in point is Major-General Sir Henry Durand, who in his capacity as the lieutenant governor of the Punjab visited the town of Tonk (now Tank in Pakistan) on New Year's Eve in 1870. His long years of experience in India had taught him that nothing impressed locals like a man of authority riding on an elephant, and he insisted on entering the town mounted on such a beast. Indians attending warned him that this was not a good idea but he dismissed their concerns, convinced of his own authority in the matter. What he did not understand was that the town gate was too low to allow an elephant with a mounted passenger to pass. He struck his head, fell, and died the following day.[45]

At the outer edges of perception is the phenomenon of illusory correlation (sometimes known as *pareidolia*), the process by which a mind can be so used to finding meaning that it sees patterns which simply can't be there. We see faces on the moon and on burnt tortillas, and castles in clouds. We hear words in birdcalls. For English speakers, a peacock calls "help"; a Scottish red grouse shouts "go back." For Icelandic speakers, the golden plover says *dyrdin, dyrdin*, which means "wonder, wonder," and is much loved as the herald of spring. The urge to find patterns in random evidence can throw off listening in a foreign policy context as easily as any other. Though one never hears of diplomats crediting failures to what borders on hallucination, it is possible to read between the lines and detect a will to perceive in many of the classic scenarios of misunderstanding, such as the institutional readings of public opinion in pre-invasion Iraq. At moments of great change, the world collectively looks to patterns in the campfire. The dominant optimistic imaginings of the extraordinary events of 1989 certainly did not fit with what was about to happen in Yugoslavia, and the collective misperception provided opportunities to those of ill will in the region. The listener does well to recall the dictum of the North American skeptic Michael Shermer that humans are "pattern-seeking story-telling animals, and we are quite adept at telling stories about patterns, whether they exist or not."[46]

Designing the ideal listening process

Once it has been established that listening is both a central duty and hard to do, the issue then arises as to exactly how it may be done effectively.

Cognitive bias is not an insurmountable problem for public diplomacy. In fact, these biases provide important avenues of approach for advocacy work. The chief answer to the challenge of cognitive bias is to accept limits on one's own ability to listen and to approach the listening process with discipline. Nobel-prizewinning behavioral economist Daniel Kahneman stresses the importance of checklists, attention to data, and routines to minimize the role of subjective factors in judgment. He notes the way in which the antenatal checklist devised by Dr Virginia Apgar back in 1953 radically improved the ability of doctors to spot babies with problems in the delivery room. Kahneman ends every chapter of his book by suggesting a way of speaking that could minimize the impact of a particular bias on decision making.[47]

One example of an attempt to minimize the impact of perception biases is the way in which some airlines teach pilots to understand that different personality types may react quite differently to the same stimulus, especially under stress. British Airways flight crew are trained to know that the other pilot in a multi crew environment may verbalize their concerns in a different way or even internalize a reaction. This is a helpful skill in a cockpit where by their nature clues from body language are minimal.[48] In a similar vein, Israeli military intelligence – alarmed by the intelligence failures of the Yom Kippur War of 1973 – resolved to design a hedge against future groupthink. The IDF Intelligence Directorate created what was known as the Red Team or Devil's Advocate Office, charged with the task of researching the contrarian view and empowered to report directly to the top without fear of retribution. Their motto is *ipcha mistabra*, Aramaic for "on the contrary, it appears that . . . ." The approach became more widely known when a fictionalized version – "the 10th man doctrine" – appeared in the 2006 novel *World War Z* by Max Brooks and the 2013 movie of the same name. Applying the doctrine allows Israel to be the only country ready for a global plague of zombies.[49] Britain's most famous listeners – the codebreakers and online monitors at GCHQ – have learned that good listening needs a diverse group of unlimited by age, gender, sexuality, or neurotype. The agency is especially proud of its record employing people with Asperger syndrome, and in 2017 it was named one of the hundred-best employers for the LGBTQ community by the civil rights NGO Stonewall.[50]

The American educational theorist Leonard Waks has argued that the worst kind of listening is what is termed *cataphatic*, which is to say overly shaped by predetermined categories. The listener who is listening for categories can easily simply check boxes, thus missing ways in which his interlocutors are straining to express something different. There is an old American joke from the 1930s which turns on this idea. A cop wades into a street battle between communists and their opponents, seizes a likely looking man, and prepares to beat him with his nightstick. "Don't beat me," cries the man. "I'm an anti-communist." The cop replies: "I don't care what kind of communist you are!" and lands his blow. The policeman had a predisposition that he would be presented with multiple categories of radical philosophy – communism, Trotskyism, anarcho-syndicalism – and was in no mood to equivocate. Waks argues that the better way is what he terms *apophatic* listening: a more open approach which avoids an emphasis on predetermined categories. As Dobson notes, a model for what this may look like can be found in recommendations for clinical best practice. Nurse and scholar Sheila D. Shipley suggests that truly effective clinical listening is marked not by superficial indicators of paying attention (the eye contact and nods that debutantes were taught to do in charm school) but a deep engagement with the subject which includes regular checks during which phrases or concepts are repeated back to confirm that the words are understood: "so what you are saying is . . ." and so forth. In this way the conversation becomes a kind of co-creation, shaped in real time by rolling feedback. A person who has been engaged in such a way will feel that they have been heard. [51]

To be effective, listening in public diplomacy should be systematic *and* consistent. Only when contextualized through comparison to data gathered over time and across a variety of locations can a current of opinion be properly understood. The listener needs to understand if things said are unrepresentative. For this reason, it can help if at least some of the listeners are people with long-term experience of a country, with a feel for currents of opinion, in order to minimize the risk of projecting patterns which fit easily from home politics.

Listening should be open and transparent so that it can be seen to be happening and the genuine interest of the listener in the population of interest can be clear. Listening needs to be seen to be responsive and open to feedback. It helps for sources to be eclectic and for listeners to be imaginative as populations are dynamic; listening only to familiar sources can be misleading and may not reveal critical change. Listening tasks can be labor intensive and wise international actors understand the value of dividing tasks with allies.[52]

Listeners should always be on the lookout for their own biases, expectations, and the distortions which can come from culture, which is a further reason to track critical populations in cooperation with others who have different biases. International actors need to be aware that if they want a culture of listening within their bureaucracy, they should build rewards for listening into their measures of performance and their systems of reward.

Some institutions have done this, as is the case with the Department of State which gives a Director General's Award for Impact and Originality in Reporting.[53] A final point to remember, however, is that, as with anything, too much listening can be counterproductive. There is a danger that an actor can be so preoccupied with listening, developing a culture of sensitivity to foreign opinion, that they neglect to act on what they have learned (Germany seemed this way in the 1990s), and an over-analyzed population can become sick of being studied and cease cooperating with intrusive listening techniques, such as opinion polls. Some western pollsters came to suspect that by 2010 the Afghan population was so weary of being analyzed that they had begun to give deliberately confusing answers when questioners called.

Not all actors are equally predisposed to listen. There seems to be a correlation between size and/or self-confidence and a willingness to listen, with the largest countries seeming to be worst at listening. It is a daunting task to teach a superpower to listen; those considering such an exercise might be better advised to teach those wishing to engage that actor to speak more effectively and hope that it has the same effect.

The emergence of digital and social media has opened undreamed-of possibilities in listening. One institution to rise to the challenge in recent years is the United Nations where in 2009 the assistant secretary-general for policy and plans, Robert C. Orr (now dean of public policy at the University of Maryland) established a digital research and innovation unit within the Office of the Secretary General. He called it the Global Pulse. The Global Pulse set out to explore how new sources of real-time digital data could help guide UN activity, as well as to test new frontiers in data collection and analysis of online media as a substitute for mass-participation surveys. A further goal was to help build up the UN's internal capacities in data literacy. It attempted to share its findings in fresh and easily understandable ways, setting high standards in its use of infographics and data visualization.

The Global Pulse unit has lived up to its promise. It has focused on real-time information and feedback and has learned the value of tracking proxy indicators in social and other online media. The unit rolled out regional innovation hubs – known as Pulse Labs – in Indonesia and Uganda, starting in 2012. In a particularly novel approach to "listening," the Global Pulse Lab in Uganda (where radio is still the king when it comes to media) built a system for automatically analyzing keywords from local radio broadcasts as a means of early warning about issues of concern to the public, most especially the kind of dehumanized discussion of enemy communities that has preceded genocide elsewhere in the region. In a similar vein, the Indonesian lab built a dashboard/tool to analyze digital media and citizen-generated online content to provide real-time information on fire and haze hotspots. Probably the most interesting piece of Global Pulse work was related to the UN's mass public opinion survey called MyWorld, in which people around the world were asked which of the UN's Millennium Development Goals they thought most important. On the surface, the result was depressing – agreement within regions but no consensus across regions over what the most important was. Some populations voted for gender equality, others for anti-corruption, some prioritized climate issues, others maternal health, and still others elder care. But remarkably there was unanimity on one issue. Every region of the world flagged education in second or even first place. The exercise had revealed a universal shared value.[54]

From the foundation of listening, the actor may then look to advocacy, the subject of the next chapter.

3   Advocacy: The Cutting Edge

In 2012, Riva Ganguli Das and her team at the Public Diplomacy Division of the Indian foreign ministry had a tough task: to find a way of advocating for India online without benefit of a substantial budget. In 2011, the ministry had enjoyed some success by challenging the world to submit three-minute YouTube videos under the title "India is. . . ." Das and her colleagues suspected that real success would come if they opened the competition to still photographers. The theory was that entrants would likely not only share their submissions with the foreign ministry but with their friends in thousands of individual online posts and the public diplomacy unit would acquire a library of images for use in its work. And so it was. The foreign ministry received thousands of submissions. The photographers shared their pictures with each other, the foreign ministry shared the winners, and the best were integrated into the print output of the public diplomacy section – all for a tiny initial investment. Every picture advocated for India.[1]

Advocacy in public diplomacy may be defined as an actor's attempt to manage the international environment by undertaking an international communication activity to promote a particular policy, idea, or that actor's general interests in the minds of a foreign public. Elements of advocacy are to be found in all areas of foreign public engagement, and its short-term utility has led to a bias toward this dimension among political leadership. There is an associated tendency to place it, and the elements of the bureaucracy most closely connected to it, at the center of any public diplomacy structure. While advocacy should not be seen as the totality of public diplomacy, it does deserve careful scrutiny as to what amounts to the activity's cutting edge. This chapter will consider: the range of language used to describe advocacy work; the types of public diplomacy organizations who do it; types of advocacy campaign and the ways they play to cognitive bias. Finally, I will consider specific examples of successful messaging.

Advocacy in history

The ancients knew the value of advocacy. As already noted, Bias of Priene urged "gain your point by persuasion, not by force." Yet from ancient times advocacy and rhetoric were mistrusted. Synonyms for advocacy over the years have included *information, policy advocacy, political communication, influence,* and (with a pejorative edge) *spin.* Around 2004, US bureaucratic jargon embraced the term "moving the needle" to evoke the payoff to advocacy, imagining a detectible target public response in real time.[2] Advocacy was expected to have impact. It is the hardest element of global engagement to disaggregate from propaganda. Advocacy is not necessarily direct. The man who reintroduced the term propaganda – Ignatius Loyola – recommended that his Jesuit order seek to influence those who would influence others. He wrote: "Therefore preference ought to be given to those persons and places which, through their own improvement, become a cause which can spread the good accomplished to many others who are under their influence or take guidance from them." This remains good advice.[3]

Visualizations of the location of advocacy within public diplomacy typically place it at one extreme. It is at the apex of the Canadian public diplomacy pyramid. For the Anglo-German analyst team of Ali Fisher and Aurélie Bröckerhoff, advocacy was one end of the spectrum of their "options for influence" (Figure 3.1)[4]

The benign end of the spectrum was listening, then facilitation, then the building of networks, followed by cultural exchange. In the middle, there

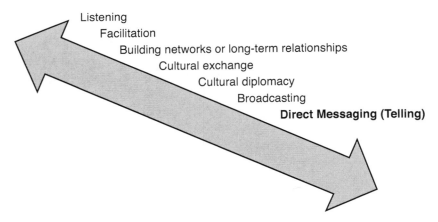

Figure 3.1 The Fisher/Bröckerhoff spectrum from *Options for Influence* (2008). Reproduced by kind permission of Ali Fisher and Aurélie Bröckerhoff.

were the more one-way activities of cultural diplomacy and international broadcasting. At the far end was the direct messaging (telling) work of advocacy. All these approaches may be used to advance policy goals, but not all were as likely to be resented by audiences or to encounter as much pushback as advocacy.

There are many kinds of advocacy organizations. National advocacy organizations are the best known. Subnational entities can have advocacy operations either speaking on behalf of their region, as is the case with the units advocating for Scotland, Catalonia, or Quebec, or partnering at the national level. Multinational groups deliver collective advocacy on behalf of their members or on issues of shared concern, as is the case with the European Commission or the press apparatus of NATO. All major international organizations have an advocacy element, top of the heap being the UN Secretary-General's Department of Public Information. At some points in its history, the UN General Assembly has created issue-specific advocacy organizations.

All advocates need credibility and not all advocates are equally credible. This is not merely a question of their track record of past duplicity but can apply to entire categories of advocate. The demon of Perfidious Albion or perfidious Uncle Sam can be succeeded by the demon of the perfidious neoliberal state. Alternate types of voice have different credibility. The subnational voice can be especially credible when aligned with the national story. The same can be said of voices that represent a minority or subordinate group within a nation, whose testimony is interpreted internationally as being less biased than that of a speaker who has more of a vested interest in the status quo. Some of the most effective advocates for the United States internationally have been African-American, culminating in President Barack Obama. International voices have a credibility that comes from their innate breadth and collective nature. NGOs have the advantage of being able to devote their attention to a single issue with less likelihood of being sidetracked by inconsistency. Friends of the Earth does not have a tax policy or healthcare system to explain. Unlike government-centered advocacy organizations, NGOs carry limited historical baggage. No one nurses resentment against having been invaded a century ago by the World Wildlife Fund. The whole NGO sector has enjoyed something of a collective aura of credibility. However, history suggests that auras are not indestructible. NGOs are vulnerable to one another's misdeeds. The variation in credibility is a major reason why so many contemporary public diplomacy actors embrace partnerships, believing that at least one member of a partnership around an issue should be credible to each sector of the population of concern.

Advocacy and cognitive and social bias

As with the process of listening, the work of advocacy is seriously impacted by the limits of human perception: the cognitive and social biases that shape the judgment of all individuals. However, while these biases are the enemies of listening, they are the mechanisms by which effective advocacy works. Public diplomacy advocates rarely think in terms of exploiting biases, but when effective work is examined, these biases can be seen to be in play. Practitioners learn from success, and working to these biases has become second nature as a result of trial and error. Understanding them is one route to building effective campaigns and avoiding unnecessary errors. In revisiting cognitive and social bias, let us repeat the segmentation into "who, what, when, where, why, in what way, by what means."

Cognitive bias: who should advocate

The study of bias reveals that some speakers are more credible than others. Audiences defer to an "authority effect," trusting experts. However, authority varies from place to place and across time. For some audiences, religious authorities have weight; for others, academics impress. The same halo effect that can cloud listening can enhance advocacy, giving a speaker an undeserved credibility even beyond their immediate area of expertise. International actors have learned the value of a celebrity spokesman.[5] A further multiplier of credibility is similarity, the perception that a speaker is the same as the audience member. This was used effectively by the United Kingdom's Foreign and Commonwealth Office in 2009 in a domestic public diplomacy campaign called "Know Before You Go." British consulates in the Mediterranean reported a spate of tourists from the United Kingdom getting into difficulty overseas because they lacked travel insurance. The FCO resolved to turn this around through communication and did some research which discovered a number of things: that most Britons traveled as couples; that it was usually left to the women to buy the insurance; and that a lecture from an official source was unlikely to change behavior. The FCO decided to work through people who would be credible to an audience of young British women and settled on the people known as "WAGs," wives and girlfriends of British soccer players. As summer approached, they discreetly suggested to a number of WAGs that when interviewed by magazines about their summer preparations – skin routines, swimsuit choices and so forth – they include remembering to buy their travel insurance on their list. The initiative worked, significantly diminishing consular problems in the following season.[6]

The bias to similarity is an obvious problem for public diplomats since they are necessarily not like the foreign audiences they wish to reach. This is why strategies that empower someone from the foreign audience to speak on one's behalf are so important.

Cognitive bias: what should be said

The element of cognitive bias which has attracted most scholarly attention is the *frame*. In foreign as in domestic policy, the public's perception of an issue is profoundly influenced by the frame or context in which the issue is presented. Political issues regularly field alternate frames to accentuate the most positive quality that can be associated with the cause. Hence the combatants in the pro-/anti-abortion debate in the United States frame themselves as pro-life and pro-choice respectively. Dueling frames in public diplomacy include the framing of a non-state actor's military campaign as "terrorism" versus a "liberation struggle" or a foreign power's arrival in another's territory as an "intervention" or "invasion" or "police action," or even "liberation." Choosing the optimal frame is like choosing the optimal battlefield in warfare and, as in a physical battle, there is a massive advantage in getting to the field first. One of the most important aspects of crisis diplomacy is to put out the best possible frame for what has happened and the worst possible for one's opponent.[7]

A significant consideration in the shaping what is said is the *availability bias* by which the most memorable piece of information or argument is the one which influences the audience. Sometimes this phenomenon is called "rhyme equals reason" as embedding an argument or claim in a rhyming couplet is one of the most effective ways to make an argument available/ memorable and thereby influential. The succinct couplet "red sky at night, shepherd's delight/red sky in the morning, shepherd's warning" is more memorable than a rambling prose remark about the correlation between sky color and weather. In the same way, a defense attorney's dismissal of a piece of evidence to the jury with the couplet "if the glove don't fit, you must acquit" can cut through all kinds of prosecution verbiage. In some cultures, folk warnings against wartime rhetoric are expressed in these kinds of couplets. "*Kommt der Krieg ins Land/Gibt Lügen wie Sand*" (When war comes to the land/the lies [pile up] like sand).[8] Spain has "*En tiempo de guerra, mentiras por mar y por tierra*" (In wartime [understand], lies [come] by sea and land).[9]

In the era of social media, special attention is paid to the role of *emotion* as a driver of bias. Arguments which connect to a listener's emotions carry much more weight than those operating on cold logic alone. Many communicators look to humor. In 2009, the British Foreign Office achieved some success in dissuading young men from getting drunk and showing off while overseas in Greece by creating a cartoon character called Dick whom they depicted in various situations of excess while his friends, Tom and Harry, looked on with disgust before walking away. The slogan "Don't Be a Dick" was provocative but to the point. The emotional element is complex, playing initially on the humor of the directness of the slogan but then introducing uncertainty as to whether the reader's own behavior might qualify.[10]

Mechanisms to harness emotion include personalization of a situation, sometimes called the *identifiable victim effect*. This effect is based on the observation that an audience may have difficulty dealing with a crisis in the abstract but can be led to strong feelings if a single identifiable victim is introduced to them. The issue of women's education in Pakistan is hardly new, but the emergence of Malala Yousafzai as an identifiable victim served to dramatize the issue in a new way. Similarly, the photograph of the child Aylan Kurdi lying dead on a Turkish beach dramatized the Syrian refugee issue as nothing before. The strongest historical example of the identifiable victim effect is probably the role of a single individual in developing understanding of the Holocaust. Six million dead was too big a number to comprehend, but the publication of the diary of Anne Frank and its dramatization on stage and screen in the 1950s made it possible to comprehend one person's experience so that the Holocaust became real. It is interesting to note that in all three of these examples, the identifiable victim is a child. While there are plenty of examples of adults whose suffering worked in this way, the image of a child is especially powerful because of both the cultural taboo on harming children and the assumption that a child is essentially innocent and above any putative provocation for the suffering in question. Female victimhood has also been used to dramatize international politics. Cases include the two young Cuban women whose stories riled US opinion in the run-up to the Spanish–American war of 1898: the genuine *cause célèbre* Evangelina Cosio and the "fake news" Clemencia Arango.[11] Gender was part of the level of attention extended to Ang San Su Kui in Myanmar/Burma in the 1990s. Publicizing identifiable victims of political persecution of all genders, races, and identities has been a central tactic of human rights NGO Amnesty International.

A final element in considering the "what" of advocacy is a caveat on content. Wise communicators know the value of sometimes understating a message to keep it credible. An artistic example of this is the decision of the advocacy-minded creators of a recent film about drone warfare – *Good Kill* (2014) – to show images from the drone's camera as having much lower resolution than in reality, as a way of remaining credible to the audience.[12]

Cognitive bias: when to say it

As noted in chapter 2, one of the strongest cognitive biases is the *confirmation bias*. There is abundant evidence that audiences are disproportionately influenced by the first information they hear about an issue: all subsequent information is filtered through this with the audience preferring material which confirms their existing idea or perception and, by the same token, resisting information which challenges it. This means that the general answer to "when" in advocacy is "as soon as possible" since otherwise a rival will establish the foundational facts of a case. Moreover, the "what" and "when" should be combined so that the most advantageous frame for the issue at hand is established as soon as possible. There is also a time-related aspect to the availability bias toward memorable information. If a piece of information is heard, it will often be more memorable. Furthermore, people tend to overvalue the last argument heard. For the advocate, this suggests that an argument once made should be regularly repeated. The approach is not necessarily a surefire winner because it is possible that an adversary could "poison the well" and establish a link between the expression of the argument and a negative agenda, so that hearing the argument again merely reminds the listener of the negative. This happened in the United States during the Iraq war when voices in the Islamic world successfully linked the US agenda to unconditional support for Israel and the shoring up of the "apostate regimes" in Egypt to such an extent that US messaging seems to have become counterproductive.[13]

Cognitive bias: where/why to advocate

Cognitive biases also play out in the relative effectiveness of methods: the kinds of channels used to communicate. As noted in the listening chapter, audiences give greater credibility to material which they discover rather than are told directly. This is the *eavesdrop bias*. A famous example of this is Britain's use of the so-called Zimmerman telegram sent by the German foreign minister to his ambassador in Mexico had an immense impact when British intelligence made it available to the US media in 1917: the experience of overhearing a suggestion that Mexico be invited to join the Great War with the promise of Texas, Arizona and other lost territories as compensation was simply explosive and served as a major element in the US entry into that conflict a few weeks later.[14]

Cognitive bias: the ways/means of advocacy

A relevant social bias is the predilection of people to be more convinced of an argument when others appear to agree. This is the *bandwagon effect*, so named because of the practice in old time US elections of candidates hiring a band to sit on a wagon and pulling it through town so that voters could literally "jump on the bandwagon" and ride along with one another to the meeting or polling place. There was an echo of this psychology in the opening line of Frank Sinatra's campaign song for JFK in the 1960 election: "*Everybody's* voting for Jack . . ." This is often exploited in domestic political advocacy through the selective quotation of opinion polling to indicate that one's own side has majority support. It has also been known to be part of international argumentation. Today's international NGOs routinely seek to either build or present a bandwagon around an issue. This is a key tactic of the online campaign platform Avaaz, which launched in 2007.[15]

The final major cognitive biases which can boost the embrace and retention of an argument are those associated with possession: the endowment effect and the participation effect. The endowment effect operates in the same territory as the confirmation bias in that it accounts for the strength of views already held by an audience. The endowment effect holds that with possessions – whether physical (like a chair) or intellectual (like a stereotype) – an individual feels a sense of ownership and will overvalue those things that they already possess, making it harder to sell them a new chair or convince them of an alternative to their stereotype. Even more powerful is an effect which kicks in if the individual had a personal role in creating the chair or had to work in some way to reach the conclusion. Behavioral economists have dubbed this the "IKEA effect," noting that people who have assembled a piece of furniture value it more highly than a piece of equivalent quality available ready-made.[16] A public diplomacy example could be the attachment which many Eastern European audiences felt to the western radio broadcasts which they had to work to receive by countering official jamming while avoiding detection. They became co-creators of the news and treasured it accordingly.

When examined, many campaigns reveal multiple biases at work in favor of the international actor. The remainder of this chapter will consider cases of advocacy looking first at the strategic level at the four core approaches and then at the tactical level, considering individual cases of successful messaging.

Four core strategic approaches to advocacy

There are four essential approaches to advocacy in public diplomacy. The first is the *direct appeal* of speeches and campaign work, which visualizes the immediate reader or listener as the object of influence. The second is the *indirect appeal* which targets opinion makers and imagines a two-step process whereby the opinion maker will pass on the message to a wider audience. The third approach is *crowding the message space*, a strategy which incorporates the other two but which distinguishes itself by an emphasis on the volume of material released. The approach aims to crowd out other approaches and to boost an argument by maximizing the audience's exposure to it, thereby stacking the deck in the debate.[17] The fourth is *partnership*: rather than the actor speaking themselves, they empower others. It can resemble the indirect appeal but participants have greater autonomy and the message becomes a co-creation. Each of these will be illustrated by a suitable example.

Direct messaging by Abraham Lincoln

During the American Civil War, Abraham Lincoln faced a major international communication issue. He knew that if he were to succeed in compelling the Southern states to rejoin the Union, he needed them to be isolated from those capable of bankrolling or supplying their war effort: he needed Europe to remain neutral. This was not an idle concern. European cotton mills were major consumers of Southern cotton, and their owners had a vested interest in continuing trade with the Confederate states. Lincoln's chief method for securing European neutrality was a direct appeal to the people of Europe through a series of open letters to European newspapers. The letters sought to work with ideas of morality which Europeans already had, reframing the Union cause not as an abstract struggle over State's Rights but as an intensely human struggle over the issue of slavery. His international reframing of the cause preceded his explicit reframing of it for domestic audiences, which can be dated from the emancipation proclamation of January 1, 1863.

Lincoln's campaign was helped by stories which resonated powerfully with European audiences, specifically the slave narratives presented in writing (and through the personal appearances by survivors of slavery) which provided identifiable victims, and no less by the dramatization of slavery in fictional works such as Harriet Beecher-Stowe's *Uncle Tom's Cabin*. These were the foundational elements which Lincoln's argument could confirm; these were the endowments in which Europeans were already invested which Lincoln could sharpen and which made the job of the Confederate advocates so much harder. European opinion – especially among working people – surged in support of Lincoln's cause and all thought of backing the Confederates evaporated from the minds of the continent's rulers.[18]

Indirect appeals: NATO and the INF deployment in Europe

In 1975, the Soviet Union began deploying intermediate nuclear forces (INF) in Eastern Europe in the form of the SS20 missile. As NATO had no equivalent missiles in place, Moscow had gained a massive strategic advantage. For the purposes of deterrence and to stimulate serious arms-reduction talks, the United States needed a counter-deployment but faced mounting public opposition to nuclear weapons across Western Europe. In 1979, NATO decided to pursue a "twin-track" policy seeking an arms-reduction agreement while deploying its own INFs in Europe. It fell to the Reagan administration to accomplish the deployment of ground-launched cruise missiles and the Pershing II ballistic missile. To manage a supporting public-diplomacy campaign, the Reagan White House convened a small interagency group, which resolved that arguments in support of the deployment made directly by the United States would be counterproductive and that the case was best made by local voices in European politics and the media. The task of delivering the campaign fell to the new US ambassador to NATO, David M. Abshire. Abshire was the founder of the Center for Strategic and International Studies (CSIS) in Washington, DC and knew not only the European think-tank circuit and key defense journalists but also senior people in the peace movement. The frame for the campaign emphasized that the Soviet SS20s were the real disruption to peace rather than America's plan. Abshire stressed that real peace was more than the absence of war, it was an international system based on respect between countries. In June 1983, Vice-President Bush made a European tour and obtained the necessary agreements for the deployments, which went ahead everywhere as planned except in the Netherlands. While follow-up polls showed that the INF deployments were unpopular, Europeans largely accepted the sincerity of the American approach and were far more worried about other issues of the day, such as the economy. The point was that opinion had shifted enough to allow the missiles to be deployed. The

United States had made a move which compelled the Soviets to negotiate and in retrospect looks like one of the decisive plays in the Cold War confrontation. Abshire received the Distinguished Public Service Medal for his role.[19]

In terms of psychological biases, the campaign's use of European proxies tapped into the power of similarity/affinity and, in the choice of proxy, authority effects. The frame was that of a response to a Russian initiative made to kick-start mutual arms-reduction talks. The campaign did well to limit its objective (tolerance of INF deployment rather than nurturing a love of the Reagan administration), to carefully select the audience (European opinion makers rather than an unwinnable mass audience), and to recruit a credible messenger – Abshire – who was already known to and authoritative for the target audience. Finally, it is also notable that the Reagan administration was not concerned that its public diplomacy be seen to be effective by a domestic American audience, nor that any credit be seen to accrue to the administration as a result.

Crowding the message space: the Blair government and climate change

By the middle of the first decade of the twenty-first century, it was clear to most scientists around the world that the earth's climate was becoming increasingly unstable and that human activity was the likely cause. For the government of Prime Minister Tony Blair in the United Kingdom, providing leadership to draw increased global public attention to the issue was one of the highest communication priorities, alongside counter-extremism, the EU, and the promotion of the knowledge economy which promised to help Britain financially. The Blair government issued a short list of strategic priorities for all elements of British global public engagement including the arms-length units, the BBC, and Britain's cultural relations organization, the British Council. Climate was prominent on the list. Important elements of the campaign included an example of reframing, terming the issue "climate security" rather than "climate change." All elements contributed, crowding the public sphere with statistics, arguments, data, and graphics to build a picture of a closed case and burying the dissenting/denying position. The Foreign Office worked with designers and scientists at the Meteorological Office to create an interactive map to show the problems that would accrue if the world's average climate shifted by only 4°C (7°F). The problems were arrayed on tabs across the bottom of the screen. The user could just click to see where there would be serious issues of fire, crop failure, water shortage, sea-level rise, marine degradation, ice melt, cyclones, and extreme heat.[20] But if there was one British addition to the debate which caught the attention of the world, it was the officially commissioned report issued under the authorship of economist Professor Nicholas Stern in 2007. The Stern Review examined climate change through the new lens of the likely cost of climate change to the world economy and the path of collective development. It was a new way of thinking about the problem which freshened what sometimes seemed like a repetitive argument.[21]

The Stern Review (and much of the material released by the government) worked with multiple forms of credibility to maximize its impact, including the authority effect of employing respected scientific experts to communicate the material and the credibility of the data themselves. The frame of climate security rose above the limits of the "global warming" frame, which was questioned in some quarters whenever there was a cold snap. Moreover, the frame located the challenge in the realm of security, traditionally the highest priority for a government and of obvious relevance to audiences at home and abroad. For all the sober scientific approach, there was an underlying emotional dimension too in the Stern Review, the 4°C map, and other messages. The prediction for a world in which nothing was done to slow the changes was terrifying.

Partnership: the struggle against apartheid in South Africa

In 1948, an election in South Africa returned an extreme government to power, The National Party, representing the white and Afrikaner-speaking minority, enacted a series of laws to ensure the separation of the black, white, and mixed-race citizens of South Africa and to build a country in which white privilege was guaranteed and race was destiny. From the beginning, the system was vigorously opposed, including by the existing party of anti-colonial resistance, the African National Congress. The ANC worked with South Africans overseas, especially in the United Kingdom, to generate international support for the cause through publicity, protest, and a boycott of South African products. In 1960, the South African government moved to clamp down on dissent. In March, police opened fire on a crowd of protestors in Sharpeville near Johannesburg, and international attention shifted toward South Africa. In New York, the United Nations not only passed resolutions censuring the increasingly rogue nation of South Africa but also set up a bureaucracy to campaign against apartheid, the UN Committee Against Apartheid. This organization, and more especially its offshoot the UN Center Against Apartheid, became the clearing house for international pressure against the regime.

The UN campaign against apartheid was at its heart a partnership. In the first instance, it was sympathetic nation-states who came together to create the center within the UN. Ukraine took the lead, with support from the newly decolonized African nations, the Eastern Europeans, and Nordic countries. The next level of partnership was with the ANC and its rival Pan-Africanist Congress as they struggled for change from exile. Third, the UN linked local anti-apartheid movements. The nature of the campaign with its emphasis on mass-participation protest and boycott was inclusive and rewarding for members. Anti-apartheid seemed to be one of the few places where the energy of the 1960s never dissipated. The campaign required infrastructure for conferences, publications, and lists to register the names of individuals who chose to break the sporting boycott and later the cultural boycott of the country. The chair of the UN operation – an Indian diplomat named E. S. Reddy – realized that the story of Nelson Mandela was one of the greatest assets the campaign possessed, and he crafted what amounted to a relaunch of the campaign in 1978 to coincide with Mandela's sixtieth birthday. "Free Nelson Mandela" became the slogan of a generation. South African government documents reveal that the challenge of the UN Center Against Apartheid was well understood. It was seen as the most serious threat to the apartheid agenda and prompted Pretoria to begin a program of its own propaganda expansion which would prove politically disastrous, leading to the humiliations of the so-called Muldergate or Information scandal.

Major advocacy strategies at play in the partnership against apartheid include: authority in the use of the UN as an imprint for materials sourced by the liberation movement, which would not have been credible if published directly; the identifiable victim effect attached to Nelson Mandela; and the participation bias inasmuch as mass participation in the marches and boycotts of the corporations with links to South Africa like Barclays Bank and Shell Oil gave an unprecedented number of individuals the feeling that they were part of the struggle. As the security situation in South Africa changed their tune and deteriorated in the mid-1980s, Pretoria's old apologists in Washington enacted economic sanctions. A path to a negotiated solution and an eventual end to apartheid duly opened.[22]

An integrated strategy: Churchill draws the United States toward World War II

By 1940, Britain had a major problem. It faced the combined strength of Germany and Italy in Europe and the threat of Japan in the Pacific all but alone. The new prime minister, Winston Churchill, knew that Britain needed US aid to survive and US intervention to win the war, but he also knew that a clumsy propaganda campaign to sell the war to the neutral American public would be counterproductive. Americans blamed Britain for its entry into the Great War and were in no hurry to return to the battlefield. Fortunately, with this in mind the British government had already launched a wide-ranging campaign of public engagement, crafted to avoid alarming the United States but to get the message across nonetheless.

The first rule of the British campaign was to avoid direct appeals. While a few were made – as when in February 1941 Churchill broadcast the message to the United States, "Give us the tools and we will finish the job" – such appeals were used sparingly and only later in the process. The British preferred to work indirectly. The Ministry of Information established a British Information Service in the United States to respond to media and public interest in the United Kingdom and its war effort, and worked to empower American voices to speak on Britain's behalf whenever possible. The most significant voice was that of Edward R. Murrow, the London correspondent of the Columbia Broadcasting System (CBS) who was given special access to allow coverage of the Blitz on London. Britain certainly crowded the media space with all manner of multimedia products dramatizing British experience and explaining the country's agenda including radio broadcasts, novels, documentary and fiction films, novels, and even poems. There was no shortage of partners in the cause. Britain found allies among the US upper class who founded pressure groups like the Fight for Freedom committee; Britain partnered with Hollywood, helping the studios create their own accounts of Britain's struggle such as *Mrs. Miniver* (1942); Britain partnered with allied governments in exile and ultimately with President Roosevelt himself. In the summer of 1941, Churchill signed Roosevelt's Atlantic Charter, committing the United Kingdom and the United States in an idealistic internationalist agenda to make the post-war world a better place.

As one might expect, the eclectic campaign capitalized on a wide range of social and cognitive biases. The American voices empowered by the British had the advantage of similarity for audiences, and for similar reasons the British looked to allied exiles to address their diaspora populations within the United States. Participation in the aid for Britain movement gave Americans a sense of ownership of a struggle that initially seemed far away. Britain was able to nullify the impact of the traditional mistrust of its imperial and classist past by emphasizing what amounted to a new brand: a people's country fighting a people's war. Churchill even took personal advantage of the eavesdrop effect. Rather than speak to America directly, he preferred to speak to the British people and arrange for the radio relays so that the US public could overhear the magnificent spectacle of his rallying his people to their duty. His hopes for a US audience bubble to the surface from time to time, as in his "fight them on the beaches" speech which self-consciously evokes the point "in God's good time" when "the New World, with all its power and might, steps forth to the rescue and the liberation of the old." Ultimately, the key to this campaign was emotion. Hitler had long since given the United States something to hate, but British engagement gave the country something to love. By the fall of 1941, US support for Britain had escalated to the level of undeclared naval war in the Atlantic. The Japanese attack on Pearl Harbor merely sealed the deal.[23]

The temptation of the covert

It is fascinating to note that all five of these cases allegedly included some form of covert activity. We now know that Lincoln certainly did not trust everything to direct appeal. The US minister to Belgium, Henry Shelton Sanford, was quite ready to bribe journalists and subsidized European newspapers that supported his cause.[24] NATO's INF campaign included smearing opponents of nuclear weapons as stooges of Moscow, which did not always help the tone of the discussion. In addition, activists were sure that CIA provocateurs had been infiltrated into such high-profile anti-nuclear activities as the women's peace camp outside the US airbase at Greenham Common in Oxfordshire to artificially divide the movement.[25] The covert dimension of the struggle against apartheid (beside the ANC's guerrilla campaign) included infiltration of propaganda materials into South Africa and rigid control of their own members. Even Britain's campaign in the United States before Pearl Harbor involved covert activity that included rigging opinion polls to try and synthesize a bandwagon effect; the faking and leaking of Nazi plans to divide a conquered Latin America; and attempts to dig up dirt on Britain's detractors.[26] Only Blair's climate campaign seems to have been wholly overt. Although the so-called "Climategate" email hack of November 2009 claimed to have found evidence that the climate scientists at the University of East Anglia, who gave the Blair government its data, were covertly manipulating material, this was found not to be the case. The distortion was on the part of those presenting the hacked material who cherry-picked quotes to undermine credibility.[27] This record of the intrusion of covert activities into overt engagement suggests that advocates need to be aware that, even within their own camp, their benign approach is unlikely to be the only game in town. Due diligence might include obtaining a guarantee from their own side against counterproductive "plan Bs." More than this, advocates should expect attacks alleging covert activity on their own part. The antidote lies in building a reputation for openness and credibility. While openness cannot be expected of the CIA or its equivalents, Britain's "Climategate" scientists would have fared better if they had been more transparent with their data. Their reputation for secrecy laid them open to people believing the worst when the hacked material was first circulated and reported.

Meet the meme: the tactical level of messaging

These examples have considered advocacy at the strategic/campaign level. What about the tactical level? Successful messages have a life of their own and it is not surprising that a helpful way of considering them should have been borrowed from the realm of biology. In his classic 1976 book *The Selfish Gene*, the evolutionary theorist Richard Dawkins suggested there should be a term analogous to the biological term "gene to refer to cultural characteristics which reproduce and spread though time." He proposed that such a cultural unit should be called a meme. The development of the digital sphere has created a fertile environment for the transmission of memes and the term has indeed become synonymous with micro-genres of humor shared online. The term need not be limited to this. A meme could be any shared or imitated cultural form including a map, a statistic, an image, and at any scale from something small (like the word "meme") to something much broader like the human practice of correlating concepts and patterns of vocalization: language itself. In biology – as Dawkins's mantra has it – "mutation is random but selection is not." This is not the case in the cultural sphere. While the appeal of some memes does seem to be random, successful memes share many qualities, and powerful messages may be designed.[28]

One readily adaptable blueprint for how an advocate might craft messages has been outlined by brothers Chip and Dan Heath in their book *Made to Stick*. In the first instance, they argue that a successful message should be simple, seeking out the essence of the issue at hand.[29] They noted that the best messages have a quality of unexpectedness to distinguish themselves from the noise competing for an audience's attention. Successful messages need to be concrete, with a clear point, and to be credible (in origin and content). As with the matrix of cognitive biases, emotion figures prominently as a multiplier of "stickiness." Messages have emotional power when they resonate with archetypes of identification pushing buttons of empathy, nostalgia, and, perhaps most potently in contemporary western political messaging, fear.[30] Finally, for a message to survive, it helps if it can be embedded in a story. Stories are memorable, rewarding to the speaker and listener, and can be easily reproduced. A message which hits all these marks is well equipped to survive, prosper, and succeed. Heath and Heath underline the point by ensuring that the initials of the qualities – Simplicity, Unexpectedness, Concreteness, Credibility, Emotional, Stories and Success – themselves spell the word "success," which fits nicely enough with their formula.

Heath and Heath's formula can be seen at work in messaging across history. Take for example the challenge faced by the anti-slavery activists a generation before the birth of Lincoln. Their most effective meme was probably a diagram showing how hundreds of slaves were packed into a slave ship. The image was simple: it was easy to work out what was going on. The unexpectedness came from its appropriation of the visual genre of a plan rather than the types of image more typically used in anti-slavery. The movement's logo, for example, was a cameo of a stylized slave in chains kneeling in petition for mercy. The plan image was concrete: a powerful statement of the reduction of fellow human beings to the level of a cargo, a cargo packed with unimaginable cruelty. The image conformed to previous descriptions of slavery's "middle passage" and hence was credible in content. It was also credible because of social context, being provided by the authority of trusted leaders and passed between fellow members of the abolitionist movement who were linked by the similarities of an existing commitment to the cause and most likely a shared religious faith. The emotional content was based on the shock of recognition of the humanity of the people shown in the diagram. The chart embodied the stories of the millions of people who had already been transported that way, and itself became part of the stories and – in time – histories. The diagram has transcended its beginnings to become a standard textbook illustration and is often presented as if it were part of an obscene how-to manual for slave traders, rather than an element in the anti-slavery campaign.[31]

A similarly powerful meme from the British campaign against American neutrality in World War II was a photograph of young girl called Eileen Dunne in a hospital bed, wounded in a German air raid, staring in shock at the camera. It was a clear image, uncluttered by surrounding details. Its unexpectedness as an image of war was that it showed a suffering civilian and not a defiant warrior in uniform. It had an unexpected and haunting directness, a tribute undoubtedly to its maker, the fashion photographer Cecil Beaton, who had redirected his talents to help the war effort. It was concrete as a picture of right and wrong. It was certainly credible;

photographs were seen as having an immediacy and an inherent reliability, and there is special credibility given to a child, a clear identifiable victim. The emotional impact was the extension of empathy for the child. It became a cover of *Life* magazine. It was used by the Allied movement as a poster and was included in war photography exhibitions. Its theme, the victimization of children in war, was echoed in Hollywood movies of the era.[32]

The emotions struck by a successful meme need not be anguished as the Canadians demonstrated during their so-called Turbot War of 1995. In March 1995, Canadian forces captured the Spanish trawler *Estai* fishing off the Grand Banks and salvaged its trawl nets which had a mesh smaller than that allowed under Canadian law. Rather than attempt to raise interest in the case through a dry press release or a speech in the Canadian parliament, fisheries minister Brian Tobin resolved to do something dramatic. He rented a barge and sailed it past UN headquarters in New York with the net hanging from a giant crane behind him and a microphone in his hand, conducting an improvised press conference. The issue was clear; the presentation was certainly surprising and the case was concrete: Tobin had the net on display. It was a credible message: Tobin had the authority of a minister and the evidence was there for anyone to see. The emotional element was in the humor inherent in the scene and the indignation that any open-minded observer would feel on reflection. It proved a winning combination. The stunt was inherently newsworthy and attracted attention to the issue. Spain and its defenders at the European Union (EU) came under unprecedented pressure to mend their ways. Spain struck back with visa sanctions against Canada and the Canadians increased enforcement at sea. As tensions escalated, the EU switched its attitude and pressed Spain to negotiate. The parties to the dispute reached a mutually acceptable settlement in mid-April 1997.[33]

Public diplomacy scholars have paid particular attention to the dimension of narrative not just as an element of a meme but as an overarching mechanism for organizing coherent communication around an issue and building shared meanings with audiences. Alister Miskimmon, Ben O'Loughlin, and Laura Roselle, who have led this approach, have called narratives at this level "strategic narratives."[34]

Advocacy today

Contemporary advocacy is especially identified with digital media as countries scramble to develop messaging for social media platforms. As of 2017, the most popular platform was Twitter with 92 percent of UN member states operating some kind of feed in the name of their leader. Facebook was second with 88 percent and YouTube third with 76 percent. While the leaders seem to prefer Twitter, with its assurance that every message can be seen by a follower, audience numbers are higher on Facebook. In 2017, the most followed leader was Pope Francis; the most prolific author was President Trump; the most retweeted leader was King Salman of Saudi Arabia. The US Department of State was the most followed foreign ministry.[35] Some actors have looked to develop connections that go beyond the one-way. Pioneers in the field include David Saranga, then spokesman of the Israeli consulate in New York, who conducted the world's first government Twitter press conference as early as January 2009 (just two-and-a-half years after the launch of the platform) at the time of a strike against the Gaza Strip called Operation Cast Lead. Exchanges included:

> *@BacklotOPS*: 1 side has to stop. Why continue what hasn't worked (mass arial/grnd retaliation)? Arab Peace Initiative?
>
> *Israelconsulate*: we R pro nego. crntly tlks r held w the PA + tlks on the 2 state soln. we talk only w/ ppl who accept R rt 2 live.

It is debatable whether the Twitter feed itself persuaded anyone but legacy media coverage of the episode helped to identify Israel with technological innovation, which helped.[36]

From 2008 on, there has been a considerable fanfare around digital initiatives from governments.[37] Scholars such as Corneliu Bjola and Ilan Manor find little evidence that the technology is yet being widely used by diplomats to build two-way relationships with audiences or do more than push out material.[38] Problems include the unwillingness of many foreign ministries to allow their diplomats full license to engage in dialogue with/on social networks. This falls short of the potential of social media, as if governments were in possession of a supersonic aircraft capable of soaring in three-dimensional space but insisted on driving round on a "two-dimensional" highway system. Yet studies of what governments say or do on social media platforms may be missing the big story: the emergence of a generation of social media creators who are able to communicate across national boundaries and build close relationships with their audiences. We already see some of these creators and their networks becoming international actors in their own right, leaving governments behind. A good example is the Love Army organized by French social media star Jerome Jarre. The organization brings together a number of fellow social media stars to promote dialogue and to raise money for and administer their own development projects, often around issues neglected by others. At the end of December 2017, Love Army was able to raise one million dollars in a single day.[39]

Even in the age of social media, some countries still look to old-fashioned techniques to get their message across. Consider Vladimir Putin's open letter to the United States about Syria placed in the *New York Times* in September 2013: it was a technique used by Lincoln. Similarly, in January and February 2011, the government of China addressed US audiences by running a sixty-second commercial in Times Square, New York built around group portraits of Chinese people who have excelled in various fields: "Stunning Chinese Beauty," "Chinese Wealth," "Award-Winning Chinese Talent," and so forth. As Jian Wang has noted, the commercial, created by the Shanghai office of the advertising agency Lowe and Partners, makes more sense as a symbolic presentation for consumption at home than an effective mechanism for projecting the country. Very few of the fifty celebrities featured in the commercial were recognizable to US audiences and an ad in Times Square is more likely to be seen by tourists than by New Yorkers, but it was an effective way of being seen to assert domestically valued aspects of China's image in a location of immense symbolic meaning to people at home.[40]

Looking at the full sweep of advocacy as an element of public diplomacy today, one is struck by the extent to which public diplomacy now requires partnership. Strategies of empowerment hold particular promise in the social media era. The key question of advocacy has shifted from "What can I say to convince them?" to "Who can I empower to convince them?" Former US Vice-President Al Gore moved beyond his Oscar-winning foray into cinematic advocacy about the climate crisis – *An Inconvenient Truth* (2006) – by using profits from the film to train a network of advocates through an organization now called the Climate Reality Project.[41] In a short cut to the same end, Ketchum, the public relations agency which placed Putin's letter in the *New York Times*, also paid writers ostensibly unconnected to Russia to author pieces encouraging investment in the country for placement in the *Huffington Post* and other online platforms.[42] Strategies of partnership and empowerment have also become central to efforts in countering violent extremism (CVE). The UK government has worked with partners like the London-based "think and do tank," the Institute for Strategic Dialogue, to generate effective online material.[43] The institute's output includes a handy how-to manual for community-based organizations looking to speak effectively online (published in 2016 and funded by Public Safety Canada).[44] Similarly, in the wake of the Obama White House's CVE summit of February 2015, the US administration announced that it would be partnering with other governments and the private sector to support the creation of civil society-led counter-narratives online.[45] Examples of good practice shown at the White House summit included a series of online animated videos created by a young British Muslim and former radical with the pseudonym Abdullah X, who, with the tag "mind of a scholar, heart of a warrior," gave an insider's view on the errors of ISIS/Daesh. Needless to say, Abdullah X was infinitely more credible to the at-risk audience than speeches from outsiders.[46]

While new media have incredible potential for a public diplomacy based on memes and the empowerment of credible voices, the techniques are equally available for an adversary and may even be more damaging if that adversary is willing and/or able to act without ethics. The reason that a massive CVE effort is needed is because jihad became a powerful meme in its own right. The core ideas that Jeffrey Halverson, H. L. Goodall, and Steven Corman termed *The Master Narratives of Islamic Extremism* have been consistent with the best advice of the likes of Heath and Heath and go a long way to explaining the success and extraordinary reach of extreme ideas.[47] This is to say nothing of the impact of disinformation and fake news whose damage to the public sphere has been such a topic of intense debate since 2016. To make matters worse cognitive biases have a final sting in the tail. The same endowment effect which can make people attached to ideas that they have co-created leads them to retain ideas with even more ferocity when they feel these are under attack. Intense advocacy against entrenched ideas seems to be counterproductive for the hardest-line audiences. This is the co-called "backfire effect" identified by Brendan Nyhan and Jason Reifler in 2010.[48]

For all the power of advocacy to address a great issue or project a nation's point of view, practitioners and scholars have long understood that international arguments are not won solely by rhetoric and that international actors benefit from a general reputation for being admirable in a wider way. The wise international actor does not limit its engagement of international audiences to advocacy but develops parallel approaches, such as cultural diplomacy.

4   Culture: The Friendly Persuader

By 2009, Alicia Adams had already distinguished herself as an unusual cultural diplomat. It was not her being a woman or African-American which made her stand out but rather that, in a field which has historically emphasized exporting culture, she was an importer. From the vantage point of vice-president for international programing at the John F. Kennedy Center for the Performing Arts in Washington, DC since the late 1990s, she has worked to enable the arts of the world to be seen in the US capital. Her platform of choice has been the arts festival, a coordinated season of overlapping events using all the Center's venues and exhibit spaces to focus attention on a single subject or, more often, location. Adams's credits included festivals introducing the arts from Africa (African Odyssey 1997–2000), Latin America (AmericArtes, 2003), and China (2005), but in the wake of the attacks of September 11, 2001 there was one festival she wanted to mount above all others: a festival of Arab culture. She wanted to do something to correct the almost total lack of exposure to Arab culture and saturation with stereotypes on the part of US audiences. Despite the possibility of political pushback – the center was funded by Congress – she secured the backing of the Center's president, Michael Kaiser, and began to wait for the right time to launch the project. By 2008, it seemed clear that there would never be a perfect time and she resolved to do the festival anyway, setting aside February and March of 2009 as the target dates. The festival would be called *Arabesque: Arts of the Arab World.*

Building the program for *Arabesque* was a daunting undertaking which required partnership not only with individual performers but also with cultural institutions such as galleries and museums and with ministries of culture across the Middle East. With a US$10 million budget, it brought together performers and exhibits presenting painting, costume, jewelry, calligraphy, and photography. There was also a unique video installation called *Exploratorium* which showcased the Golden Age of Arabic sciences. Theater included *Alive from Palestine: Stories under Occupation* by Ramallah's Al-Kasaba Theater and Cinematheq. Dance companies performing included the Whirling Dervishes of Aleppo and Lebanon's Caracalla Dance Theatre. Music ranged from soloists and small ensembles like Grammy Winners Fathy Salama and Youssou N'Dour of Egypt to the entire Qatar

Philharmonic Orchestra with its resident composer Marcel Khalif, which performed under the baton of Lorin Maazel. Some performances were themselves cultural exchanges, as with *Richard III: An Arab Tragedy*, adapted from Shakespeare by the Kuwaiti writer/director Sulayman Al-Bassam, or the dance performance created by French company Cie La Baraka, whose piece *Allegoria Stanza* mixed contemporary and hip-hop dance with video. Adams's key frame for the festival was to focus not on the idea of the Middle East as distant or exotic but to emphasize shared humanity. She felt this was most clearly demonstrated in a static exhibit mounted in the long gallery at the Center which featured a collection of wedding dresses from across the region. The exhibit presented something that was clearly recognizable and part of a shared experience but also in such diversity as to challenge the notion that Arab culture was any single thing.

One festival cannot work a miracle but Adams was sure that it had an impact. The Kennedy Center itself was sufficiently convinced of the value of the festival format to follow up swiftly with similar festivals focused on India, the Nordics, and Ireland. Sadly, within a few years, repeating a festival of Arab culture became impossible. The upheavals of the Arab Spring left only a few states in the region with strength or self-confidence to participate in international artistic exchanges.[1]

Cultural diplomacy is an actor's engagement of a foreign public through intervention in the cultural field which may include facilitating the export of an aspect of the actor's cultural life.[2] This chapter will consider the historical foundations of this practice, some varieties of terminology and practice, some major instances, and some recurring problems.

Terminology

The initial problem in discussing cultural diplomacy is that "culture" itself is a contested term. In the English language it has evolved over time from early articulation which thought of culture in a qualitative way as the most admirable expressions of a society's beliefs and practices (what is now termed high culture) to include a much broader swathe of the expression of the lived experience of an actor (what is now termed popular culture). The study of its extension onto the diplomatic stage is further complicated by the absence of a single agreed vocabulary.

A variety of terms is used in the field to describe foreign public engagement through culture. The preferred American term – *cultural diplomacy* – emphasizes the relevance of the activity to the mainstream purposes of foreign policy. The preferred UK term – *cultural relations* – implies a more organic process in which the government's role is more facilitative and outcomes may be loosely beneficial rather than specifically goal oriented. In Japan, the preferred term is *cultural exchange*, which emphasizes an idea of mutual learning rather than the assertion of geographically specific human idiosyncrasy as superior. All of these terms act in some way as frames directing arguments in the minds of audiences, funders, and practitioners alike. All cultural diplomacy is seen as an important tool for developing soft power. As outlined in the introduction, the present author sees culture as one of the five core categories of foreign public engagement or public diplomacy. In some countries, the distance from the short-term purposes and structures of advocacy are such that practitioners and local theorists alike assert that their approach to cultural diplomacy is not a subfield under the umbrella term "public diplomacy," but an entirely parallel practice. This claim is an important aspect of Mexican cultural diplomacy, which springs from a society in which the element of intervention in the affairs of another country implicit in the frame of public diplomacy breaks a major historical policy taboo.[3] In terms of international relations theory, cultural diplomacy is an obvious attempt to maximize a nation's soft power of culture and values. In terms of the psychology of bias, it may be seen as working with the halo effect: the phenomenon whereby a perceived excellence in one area encountered first brings benefit to an unrelated area. Edward Corse has even suggested that cultural diplomacy might be a manifestation of the kinds of display used in the animal kingdom to entice mates, ward off rivals, or establish dominance: a peacock's tail.[4]

As with the practice of public diplomacy, the terminology is relatively recent. The concept of a nation building its power through cultural projection was part of German discourse at the start of the twentieth century, though it was termed either *Auswärtige Kulturpolitik* or *Auswärtige Kulturbeziehung* (foreign cultural policy or foreign cultural relations).[5] There are isolated examples of writers using *Kulturdiplomatie* (cultural diplomacy) and the English language translation surfaces in writing from prewar Japan.[6] Its earliest use in English text seems to be in 1954 in a *New York Times* piece by the art critic Aline B. Louchheim, in which she commiserated over the absence of an American presence at that year's Brazilian art biennale. It was one of many pieces on the need to upgrade the official US use of high culture in the Cold War. The extensive cultural interventions of the early Cold War ensured that a term was needed and by the end of the decade the term was used inside the State Department. In 1959, diplomat Robert Thayer wrote a report once again calling for an improved US effort at representing its life and art internationally. The term was widely used within the United States in the 1960s and spread to the United Kingdom in the 1970s where it figured in debate over the need to preserve Britain's mechanisms of cultural engagement in the era of détente and consideration of how joint European cultural outreach might work.[7] But the practice has deeper roots than the terminology.

A short history of cultural diplomacy

Culture is not a static category and, while geographies and proximities have created locally distinct collections of belief and behavior (a specific culture), these local units are always in some kind of transition usually through their relationships with neighbors. From the earliest times cultures have influenced one another. Elements of material culture were transmitted by trade; practices were extended as an intended or unintended consequence of conquest; individuals brought their culture with them when they were part of migrations; and from time to time particular rulers have determined to spread an element of culture to other places. While many of these examples relate to cultural extensions within a territory (such the Roman Emperor Constantine's support for Christianity within his imperium), there are also ancient examples of rulers deliberately extending cultural practice to neighbors, as with the Indian ruler Ashoka the Great's attempts to export Buddhism to neighboring kingdoms including Sri Lanka and Burma/Myanmar. In fact, when examining a culture, the reality is generally based on a history of mixing and exchange with neighbors, even though mythologies tend to emphasize distinctiveness and even purity. The scholar need only consider eclecticism in diets around the world, and the many mutual borrowings of language and syncretism in religion, to realize that humans are borrowers and sharers even if they imagine otherwise.

A key moment for any historian of cultural diplomacy must be the point at which the commonalities of everyday life and belief become of explicit concern to the state. The key European case is that of France. It is a sign of the ultimate triumph of French cultural nationalism that outsiders tend to forget the centrifugal forces within the geographic boundaries of France. The lands north of the Pyrenees and west of the Rhine which roughly define France included extraordinary linguistic variation, including entirely distinct languages like Breton, Catalan, and Basque and the family of languages across the south known as the *langues d'oc* or languages of "oc" (their word for "yes").[8] This diversity led successive governments to seek to regulate language use in the country: milestones include the ordinance signed by Francis I in 1539 establishing French as the language of legal affairs (rather than Latin) or Cardinal Richelieu's decision in 1634 to create the Académie française: the body of forty of the most respected writers and thinkers charged with ensuring the integrity and thereby the "immortality" of the French language. In the royal patent, King Louis XIII cited Richelieu's view that "one of the most glorious proofs of the happiness of a realm is that the sciences and arts flourish within it, and that letters as well as arms are held in esteem, since these constitute one of the chief ornaments of a powerful state."[9] From the days of the revolution of 1789 onward, the repression of alternative languages became a major preoccupation of a state which saw the need to bind its people together in as many ways as possible. The internal stories told about France, its Enlightenment, and the value of its way of life had external consequences. It was a logical extension of decades of projects to bring the residents of France into a single language to adopt policies to extend that language, and the culture associated with it, beyond the borders of France in what became known as the *mission civilisatrice française* (the French civilizing mission). From the nineteenth century on, France has paid the closest attention to cultural projection overseas and cultural protection at home. No other country has attempted such sustained expenditure to match France with its centuries of effort to build and preserve a French-speaking community around the world.[10]

Nineteenth-century foundations

France merely led the way. Nineteenth-century Europe was characterized by many peoples embracing those who shared common cultural traits as compatriots and building nations. The agenda was predictable. They took (or sought) control of the government of their territory through reform or revolution; they embraced a politics which emphasized the superiority of their nation over their neighbors; they worked to extend the "blessings" of their way of life to others. Religious revivals drove missionary movements, and European churches looked to Asia, Africa, and the Pacific for converts. There were intellectual projects to establish schools for nationals living overseas which morphed into mechanisms to model local populations in the image of the cultural source country. There were full-scale imperial projects which explicitly imagined hierarchical structures of authority in which political beliefs and values were harmonized from the top to the bottom. The vocabulary of commonality, which evolved in the fragmented German lands of the eighteenth century around the concept of *kultur*, finally crossed into English. Where once it had been a verb referring to the nurture of a plant, now "culture" became a noun. Writing in his 1873 book *Literature and Dogma: An Essay Toward the Better Appreciation for the Bible*, the poet and critic Matthew Arnold used the term repeatedly and defined it for unfamiliar readers as "the acquainting ourselves with the best that has been known and said in the world, and thus with the history of the human spirit."[11] In 1875, the *Oxford English Dictionary* included the term in this sense.

As culture played a prominent role in national self-imagining, it was only to be expected that it would become a site of rivalry. It is sobering to note that the first phase of systematic international cultural outreach was plainly driven by cultural insecurity and feelings that one's special way of life and its advancement was threatened by the activity of others. The driver was not the government. Private cultural organizations pushed for the extension overseas of cultural markers like language and – as Jessica Geinow-Hecht has documented for Germany – music.[12] The first major organization to preserve and develop a European language and culture abroad was the Alliance française (AF), which was established in 1883 by concerned French citizens, including the writer Jules Verne, scientist Louis Pasteur, and veteran diplomat and father of the Suez Canal Ferdinand de Lesseps.[13] The concept was to create and support a network of citizen schools in cities around the world to provide classes in French language and culture for the children of French families living abroad and their neighbors too. The success of the AF may be judged by the speedy appearance of similar organizations in France's European rivals, such as the Italian *Società* Dante Alighieri, established in 1889. In 1881, private citizens in Germany had already established the Allgemeine Deutsche Schulverein (General German School Association) to run schools overseas for expatriate Germans. This now kicked into high gear. Supporters included the great classical historian and Nobel prizewinner for literature, Theodor Mommsen. From 1908 onward, this society adopted the name it still uses: VDA (Verein für das Deutschtum im Ausland/Association for Germanness Abroad). So began an educational arms race.[14] The impulse to rivalry was so strong that an organization which sought to use the culture of sport as a mechanism to bring people together – the International Olympic Committee, established in 1894 by Baron Pierre de Coubertin – became almost instantly a lightning rod for nationalism. The surge of national feeling that followed the victory of a Greek marathon runner at the 1896 Athens games swelled the ranks of extreme Greek nationalists and hence must be counted among the causes of the war which Greece launched and lost against the Ottoman Empire a year later.[15]

The United States was not above these impulses. American missionary projects, such as the foundation in Beirut in 1866 of the Syria Protestant College (known since 1920 as the American University of Beirut), were as interested in broad cultural influence and development as specific Christian proselytization. Many foreigners were exposed to elements of American culture through commercial channels such as the publication of internationally known writers as Mark Twain or through the showmanship of entrepreneurs such as Buffalo Bill Cody who capitalized on international interest in American life abroad by touring his Wild West Show. The international tours of the African-American choir, the Fisk Jubilee Singers, taught the world of the 1870s such songs as "Swing Low Sweet Chariot" and "Joshua Fit the Battle of Jericho." It should also be noted that one of the drivers of European interest in asserting its cultures for audiences around the world was a mounting impression that the United States was a waking giant of influence and that the story of the coming century would be one of resistance to American influence.[16]

The era of the world wars

In the run up to the Great War, culture became even more prominent in world affairs. American foundations joined the ranks of actors, sponsoring programs with cultural agenda in such fields as education and health. On the outbreak of war, culture was immediately weaponized, with Britain particularly working hard to trade on cultural connections in its bid to draw potential allies away from neutrality. Britain's great writers, including Rudyard Kipling and John Galsworthy, were encouraged to send letters to all and every international acquaintance, stressing the importance of Britain's cause in the hope of capitalizing on their social networks. It was Facebook diplomacy in pen and ink. It helped that the tercentennial of the death of William Shakespeare fell in 1916, giving Britain an extra reason to remind the world of his home country's significance.[17] Following its entry into the war in 1917, the United States took steps to build cultural influence too, opening libraries in some of its most important diplomatic posts and, hardly less interestingly, taking steps to limit the enemy's cultural reach in a form of negative cultural diplomacy. German film distributors found former foreign outlets in Latin America and even Scandinavia suddenly closed to them: a price extracted by the US government to permit the access to such sought-after Hollywood material as the films of Charlie Chaplin.[18]

In the aftermath of the war, international cultural outreach became a major element in reconstruction. There were programs to promote mutual cultural understanding associated with the League of Nations but, more ominously, individual countries explicitly saw culture as a way to build (or rebuild) international prestige. The French government launched a cultural wing of its foreign ministry, Service des oeuvres françaises à l'étranger; Mussolini's Italian government unveiled a network of Italian cultural institutes; and in Moscow the new Bolshevik regime worked through such cultural forms as music, writing, cutting-edge cinema, and exchanges with foreign cultural figures to advance its international agenda. When the regime of Adolf Hitler secured power in Germany, it launched a number of international cultural gambits including outreach to ethnic Germans living outside the country's borders. The multiple threats prompted Britain's decision in 1934 to create a British Council on Cultural Relations Overseas, with an emphasis on teaching English and promoting the culture of parliamentary democracy. US government cultural work was initially limited. The US government didn't initiate a cultural program until the foundation for the State Department's Division of Cultural Relations in 1938, and even then the new unit focused only on building links with Latin America to counter Nazi adventurism in the hemisphere.[19]

Cultural diplomacy came of age during World War II. The combatant powers all sought to use culture as a way to appeal to neutrals and to cement relationships with allies. The Allied governments understood that there would be cultural friction between partners and took steps to explain the nature of one society to the other. Once involved in the war, the United States began adding cultural attachés and libraries to certain embassies, with especial concern for posts in places like Turkey, Iran, and Afghanistan which it suspected would be significant in the post-war period. Of course, it is difficult to credit specific achievements to cultural work. A guest lecture by T. S. Eliot could not have the decisive impact of a beach assault or the capture of a strategic bridge. Edward Corse has uncovered one rare exception, noting that the Swedish foreign minister was so moved by the music at a British Council chamber concert that he agreed to give the British government a prototype of the German V2 rocket which had recently crashed on Swedish territory.[20]

The cultural Cold War

Culture played a prominent role in the Cold War. From the outset, the contending powers realized that they were engaged in a struggle not just for territory but for imagination, and assumed that an idea implanted by or in support of their "side" was a victory. The Soviet Union stepped up its export of music and dance and worked to ensure that, once it had joined the international Olympic movement, sporting success was seen as a testament to the superiority of its system. The United States not only worked to engage international audiences with overt cultural projects like the famous tours by jazz musicians but also attempted covert interventions via the newly created CIA to strengthen the impression of a dynamic non-communist left wing in Western Europe. Secretly subsidized activities included the grouping of writers and thinkers called the Congress for Cultural Freedom and such literary magazines as *Encounter*. The success of these activities was not worth the embarrassment of the exposure of the CIA's role ten years later. Expo grounds became the showcase of Cold War cultural achievement, with the architectural splendor of the exteriors dueling with the treasures on display inside to project an overall picture of the nation. High points included the US pavilions at the Montreal Expo of 1967 and Osaka of 1970, when the architects and designers had the budgets they needed and the US government had space hardware and (in 1970) a moon rock to show. The United Kingdom's big expo hit of the era was getting Mary Quant to design the outfits of its hostesses in Montreal, introducing miniskirts to a global audience.

As the Cold War thawed in the era of détente, there were attempts to use culture as a meeting point – even a joint Soviet–American feature film – and a stepping up of exchanges.[21] In Western Europe, cultural diplomacy became less of an element of Cold War strategy and reinvented itself as a part of the export drive and international development agenda. Agencies also found that they could charge clients for certain services, loosening dependence on government funding. The renewed Cold War of the Reagan years underpinned a final push of activity by the United States but apparent success in the collapse of the Soviet Union at the end of the period left the United States Information Agency without the best justification for its existence and, despite no shortage of work still be done, the US public diplomacy budget went into steep decline.

The era of soft power

The post-Cold War era was not a happy one for US cultural diplomacy. Cultural programs seemed especially hard to justify on Capitol Hill and serious downsizing began. Yet, even as the United States retreated from cultural diplomacy, culture became increasingly central to the discourse of international relations. In 1993, Samuel P. Huntington went so far as to characterize the future of the international system as a "clash of civilizations."[22] Other voices, including the Iranian president Mohammad Khatami and the UN's General Assembly, preferred to speak of a need to facilitate a dialogue of civilizations. In terms of practice, the two most potent ideas were undoubtedly Joseph Nye's soft power and Simon Anholt's recognition of nation brands. Both provided a logic for cultural outreach and underpinned work by familiar players and the exertions of rising powers like China, South Korea, Turkey, Kazakhstan, and the United Arab Emirates, all of whom put immense energy into exhibiting at, and seeking to host, expos. In the twenty-first century, when nongovernmental actors moved to respond where government budgets could not, it was clear that cultural diplomacy remained a significant element of public diplomacy practice.

Evaluating cultural diplomacy

Evaluation of cultural diplomacy has historically been bogged down in the measurement of output rather than outcomes, or a focus on the efficacy of a particular program in a specific location. The British Council did well when, in 2012, it ran a major evaluation exercise under the title *Trust Pays*, which sought to explore not only whether exposure to the United Kingdom's cultural diplomacy outreach increased a foreign individual's trust in the United Kingdom, but also if that correlated with a likelihood of trading with or investing in Britain. The subtitle of the final report summarized the central finding: *How International Cultural Relationships Build Trust in the UK and Underpin the Success of the UK Economy.*[23] The data were collected by polls (mostly online) conducted by Ipsos MORI and YouGov of groups of around a thousand people in ten different countries. The Council was delighted with the results which suggested a dramatic correlation between exposure to the Council's cultural work and trust in the United Kingdom. People who had taken part in some kind of Council programming had levels of trust that were 16 percent higher than that of their peers. In Pakistan, the difference was as high as 26 percent. Moreover, the findings also pointed to a strong link between trust in the United Kingdom and business with it. The correlation between cultural diplomacy work and benefit was sufficiently clear for the report to have been part of arguments in support of cultural work by other countries, suggesting the value in a broader stocktaking in public diplomacy activity for the entire sector and not just the commissioning country.

In a similar vein, in 2017 J. P. Singh of Edinburgh University led a study for the British Council entitled *Soft Power Today: Measuring the Influences and Effects* to see whether strength in the field of soft power (including cultural diplomacy activity) correlated with tangible measures of foreign policy success such as the ability to win votes in the UN General Assembly. His results were dramatic. He found that a country's cultural rank translated into more inward investment and had much the strongest correlation to its ability to win support at the UN compared to hard-power measures of strength. He concluded that "great power influence in international diplomacy is less dependent on their hard power and more on their soft power including their cultural rank and lack of political restrictions." The British Council considered the case for cultural relations work well made.[24]

Types of cultural diplomacy actor

As with other activities in the public diplomacy universe, cultural diplomacy is practiced at multiple levels. National cultural diplomacy agencies are charged with advancing the ends of foreign policy in a general or specific direction through cultural work. The most recent major addition to the lineup is Fond Russkiy Mir (the Russian World Foundation), established in 2007 by President Putin to promote Russian language and Orthodox Christian values around the world. Nation-states have found a range of homes for this kind of work. Some, like the US State Department, entrust culture to a bureau within the foreign ministry. Others, like most European countries, have arm's-length agencies for the purpose, such as Spain's Institute Cervantes or Britain's British Council, which accept loose guidance and partial funding but not editorial control of their output. Germany has both kinds of institution: there is a section for culture within the foreign ministry to oversee the network of embassy cultural attachés,[25] and there is an arm's-length agency – the Goethe Institute – which has promoted German culture and language abroad since 1951. State agencies further afield include the Japan Foundation and the Korea Foundation.

Below the national level are regionally constituted organizations which have historically served to represent minority voices overseas. Some of these organizations are expressions of independence or autonomy campaigns. The international cultural work conducted by Catalonia and Quebec over the years has had this flavor. The German region of Baden-Württemberg (home state to Stuttgart) has an Institut für Auslandsbeziehungen (Institute for International Relations). Despite its local origins, it runs a host of educational and exchange projects around the world as an adjunct of the federal German foreign policy agenda.[26] Scottish cultural initiatives have fallen somewhere between the two and often reflect a branding agenda to promote inward investment. Still more locally, there are many cities which work in the international cultural field, most often as hosts of globally significant cultural events along the lines of the Venice Biennale of Art (established in 1895), which provides a showcase for artists from many locations but is always a showcase for Venice itself.[27] Some individuals have such cultural significance that they can operate as cultural diplomatic actors in their own right: a good example is that of the Canadian pianist Glenn Gould who traveled to the Soviet Union in the 1950s on his own initiative and improved relations between Canada and the USSR in the process.[28]

There are multinational cultural diplomacy actors, like the partnership platform created to promote cooperation between the cultural organizations of European Union members, EUNIC (European Union National Institutes of Culture), which organizes joint European cultural events in many cities around the world. The EU has made an explicit commitment to reaching out through culture. In June 2016, the High Representative of the European Union for Foreign Affairs and Security Policy, Federica Mogherini, declared:

> Culture has to be part and parcel of our foreign policy. Culture is a powerful tool to build bridges between people, notably the youth, and reinforce mutual understanding. It can also be an engine for economic and social development. And as we face common challenges, culture can help all of us, in Europe, Africa, Middle East, Asia, stand together to fight radicalization, and build an alliance of civilizations against those trying to divide us. This is why cultural diplomacy must be more and more at the core of our relationship with today's world.[29]

In a similar vein, there are cultural actors formed around shared language like the Organisation internationale de la Francophonie (OIF) which grew out of the Agence de Coopération Culturelle et Technique (Agency for Cultural and Technical Cooperation) established by 21 former French colonies in 1970.[30]

There are global international organizations working in the cultural sphere. UNESCO (the United Nations Educational, Scientific and Cultural Organization) works on cultural projects of collective value, including those related to cultural development, preservation, and protection.[31] While its constituent members are nation-states, some of its programs engage at the more local and intimate level: for example, UNESCO sponsors an NGO made up of member cities with a special connection to intangible cultural heritage: the intercity Intangible Culture Cooperation Network. The ICCN began in 2004 to support city-level celebrations of cultural forms like music, dance, theater, and cookery. Members include Dubrovnik, Isfahan, Bethlehem, and its founding city of Gangneung in South Korea.[32] There are also international organizations with a smaller remit to work on and through one particular aspect of culture, such as the International Olympic Committee.

In parallel with the international organizations, there are also bilateral cultural diplomacy structures which link two specific countries. Some of America's most important relationships are promoted by such structures, including those with its wartime adversaries/post-war allies Germany and Japan. The US–German relationship is helped by a German–American part-nership program jointly operated by the State Department and the Goethe Institute.[33] The US–Japanese exchange which includes the biennial US–Japan Conference on Cultural and Educational Interchange (CULCON) and the Japan–US Friendship Commission.[34] Similar platforms have been created to help US–China and US–Korea relations.

Nongovernmental organizations have a long history of work in the cultural sphere. The Alliance française is the best example. Since the 1920s, US cultural diplomacy has been helped by so-called binational centers established by expatriate Americans and local community leaders to teach English, run libraries, and promote connections between the host city and the homeland. The first seems to have been in Bangkok in 1925. The centers were especially significant in South America, beginning with a center in Buenos Aires in 1928. By the 1990s, the network included more than a dozen institutions in Argentina alone.[35] The Asia Society, founded in New York in 1956 by Nelson Rockefeller with an agenda which, including the promotion of intercultural understanding between Asia and the West, is able to mount exhibitions and cultural events quite beyond the capacity of state-based actors like the US embassy in Beijing. Asia Society triumphs include its US–China Forum on Arts and Culture, held in Beijing in November 2011, which enlisted the participation of American artists including Yo-Yo Ma, Meryl Streep, and dancer Lil Buck.[36] New cultural diplomacy NGOs spring up all the time to reflect both currents of popular interest and activity and opportunity. Recent additions include an NGO which works to bring together young people in the United States and Cuba who share a love of skateboarding: Cuba Skate.[37] Of course, broadly defined religious organizations can also be considered cultural NGOs.

In recent years, commercial actors have begun to work explicitly in the cultural space, associating themselves with international cultural projects and events as a way of enhancing their brand, sponsoring projects as diverse as sporting events and symphony orchestras. Some brands have gone so far as to actually sponsor the creation of cultural material as an extension of their corporate social responsibility or as elaborate exercises in advertising. An example of the latter occurred in 2001 and 2002 when BMW com-missioned a series of eight short films for internet download directed by well-known directors including Ang Lee, Alejandro González Iñárritu, Guy Ritchie, and Tony Scott. The series starred the British actor Clive Owen as a mysterious driver of a different BMW model in each episode, under the umbrella title *The Hire*. The result attracted an online cult following. Car sales picked up and it provoked prompt imitation in the mainstream film world in the shape of *The Transporter* franchise (also showcasing BMWs as blatant product placement). BMW also engineered its own follow-up in a series of comic books with the publisher Dark Horse. There was, however, a notable absence. Given the close connection between the historical image of the BMW brand and Germany's reputation for excellent engineering, it is fascinating to note that no Germans were involved in the project either on screen or off as actors, directors, producers, composers, or editors, and not a word of German was spoken on screen. The milieu was one of a rootless global culture, as if BMW were embracing a post-national identity.

Finally, as with so many elements of public diplomacy, partnership is an increasingly significant part of cultural diplomacy. Actors increasingly build coalitions, including some or all of the players presented above. The phenomenon is of sufficient importance to be addressed in chapter 8.

But what of the content of cultural diplomacy? What are the core approaches to emerge from decades, or even centuries, of practice?

Core approaches to cultural diplomacy

1 Cultural gift

The most basic approach to cultural diplomacy is the cultural gift. This is when an international actor selects an element of its culture to present to a foreign audience in the hope of exciting admiration or appreciation. Well-known US examples have included tours by such writers as William Faulkner or the Boston Symphony Orchestra's famous visit to Eastern Europe in 1956. A Canadian example would include the art gallery 49th Parallel which the government operated in New York City for some years.[38] An example in British arts diplomacy would be the British Council sending the National Theatre production of *Hamlet* to Belgrade in 2001 or presenting *A Winter's Tale* in Tehran in 2003, complete with "culturally sensitive" staging to ensure no men and women touched on stage,[39] or when the Chinese government sent the classic of Beijing opera – *The Peony Pavilion* – to Sydney Opera House in 2013. The drawback of this approach is that it tends to play into stereotype and that an artistic or cultural element valued by the giver may not necessarily be appreciated or even understood by the recipient. Of course, the "gift" might be chosen to send a message. On the eve of World War II, the British Council sent the Old Vic's productions of

Henry V and *Hamlet* to Mussolini's Italy. Some saw a gesture of appeasement but others read a warning, noting that *Henry V* is Shakespeare's most martial play and the Old Vic's *Hamlet* was played in such a way as to warn Italy of how a peaceful prince (read British society) might react when roused by the sustained injustice of a tyrant (read Mussolini). Either way, there are more reliable ways of sending messages.[40]

2 Cultural information

A second approach to cultural diplomacy is that of cultural information: sharing an unknown dimension of your culture overseas to correct an image. A classic US case is its use of the arts to counter a reputation for racism, as with the officially funded Mediterranean tour of George Gershwin's *Porgy and Bess* in 1954 and 1955.[41] Canadian cases include the international circulation of National Film Board material depicting First Nations' lives and culture.[42] A British Council arts diplomacy example might be an international tour by a new writer, perhaps reflecting a minority community in the United Kingdom. A Chinese example might be work to help foreigners understand the diversity of China so underappreciated internationally. An example of this was the exhibiting of wedding costumes from China's many regional and linguistic groups which formed part of the Festival of China at the Kennedy Center in Washington, DC in 2005. This approach has the advantage of its novelty and challenge to an audience's assumptions but may suffer from a dynamic of being (like the gift) overly one way in its approach to its public. Also, many cultural agencies have encountered political problems when sending cutting-edge material overseas. The frustrations of the State Department, when it attempted to send modern American art overseas in 1946, are well known. Other cases of difficulty include the domestic controversy attending the British Council's export of a provocatively titled play by Mark Ravenhill in 1998. Tony Blair's Minister of Education, David Blunkett opined "I understand it's full of foul language . . . Shakespeare didn't need that, did he?" Blunkett added that even a penny for the British Council was "too much." The British Council defended the play as "great British writing."[43]

3 Cultural capacity building

One important way to ensure relevance to the international audience is to identify and meet one of its needs through a program in cultural capacity building, which can in turn promote understanding, build links and – depending on the field – promote development. The best-known form of this is, of course, language education, a field in which China's Confucius Centers have been making headlines in recent years.[44] In the field of arts diplomacy, the State Department has supported international artists working under the mentorship of the Kennedy Center to learn modern methods of arts management and corporate sponsorship. Canada sponsored university programs in Canadian studies for many years. The British Council has often been involved in wider forms of cultural capacity building; again in theater diplomacy, one could cite workshops for emerging political writers in the Baltic states, or a remarkable visit by Peter Brook to California in 1973, during which he helped to nurture the political theater of California's Mexican-American community: El Teatro Campesino (the theater of the fields). The troop went on to tour internationally on behalf of the US cultural program in 1976.[45] The British Council has a partnership with the Royal Court Theatre in London to develop playwrights around the world based on an annual summer school and projects in foreign locations, including Uganda and Palestine. One does not have to be a national actor to develop capacity. In the 1990s, George Soros's Open Society Foundation and the United Kingdom's National Theatre created the "Seeding a Network" project to build theater and culture among the newer democracies of central and eastern Europe, with events both in London and in the region.[46]

4 Cultural dialogue

The final way in which cultural diplomacy can work is by using culture as a site of exchange and dialogue. Unlike other approaches, the cultural dialogue approach is explicitly two-way and requires the active participation of the other party. Chinese examples include the project called West Heavens which brings together thinkers from India and China to consider the impact of Indian thought on China over the centuries, or indeed the Sino-Indian co-produced film on one of the great characters from that historical exchange the seventh-century traveler and monk Xuanzang.[47] In Canada, the Canadian Fund for International Understanding through Culture (Can4Culture), a nongovernmental alliance, including some of the country's leading museums, has organized a series of four cultural dialogue conferences with China.[48] Recent US State Department initiatives have included funds to bring international performers together in locations like the University of California Los Angeles (UCLA) Center for Intercultural Performance and support for the Pegasus Players project which has brought small groups of youth arts professionals from the Middle East to the United States, and sent their American counterparts to Jordan and Morocco to create work in dialogue with local youth theaters for one another to perform.[49] Building dialogue into cultural diplomacy and cultural diplomacy into dialogue has long been a standard approach of the British Council.[50] Arts festivals are a long-standing venue for the best intercultural cross-fertilization and dialogue. The connection between festivals and cultural diplomacy was explicit in the creation of the Edinburgh International Festival in 1947. The British Council's Scottish representative Henry Harvey Wood co-founded the festival with the Austrian-born opera impresario Rudolf Bing.[51] The drawback of a strategy based on dialogue is that it can be hard to sell to political masters looking for quick wins and unilateral successes.

A well-planned piece of cultural diplomacy can hit all four of these marks.

Genres of cultural diplomacy

There are multiple genres of cultural diplomacy. Arts diplomacy works through such forms as music, fine art (including contributions to international exhibitions), theater and dance diplomacy, and the hosting of international festivals. Current State Department programs working to take American culture overseas include American Music Abroad, DanceMotion, and SmARTpower. Arts diplomacy does not have to be export focused. Many international actors work to bring performers into their own countries. Current US inbound programs include the Center Stage program to bring selected foreign performers to US regional theaters; OneBeat, a musical program which brings international musicians to the United States to learn from one another and then tour (in what its organizers call a blending of two great US institutions: the band camp and the road trip); and the International Writing Program, which brings promising writers from overseas to Iowa to develop their skills and learn something about the United States in the process.

Sport diplomacy can include hosting events, expressing national culture through the propagation of an activity (as Japan, South Korea, and Brazil have done effectively through martial arts) or codifying rules of existing sports (which Britain did a lot during the nineteenth century). Sport can be used as a safe sphere to begin interaction between formerly estranged countries (the US/China ping-pong exchanges are the best-known example), and it is a source of internationally recognizable individuals who can be part of a country's formal or informal soft power, from the professional athlete accepting an embassy speaking tour to the good feeling generated by a particularly friendly group of supporters, like the famous Estonian ice hockey fans.[52]

An important dynamic within cultural diplomacy is heritage and programs based around the recognition and preservation of the cultural value of the engaged society. Heritage projects are sometimes collective, as when UNESCO extends recognition to a site or a particular treasure or – since adopting its Convention on Intangible Cultural Heritage in 2003 – a cultural practice such as dance or handicraft. National actors have long used heritage as a gambit. In early twentieth-century Lebanon, the great powers competed to excavate and preserve elements of the ancient past. Kaiser Wilhelm II personally dispatched a team of archeologists to Baalbek, following a visit in 1898.[53] The United States has long worked to enforce cultural protection conventions. One of its first uses of online cultural diplomacy was a USIA website and database to fight antiquity smuggling. Today, the Department of State maintains an Ambassador's Fund for Cultural Preservation which, while small, has an excellent track record for well-placed interventions. At a time of ongoing tension between the United States and those who claim to speak for the Islamic world, it is especially significant that US funding has been seen to go to the preservation of ancient mosques and Islamic texts.[54]

Other subfields of cultural diplomacy include gastro diplomacy – which works with international actors' culinary cultures. Initiatives might include sending chefs on training/speaking tours of the great culinary institutes, awarding prizes or certification to international-based exponents of one's cuisine. Countries which have placed an especial emphasis on this approach include Thailand and Peru.[55]

Despite its track record, which includes some spectacular successes, cultural diplomacy is prone to a number of recurring problems. Some of these arise from the nature of culture itself. Culture will always be as complex and contradictory as the humans who create and live it and, by this token, frustrating for bureaucracies to manage. In the West at least, there will always be a voice somewhere in society objecting to the spending of public funds on something so frivolous or so connected to this or that "undesirable" trait. Socialism, atheism, and LGBTQ issues have all drawn fire in their time. Senators have attacked the State Department for sending comedians on tour, while the British Council has endured nearly eighty years of bombardment from the *Daily Express*. This is not to say that actors should avoid cultural diplomacy but rather that they should expect criticism and that a firewall of the kind that insulates the British Council and the Goethe Institute from their governments is an excellent idea. For many actors, the implementation of cultural diplomacy has been compromised by political agendas which seek to impose a short-term advocacy agenda on work that would be better presented in an apolitical way, and yet, perhaps because it is difficult to orientate cultural diplomacy to advocacy, it has often had to struggle for funding. The cultural program budget is one of the least supported elements of US public diplomacy, remaining in the vicinity of US$10 million for programs, while broadcasting and exchange have attracted around three-quarters of a billion dollars each.[56]

Cultural agencies have to make difficult choices. A familiar question is where to draw the line between working with an actor's best-known cultural exports and its less-known work which may initially have less appeal to audiences. A country like the United States is many things to many people. Barry Sanders has argued that it is a kind of "avatar" of their fantasy, positive or negative, and in that circumstance reinscribing the same culture that is available through commercial channels may simply be deepening the country's image problems.[57] In a related issue, international actors need also to consider the question of cultural imperialism. A nation which approaches its cultural diplomacy by overemphasizing the "gift" and which perpetually promotes its own cultural excellence may find that it alienates as many people as it attracts.

The advent of digital and then social media has changed the terrain of cultural diplomacy, opening new possibilities for collaboration, new platforms for engagement and, perhaps most seriously, new challenges and obligations to help one's neighbors' citizens cope with the digital world. National agencies, NGOs, and international actors like the Organization for Security and Co-operation in Europe have been involved in projects to build media culture in vulnerable parts of Europe such as the Western Balkans, working to improve media literacy as a hedge against propaganda. To this end, the British Council has expanded the capacity-building elements in its work far beyond the simple teaching of English sees the promotion of "twenty-first-century skills" as a major element in its activity. These skills include: critical thinking and problem solving; collaboration and communication; creativity and imagination; citizenship; digital literacy; student leadership; and personal development.[58]

The final issue for cultural diplomacy is that of the artists or cultural figures themselves. Artists are by their nature protean figures whose creative energy is the antithesis of the cautious approach of formal foreign policy. There is a long history of cultural diplomacy headaches arising from the unexpected behavior of artists. Many of the British Council's worst nightmares were interpersonal. The actor Ralph Richardson and novelist Colin MacInnes both earned spots on a blacklist for bad behavior overseas (one was too rude, the other too drunk and indiscreet). The US nightmares were political. Famous examples include the case of the artist William Weege whose printmaking display at the Venice Biennale of 1970 included his creating and handing out a poster reading "Impeach Nixon."[59] Today, as at its inception, a cultural diplomacy agency is helped if it has a mandate to represent the culture whatever its currents may be rather than to please policy makers. A firewall between a government and its cultural diplomacy arm can head off a world of misunderstanding.

In conclusion, while there is always value to be had from using culture only as a mechanism for self-promotion, to do so is to neglect some of the deeper power in the field. We know that people learn best through participation and develop attachments the same way. Well-chosen projects of collaboration in the cultural field can be the building blocks of peace in some of the most unpromising of situations: the most obvious example is the East–West Divan Orchestra founded by Daniel Barenboim and the late Edward Said to unite musicians of Arab and Jewish origin. The German NGO the Robert Bosch Foundation has worked to encourage such collaborations by awarding an annual film prize specifically for projects made by cross-cultural teams.[60] Cultural agencies have the potential to act as intermediaries empowering others to express themselves and, in so doing, to communicate not the superficial charm of their own culture but to extend its underlying meaning as a system of self-realization. In recognition of this, many international actors have come to emphasize cultural programs which foreground collaboration and, of course, the parallel category of exchange and educational work.

5   Exchange and Education: The Soul of Public Diplomacy

June McMullin had a reason to hate. A citizen of Northern Ireland, in September 1981 her first husband – a police reservist named John Proctor – had been shot dead by terrorists as he left a maternity hospital in Derry/Londonderry where June had just given birth to their second child. But by the time her kids were teens, she had come to realize that something had to change. She enrolled her eldest in a program called the Children's Friendship Project for Northern Ireland (CFPNI), which paired kids from adjoining districts but opposing faith communities in that divided province and sent them to live together in the United States for the summer. The theory was that, amid the alien corn dogs and baseball games, the teens would realize how much they shared with one another and begin friendships that bridged the divide between Catholic/Nationalist and Protestant/Loyalist. So it proved. Moreover, the CFPNI went beyond simply linking the kids. The NGO arranged meetings between their parents following their return to the province and helped to build links across community lines that were as raw as any in the world, ultimately preparing alumni of the program for future leadership roles. The CFPNI had a capacity to take 100–150 children each year, but for a small place like Ulster that soon added up to a significant number. For Mrs McMullin, the program offered a way forward, separating the crime and the man who murdered her husband from the community to which he belonged. After her son's return, she became a volunteer with the Children's Friendship Project, serving from the mid-1990s until her retirement in 2008. For the US civil society backers of the CFPNI, her story was an exemplar of the power of their project; it also speaks to the value of exchanges as tools of public diplomacy.[1]

Human societies have long understood that one of the most effective ways to communicate something really significant and complex such as a culture, a value system, or a skill to an outsider was to embed that outsider in an environment rich with that attribute and help them to absorb it through lived experience. Such activity engineers for outsiders the natural process by which insiders had acquired the culture, value system, or skill in the first place. Languages have often been taught this way. The advantage of this approach of teaching through lived experience is twofold: the first advantage is the depth of the learning made possible as lessons are internalized by the participant and become second nature; the second advantage is the personal bond created between individual participants. There is no shortage of diplomatic case-study literature to underwrite this phenomenon. This being so, one might ask why it isn't more prominent an international tool. The obvious disadvantage of this exchange approach is in the level of financial resources and especially the time required to accomplish the process, but many still consider the investment not only worthwhile but essential to their long-term wellbeing. The exchange approach is of such significance to the United States government that in the age of Twitter and Facebook it still typically devotes over half a billion dollars of the State Department's budget each year to the work. When exchanges funded by the Defense Department and Department of Education are included, the total exceeds US$1 billion per year.[2]

Foundations

Exchanges are, in terms of the Canadian public diplomacy pyramid, the broad, foundational "relationship building" layer at the base of the entire foreign engagement structure. They operate in the long term. The government role can be active – planning, funding, directing, overseeing – but it is not as intrusive as the role in advocacy or as conductive as that necessary to run a cultural program. Exchanges draw their credibility from their mutual aspect and inherent educational benefit and, if properly designed, minimize the dangers of backfire and other unintended consequences that are part of more high-pressure advocacy approaches. They feel like life because they work through life. Experiences acquired through exchanges become part of the identity of those involved. In terms of cognitive and social biases which work in support of exchange, they trade with similarity and affinity, connecting peers; they trade in participation, making individuals an active part of their own acculturation; and they trade in the endowment effect, positive views established during exchanges that have been shown to last.

Exchanges and international education are offered by many kinds of international actors. The programs run by nation-states are some of the best-known components of public diplomacy. Subnational units like regions and cities can have their own exchange programs. "Sister city" links have sometimes run ahead of national policy or even in opposition to national policy, as with the defiant twinning of cities in the United States and United Kingdom with socialist Nicaragua during the Reagan/Thatcher years.[3] Some international organizations use education and exchange. The United Nations has established the UN University in Tokyo, the University of Peace in Costa Rica, and has a wealth of programs overseen by UNESCO; the European Union has developed procedures to facilitate exchange within the EU and with the world beyond. Private and nongovernmental organizations have always had an important role in exchange – Rotary International has been running youth exchanges since 1929 – and universities often operate as actors in their own right in international space. Finally, exchange and education are areas in which the individual and their choices are of especial significance. People make unilateral decisions to expose themselves to international experiences as scholars, travelers, hosts, and tourists. Bilateral cultural relationships between great nations are built of a multiplicity of such interconnections. Historically, individual exposure and return has had a profound impact on cross-cultural learning. Consider the story of the Japanese nineteenth-century traveler Fukazawa Yukichi. His personal decision to explore Europe and the United States gave him a unique vantage point to interpret the West to Japan and steer Japanese education in new ways.[4] Consider the way in which the great reformer and seventh president of Argentina, Domingo Faustino Sarmiento, brought home his experiences as a traveler/refugee in the 1840s and as Argentina's ambassador to the United States in the 1860s and applied those insights as a pioneer of public education not just in his own country but across his region.[5]

Scholars like international historian Giles Scott-Smith have long noted the ability of exchanges to create valuable networks along which influence and understanding can flow.[6] The nature of contemporary society makes this network aspect of exchanges especially relevant. In today's network society, communication has shifted away from its essentially vertical twentieth-century arrangement whereby information flowed down to the public from particular information providers: governments and media empires. Now information travels horizontally across networks of essentially similar people: doctor to doctor; mother to mother; teenager to teenager; white supremacist to white supremacist; *Star Trek* fan to *Star Trek* fan. Information received in this way is treated less critically than information from old media sources as humans reserve a special credibility for "someone like myself," and a friend's endorsement assists a story from a traditional source. Of course, there are points when the peer-to-peer circles overlap and an individual who exists in two different networks – doctor and *Star Trek* fan – can credibly introduce information from one circle into another. Manuel Castells refers to such an individual as a "switch." International exchange is a mechanism for creating "switches": taking someone from a network of which you are not a member, inducting them into one's own network, and empowering them to speak credibly to their old network on behalf of the new.[7]

Despite the power of the network in the contemporary world, many sponsors of exchanges have failed to understand the need to maintain their networks. They operate with the hope that the network will somehow become self-sustaining and are slow to invest in the maintenance work required to ensure its survival. Attention to simple activities like maintaining an alumni database for the network is an excellent place to start. The cost of such work is a mere fraction of the outlay required to organize the initial act of exchange.

The origins of educational exchanges

The exchange approach has a long and distinguished history. There is a remarkable story told of Bias of Priene which anticipates their power: at a time when Ionia was at odds with the kingdom of Messina, Bias purchased a number of captive Messinian girls in the slave market. To the surprise of his fellow citizens, he educated them as if they were his own daughters and – after some years – sent them back home to their own families. The Messinians sought in return to honor this wise and generous act, but Bias refused their gift of a ceremonial tripod, insisting that the wisdom was that of Apollo and not his own.[8] Centuries later the Roman Republic understood the cultural value of bringing the heirs to neighboring kingdoms to Rome for their schooling. These foreign princes learnt Roman values even as they also served as a kind of hostage. The problem with educating the sons of friendly kings of course was that this merely connected the Republic to the elite in neighboring countries and opportunities for mutual learning were limited.[9]

As centers of learning developed, they became focal points for international exchange and a level of mutual learning. Non-Greeks attended the centers of philosophical education in Athens four centuries before the Common Era. The Greek Empire then exported a great center of education and exchange in the form of the library of Alexandria as part of its effort to spread its civilization around the Mediterranean. The Roman Empire built a chain of schools of law as a way of exporting Roman culture: Alexandria, Athens, Beirut, Caesarea, and Constantinople all had colleges, though the preference still seems to have been for an education in the Eternal City itself. By 370, the numbers were such that the empire needed special laws to cope with the influx of unruly students from Gaul and other outlying areas. Rome was not alone. Other great centers of learning also pulled in scholars from the periphery. In China in 639, the wise Emperor Taizong founded an Institute of Higher Learning which is said to have drawn 8,000 students from among the "barbarian peoples" beyond his empire's borders. India had such institutions as the great monastery at Nalanda which by the 600s drew scholar/pilgrims from China and even Korea to study, including such famous travelers as Xuanzang and Yijing. Similar stories emerged in Islamic lands with institutions such as the university attached to the El-Azhar mosque in Cairo, founded in 975.[10] Northern Europe began to develop its universities in the twelfth and thirteenth centuries. As Helen Waddell revealed in her classic book *The Wandering Scholars of the Middle Ages*, schools were specialized so scholars often moved from one institution to another in search of knowledge in multiple areas.[11] Of course, these institutions still reached only specialists. Contact with ordinary people was found in cases of missionary activity, such as the work of Cyril and Methodius in the Balkans in the late 800s, but their work was the very definition of a one-way cultural process.

Examples of exchanges that were both two-way and at grassroots level can be found in the ancient practice of fosterage. This is seen in many tribal societies around the world and consists of sending children aged seven or so to neighboring villages to be raised to young adulthood and accepting the other villages' children in exchange. The practice was much in evidence in Celtic and Nordic communities and was called *fostir* in Norse language. This is the source of our contemporary English term "foster child." It seems to have helped the transmission of skills and promoted the stability of a shared cultural area held together by bonds of friendship and even intermarriage. Even in the most one-sided examples, the term "exchange" is applicable as the sustained personal contact involved the exchanged person in both learning and necessarily teaching about their culture, heritage, and identity.[12]

There are examples of bilateral exchanges taking place between entire cities. One special example is that of the relationship between the city of Paderborn in Germany and Le Mans in France. Although geographically separated by some 860 kilometers, in the 800s they were both bishoprics of the Frankish Empire, and in 836 their respective bishops, being friends and seeing mutual benefit in a connection, signed a document of *fraternitas Caritatis perpetua*. Paderborn sealed the deal by sending Le Mans the gift of holy relics. What makes the relationship interesting was that the cities remembered their connection and took the trouble to renew it in the 1200s. Moreover, four hundred years later in 1656, when relations between France and the people of German lands had hardened into enmity and French forces were waging the Thirty Years War to the east of the Rhine, the French throne guaranteed the independence of Paderborn. The relationship was marked in the nineteenth century and renewed again with a secular agreement in 1967. It is now celebrated as the most enduring of the intra-European twin-city relationships.[13]

The emergence of modern international education and exchange

By the modern period, international experience was a regular part of a European elite education. Young people from Britain, France, and Germany made a grand tour of the great cultural centers of Europe to round off their knowledge of the world. For countries on the periphery, travel was an essential part of the process of gaining knowledge for national development. The best-known case is that of Tsar Peter the Great, who early in his reign took eighteen months to conduct a Grand Embassy to Western Europe, traveling as incognito as possible for a 2-meter-tall monarch, to study European ways and learn what he could of ship building and other naval arts.[14] Young men from the American colonies also came to glean what they could.

During the nineteenth century, Europe moved actively to export its ideas. The Jesuits had led the way, playing a key role in the two-way movement of ideas between Europe and China.[15] Protestant missionaries followed suit by founding a global network of schools from universities to local primary schools.[16] If the missionaries started the process, governments were not far behind. Imperialism often included the establishment of schools or, as in the case of Thomas Babbington Macauley's tenure on the Supreme Council of British rule in India from 1834–8, a complete redesign of an educational system. Macauley founded universities and technical colleges and also successfully pressed for the imposition of English as the medium of instruction in India, summarily dismissing Indian civilization's learning to date. Indian nationalists still speak bitterly of Macauleyism.[17]

In time, some Europeans looked to a process of mutual learning. The case of Denmark is instructive. Many Danes of the nineteenth century realized that their country needed to learn from its neighbors and looked for opportunities to exchange rather than assert. The entrepreneur J. C. Jacobsen, for example, traveled extensively, learning foreign brewing techniques which he then applied in his business, Carlsberg. Having perfected "probably the finest lager in the world," Jacobsen then plowed the fortune he had made into promoting scientific and intellectual exchange, establishing the Carlsberg Academy in Copenhagen as a permanent site for this. His thinking chimed with an emerging philosophy which considered that there were better ways of conceiving of the world than conquest. Bishop N. F. S. Grundtvig pioneered a vision of practical education for collective betterment at home and abroad. Danish migrants carried his ideas of life-long learning and folk high schools to the New World. In the twentieth century, his approach inspired his countryman Folmer Wisti to establish the Danish Society, not as a mechanism for national assertion – such would have been absurd in 1940 – but rather as a channel for exchange. In 1947, the organization opened branches overseas. In 1989, it changed its name to the Danish Cultural Institute.[18]

The educational heavyweight of educational outreach in the later nine-teenth century was Imperial Germany. The country saw its historically strong university sector as a mechanism for building international influence and spoke of *Auswärtige Kulturpolitik* (foreign cultural politics) as a dimension of foreign policy. Young American scholars eagerly enrolled at German institutions to complete the coveted doctor of philosophy degree, and US schools were developed along German lines and German professors occupied the pinnacles of US learning. Harvard's German psychology pioneer Hugo Munsterberg was the celebrity intellectual of the day and seemed always to be in the US newspapers.[19] Britain feared a loss of influence and eventually opted to create its own system of PhD degrees to try to divert some of the traffic.[20] The atmosphere of competition frustrated some, most especially those who saw history in racialized terms. For Cecil Rhodes, British imperial entrepreneur, the cause of Anglo-Saxon ethnic solidarity was worthy of his fortune. His will endowed the Rhodes Scholarship program to bring young men from the United States, Germany, and the British Empire together at the University of Oxford to study in the belief that they would coalesce into a super elite who could run the world. In time the Rhodes Scholarship evolved along less racist lines including non-white male students from the United States surprisingly early and women, and black Africans disgracefully late: The African-American poet Alain Locke won in 1907, but women were eligible only in 1977 and the first black South African, mathematician Loyiso Nongxa, was selected only in 1978.[21]

The case of the twentieth-century United States

The twentieth century saw the emergence of the United States as a player in international education. The private foundations of the Progressive Era – Carnegie, Rockefeller, and so forth – soon ventured into global educational projects. Early government interventions included the Boxer Scholar program. When the international community imposed a fine on China in punishment for the anti-foreign Boxer Rebellion of 1899–1901, Theodore Roosevelt's administration resolved to spend its share of the money on educating Chinese people. Chinese scholars traveled to the United States to attend universities and American-administered colleges were established in mainland China, one program evolved into Tsinghua University, today one of the most prestigious schools in the world. For a generation, the Boxer Scholars provided a living link between the United States and China; its alumni were prominent in the nationalist leadership of the Chinese Republic. The outcome of the Chinese Civil War in 1949 reduced the value of that investment to the consolation prize of a special relationship with the nationalist government's location of refuge, Taiwan, but the principle was sound.[22]

As with US cultural outreach, the drivers of US exchange before World War II were nongovernmental. As the Great War ended, private organizations like the American Council on Education, the International Institute of Education, and the American Council of Learned Societies sprang up to connect American colleges with the world. Established groups like the American Libraries Association also looked to exchange internationally. They found eager partners on other continents, including the educational offices associated with the League of Nations such as the International Bureau of Education established in Geneva in 1925 and the International Institute on Intellectual Cooperation established in Paris in 1926. By the 1930s, the United States was well established as a destination for students especially from East Asia, and the junior year abroad had begun to be a feature of colleges at home, albeit mainly women's colleges. It was only in the later 1930s that the US government got involved in the process. In 1938, the State Department established a Division of Cultural Relations to develop bilateral relations with Latin America. Its founder Ben Cherrington believed in mutual learning but found himself swimming against the tide as the US government began to see education and exchange as one more element in the extension of American power.[23]

The conclusion of World War II provided a second opportunity for spending a windfall in the cause of international education. A junior senator from Arkansas, William Fulbright, whose life had been transformed by his time at Oxford as a Rhodes Scholar, recognized the potential locked in the US surplus war material remaining in theaters around the world. In the summer of 1946, he added an amendment to the Surplus Property Act of 1944 to allow these funds to be spent on mutual education projects that saw students from partner countries traveling to the United States and US citizens studying overseas. The aspect of mutuality was important. Fulbright understood that his own countrymen were in as much need of education about the world as the reverse. He also understood the domestic political realities of the scheme and the danger that it could be politicized and had the foresight to insist on each bilateral exchange relationship being administered by an apolitical board. As the program developed, its insulation from the excesses of Cold War propaganda was largely preserved. The Fulbright program expanded dramatically in 1961 and in some cases became explicitly bilateral as some major partners, including Germany and Japan, sought to develop a more equal relationship. Thus exchanges established themselves at the core of the US approach to public diplomacy, consolidating connections to strategic partners, building relationships with emerging nations, and even opening new doors with adversaries.[24]

The Cold War thaw of the later 1950s opened the possibility of exchange playing a role in the US relationship with the Soviet Union. Early beneficiaries of Soviet–US exchange included Alexander Yakovlev, who studied at Columbia in 1958 and went on to bring the perspective he gained to bear first as the Soviet Union's long-term ambassador to Canada in the 1970s and then as a key reform-minded member of Mikhail Gorbachev's Politbureau in the 1980s.[25] The East–West Helsinki Accords of 1975 may have recognized the Soviet Union's dominion in the eastern part of Europe but did so at the expense of much wider educational and cultural exchanges. This ensured that, coincident with the stalling of the Soviet economy, a wider cross-section of Soviet citizens had contact with the outside and personal knowledge of the West. Scholars such as Robert English and practitioners like Yale Richmond have seen this as an essential driver of the political changes of the 1980s. It was a massive payoff for US investment in exchanges.[26]

Franco-German reconciliation

Some of the most historically significant exchanges have played out as an accumulation of the efforts of multiple kinds of actors at multiple levels of government. The post-war Franco-German exchanges which laid the human foundation for the political reconciliation and collaboration that became the cornerstone of the European Union began with individual initiatives. In 1945, a Jeusit priest named Jean du Rivau founded a Bureau International de Liaison et de Documentation (BILD), with a German equivalent Gesellschaft für übernationale Zusammenarbeit (GüZ), to promote Franco-German knowledge and understanding. BILD pioneered the exchange of schoolchildren. Around the same time, city leaders looked to be part of reconciliation. In 1947, French and German mayors came together in a Union Internationale de Maires (UIM), who in turn devised a network of "twinning" agreements (called *jumelage* in French and *Städtepartnerschaft* in German). These agreements linked French and German towns of similar size, history, or industry. The first such agreement came in September 1950. In 1948, three German politicians, Carlo Schmid, Fritz Schenk, and Theodor Huess founded a Deutsch-Französisches Institut to work on the relationship. It was only after more than a decade of exchanges, church meetings, sports fixtures, and civic links that the national governments finally sealed the deal. In January 1963, German Chancellor Konrad Adenauer and French President Charles de Gaulle signed the Elysée Treaty which led to the creation of a Franco-German Youth Office (Office Franco-Allemand pour la Jeunesse/Deutsch-Französisches Jungendwerk). Annual participation topped 300,000, and by 1997 five million students, around 70 percent of whom were high-school age, had been exchanged. One analyst called it "the greatest mass migration ever."[27]

Dangers of exchanges/international education

Historical examples are more than precedent for contemporary exchange; they also serve to flag potential problems. Recipients of Roman education have included a number of bona fide villains, such as King Herod Antipas of Judea (bad guy in the Christian Christmas story) and the notorious Seleucid king, Antiochus IV Epiphanes, known as Antiochus the Mad (bad guy in the Jewish Hanukkah story); neither king reflected credit on their Roman mentors, and it is possible that their Roman experiences contributed to their unstable behavior. In our own time, there are cases of the exchange process backfiring. The most notorious case is probably that of the Japanese student Issei Sagawa who suffered a breakdown while studying for a PhD at the Sorbonne in Paris in 1981 and murdered and partially cannibalized a fellow student from the Netherlands. The Japanese government's decision to release Sagawa shortly after his repatriation did little to help Dutch–Japanese relations.[28] Such stories underscore the importance of a careful selection process with an acceptance of the potential psychological strains of exchanges.

The tribal fosterage system also includes a warning. Celtic law stressed the responsibility weighing on the foster parent when they took on the care of another family's child and made it clear that personal honor was at stake if anything went wrong. The ancients understood the potential for neglect or exploitation inherent in the exchange process and took steps to ensure that the welfare of the exchanged person had the utmost priority.[29] In many modern analogues, such as contemporary international study, other issues frequently take priority. Whether in digital-age California or

Iron Age Ireland, exchanges must make the welfare of the exchanged person an absolute priority and point of pride. Australia has placed great store in international education, setting it at the core of its famous Colombo Plan in 1968 and renewing the initiative in our own time, but such initiatives are fragile. In 2009, the violent harassment of Indian students in Melbourne led to a wave of bad feeling in India. Indian filmmakers went so far as to make Australian antisocial behavior the subject of a Bollywood film.[30]

Finally, an enduring problem inherent to exchanges is that a negative experience of the exchanged person can be amplified. There are many examples of people who experienced international education *without* falling in love with the host culture. Members of the African National Congress in exile would joke that a spell in education in the eastern bloc was a surefire way for a person to develop a love for the West and vice versa. Some recipients of exchange grants become actively hostile, the most famous example being the Egyptian nationalist Sayyid Qutb, whose experiences as an exchange visitor in Colorado in 1948 both exaggerated his alarm at US culture and – by turning him into an eyewitness – made him a more credible authority on the subject of the United States.[31] It is difficult to pinpoint the policy implications of the Qutb syndrome. Perhaps he should not have been picked in the first place, but only selecting people who already agree with you seems a rather limiting strategy. Certainly he should have been more carefully programmed and mentored, guided to see life in Colorado in a broader context. Perhaps he should have been listened to during his visit. His experience of racism in segregated 1940s America demonstrated a genuine limit on the international outreach of the United States. His case highlights a real risk that an exchange experience can increase the appeal of one's culture of origin and push the exchanged person back onto the most extreme version of their home culture. An example of this would be the impact of study in Hamburg, Germany, on Mohammed Atta and the so-called Hamburg cell of 9/11 hijackers.[32]

One serious problem with any international experience, from a diplomatic posting to a foreign education, is the challenge of culture shock. While the end result of exposure to a foreign culture is overwhelmingly positive, the path to this desired state is not smooth. There is a distinctive roller-coaster which a traveler must ride as their culture-crossing experience unfolds over time. The initial experience is exhilarating, delivering a two-to-three-week period of stimulating contact with the new culture. There is then a leveling off around a month in, followed by a precipitous decline and a negative reaction to the culture at around the three-month mark. The experience slowly improves until after about a year the person is doing well and performing with all the advantages of knowledge of both their old and new cultures. If they have to return to their culture of origin, the entire curve is repeated in a process of reverse culture shock so that the experience looks like an extended letter "w."[33] The problem is that decisions about the length of an exchange are typically not taken with an awareness of the culture-shock trajectory but with an eye to the budget. The thinking runs like this. If a year-long educational exchange is positive for one person, then four three-month-long exchanges for four people will be better. Culture shock suggests that the opposite is true. Four three-month exchanges will guarantee that one positive experience will be replaced by four negative ones. This is serious as it empowers four people with the authority of firsthand witnesses on their return to their home country. Unfortunately, as budgets shrink a number of international actors are favoring the shorter semester-long experiences.

Pondering these negative examples, we can isolate four commandments of exchange: (1) select candidates carefully; (2) protect candidates from exploitation; (3) design and structure their experience and mentor them to increase the likelihood of the desired policy objective coming to pass, including expectations of culture shock; and (4) understand the value of the relationship which has been established and so keep in touch after the person has returned home.

Types of exchange

Modern exchanges fall across a range of types: (1) higher educational exchanges; (2) leader exchanges; (3) professional exchanges; (4) third-party facilitated exchange; (5) youth exchange and mentorship; (6) online exchanges; (7) development/work experience. The nature and merits of each of these will be considered in turn, with particular reference to their use by the United States. A final section will consider how (8) tourism fits into this matrix of activity.

1 Higher educational exchanges

Educational exchanges are a programmed experience for a young adult which include a period of time in an educational facility in the host country or a specially created educational experience. These began as private-sector activities but in the course of the twentieth century became central planks in the international engagement strategies of many states. In the aftermath of the Great War, academic outreach was one of the techniques that Germany used to rebuild its place in the world. In 1925, the Weimar Republic created a special bureau for the purpose in Berlin known as the Deutscher Akademischer Austauschdienst (German Academic Exchange Service), which – with offices around the world – remains a major element in Germany's public diplomacy. The post-war USSR established Patrice Lumumba University (named for the martyred leader of Congo's independence), now known as People's Friendship University of Russia. Notable graduates include Daniel Ortega, president of Nicaragua, and Mahmoud Abbas, president of the Palestinian Authority. As recent work by Alexey Fominykh has shown, a Russian education continues to exert a considerable pull, especially in Central Asia.[34]

New kinds of educational programs include student mobility projects, such as the European Union's ERASMUS program, which have made universities across the region mutually accessible to study. Also significant is the creation of international campuses of well-known western institutions which have begun to spring up in overseas locations. Milestones include the founding of the United Kingdom's Nottingham University campuses in Semenyih, Malaysia (1999), and Ningbo, China (2004), Australia's Monash campus in Johannesburg, South Africa (2001), and New York University's campus in Abu Dhabi (2008).[35]

2 Leader exchanges

Leader exchanges are a programmed experience for a person identified as having present or future influence in a target society. The experiences tend to be short, typically two or three weeks only. The exchanged persons incorporate a wide range of influential people, though emerging politicians, journalists, and writers are favorite subjects. Leader visits began in an ad hoc way. Early US examples include the so-called "excursion," a six-week long, 41-city, 9,000 kilometer tour of the United States by special train which the US government provided for the leaders of Latin America and the Caribbean in the autumn of 1889 in the run-up to the first Pan-American conference that winter.[36] The Inter-American office created during World War II under Nelson Rockefeller brought South American journalists to the United States for visits but regular State Department use of this genre of exchange dates from the occupation of Germany following the end of World War II when it was used as a way to build links to the country's leaders. Its logic was clear from a State Department survey from 1952, asking which sources of information about the United States Germans found to be the most credible. Fifty percent named "other Germans who have visited" as their first choice. In a climate in which credibility rested with people of the same nation, it made most sense to channel resources into exchange programs that enabled as many influential Germans as possible to speak authoritatively as "Germans who have visited." Educational and leader visits flourished to such an extent that, ten years later, 31 percent of the Bundestag, 53 percent of the Bundesrat, and 70 percent of the West German cabinet had visited the United States on some sort of exchange program.[37] Following its success in reintegrating West Germany into the alliance, leader visits became standard across the map.

Famous recipients of US International Visitor Leader Program (IVLP) grants while still rising stars include Margaret Thatcher and Tony Blair of the United Kingdom, Nicolas Sarkozy of France, Morgan Tsvangirai of Zimbabwe, F. W. De Klerk of South Africa, Anwar Sadat of Egypt, Felipe Calderón of Mexico, and Hamid Karzai of Afghanistan. Incumbent alumni include President Cyril Ramaphosa of South Africa (a visitor as a trade union leader in 1983), Erna Solberg, prime minister of Norway (1996), Donald Tusk, president of the European Council (who visited from Poland in 1995), and Theresa May, prime minister of the United Kingdom (2004). There are examples of cabinets in which half or more of the members are exchange alumni. Indonesia has been especially well served. Chilean politicians may seldom find agreement but in the summer of 2015 representatives of all parties passed a resolution acknowledging gratitude for the IVLP program and its role in supporting Chilean democracy.[38] Purists may question the extent to which such programs are exchanges, given that they are so clearly tools of cultivation; however, the visits are structured to include exposure to ordinary US citizens, who act as volunteer hosts, and connection to peer networks within the United States, both of which add a dimension of local learning to the picture. Recent leader exchange initiatives include the Bush-era Murrow Fellow program to cultivate journalists and the Obama-era launch of YALI (the Young African Leaders Initiative), which pays particular attention to emerging entrepreneurs. Southeast Asia is served by YSEALI (the Young Southeast Asian Leaders Initiative) launched in 2013.

The effectiveness of the leader exchange approach may be judged by its adoption by many countries and institutions, including the United Kingdom with its Chevening Program, the European Parliament, and Israel, which has recently initiated a program to seek out bloggers and other opinion formers connected to specific national strengths and bring them to the country, understanding that this is the best way of strategically building knowledge of those elements in Israel's life, such as food, wine, or LGBTQ freedom, which might help build Israeli soft power.[39]

3 Professional exchanges

Professional exchanges are a programmed activity of work or study aimed at a particular career group. Beyond academic exchanges, military links have been especially significant. The Cold War US budget for military exchange at some points overtook even that of the Fulbright program. Today, the United States spends US$100 million per year on its IMET (the International Military Education and Training) program. Indications of value include the fact that many graduates go on to head their own militaries at home.[40] Concerns include the extent to which the United States is hostage to what alumni choose to do in their careers. The US training of military leaders in Latin America in the Cold War remains a source of resentment in countries like Chile, Brazil, and Argentina whose citizens suffered at their hands.

Civilian skills are supported. The United States offers Humphrey Fellowships for mid-career professionals engaged in development work. Another US program – TechWomen – brings women involved in technology in the Middle East and North Africa to Silicon Valley, California for a five-week-long program of mentorship and exchange at the leading US technology companies. The program includes a visit to Washington, DC and was begun during Hillary Clinton's tenure as secretary of state as a way to bring gender issues into public diplomacy. It worked well enough to justify expansion to include women from sub-Saharan Africa.[41]

Programs linking or mentoring professionals operated by other countries include such science- and development-oriented programs as the ITEC (Indian Technical and Economic Cooperation Program) for India, the Nigerian Technical Aid Corps, and Brazil's Science Without Borders program. Some professional programs double up as cultural diplomacy. Cases include the State Department's famous International Writers Program hosted at the University of Iowa, Iowa City. Since 1967, the IWP has brought 25 or so creative writers from around the world together each autumn to develop their own work while getting to know each other. They present their own work in readings and lectures, engage literary communities in the Iowa region and across the United States, and are brought into US publishing networks in a loose program of professional empowerment. Alumni include Nobel laureates for literature Mo Yan of China and Orhan Pamuk of Turkey, participants early in their careers.[42]

4 Third-party facilitated exchange

A third-party facilitated exchange is when an international actor selects representatives from two or more communities that the actor wishes to reconcile or connect with one another. Programs in this category include the Children's Friendship Project for Northern Ireland or the Seeds of Peace camp in Maine, founded by journalist John Wallach in 1993, which each summer brings together children from opposing sides of the Israel/Palestine conflict.[43]

The history of British public diplomacy includes a remarkable case of facilitated exchange: Wilton Park. To begin with, Wilton Park was a prisoner-of-war camp located in a country house not far from London and part of Britain's attempt to turn Germans toward liberal democracy. Camp activities included long discussion sessions for those who were not irredeemable Nazis about how best to build a plural society. When the war ended, prisoners asked for the POW camp to be preserved as a safe space for the rising generation of Germans to discuss politics. The premises were switched to Wiston House, close to Brighton in Sussex, and the conversion went so well that just a few years later the focus changed to include at first French leaders within its scope and then the wider European political class. Wilton Park remains an element in Britain's public diplomacy apparatus, with a mandate to host off-the-record international meetings around the global issues of the day.[44]

5 Youth exchange and mentorship

Youth exchange and mentorship projects provide school-age participants with structured international learning experiences, short of a university-level degree. In recent decades, US exchanges have been targeting younger participants, in part because international travel for younger students is less accessible and in part because of a theory that political ideas can form early in a student's career and a quicker intervention can head off later negative ideas. This could be seen as an attempt to establish a confirmation bias in the mind of the exchanged person for the rest of their life. This has long been the approach of the Rotary Fellowship but is also seen in the US government's FLEX (Future Leader Exchange) programs aimed at post-Soviet Europe and Eurasia since 1993, as well as the Kennedy-Lugar YES (Youth Exchange and Study) exchanges which have been sending teens to and from Muslim countries since 2003. More recent additions include the TechGirls program designed to "empower young girls from the Middle East and North Africa to pursue careers in science and technology." This program includes time learning in the United States through "hands-on skills development" and follow-up sessions at home developing and eventually presenting projects to their own communities. The tech industry support makes TechGirls a case of public/private exchange initiative.[45]

Other kinds of youth exchange include programs focused on reconnecting people from a diaspora with their "homeland." The approach was pioneered by a program called "Birthright Israel" which launched in 1999 and aims to provide any young person of Jewish descent with an opportunity to visit Israel. The model has been taken up elsewhere with copycat programs starting up to serve the Armenian, Greek, Hungarian, and even Palestinian diasporas.[46]

6 Online exchanges

Online exchanges are exchanges based on connection via online platforms (VoIP) or other virtual presence technologies. The coming of online media has raised great hopes of programs being able to deliver exchange-type impact but without the immense cost. The US State Department began experimenting with programs to connect US and foreign classrooms online as early as 2005. The most fruitful approach seems to be to blend online and face-to-face encounters as did the virtual exchange program called "Kansas2Cairo," which introduced architecture students in Cairo to those based at the University of Southern California in Los Angeles. The students worked together in Second Life for three months before meeting in person for a week of direct contact, and connected far more effectively as a result.[47] More than this, the United States has added virtual extensions for some of its best-known programs. The Iowa Writers Program now has a massive open online course (MOOC) to carry some of the experience of Iowa further afield. The State Department has also developed online communities for people who apply to programs like TechGirls or YALI, realizing that the many, many candidates who don't win one of the few exchange places can still be a public diplomacy resource for the United States. The YALI online community includes a blog presenting helpful ideas from experts on such subjects as entrepreneurship.[48]

7 Development/work experience

Certain hybrid forms of exchange have emerged where travel is officially associated with development work of some kind but which also has a secondary public diplomacy impact, building personal links between participants and the destination/recipient country. Such programs include outward-facing national government programs such as the US government's Peace Corps, launched in 1961, or equivalents like Norway's Fredkorpset, now known as FK Norway; supranational programs like the EU Aid Volunteers or UN Volunteers; or private NGOs like Voluntary Service Overseas, launched in the United Kingdom in 1958. Inbound programs include the hosting of foreign volunteers on Israeli kibbutzim. While the kibbutz collective farms had long been part of Israeli life, they became a significant international destination for young people from around the world in the years immediately following the Six-Day War of 1967 and grew to include an estimated third of a million people across two or more decades. The phenomenon included non-Jews and seems to have owed something to a collective desire to make up for mistreatment of Jews in Europe in the past as well as a desire to be part of a collective living experience.[49] Remarkably, some countries have failed to spot the contribution of inbound volunteer and educational projects to their international image. The Japanese government saw its JET (Japan Exchange and Teaching) program as a source of foreign-language teachers and was surprised to learn that participants often developed lifelong attachment to Japan and had become what Emily Metzgar has called a "goodwill goldmine."[50] Evidence of effectiveness may be read in the fact that China launched its equivalent under the auspices of the China Education Association for International Exchange in 2005.[51] The softest end of the development travel spectrum is what has become known as "voluntourism," a practice of spending a week or two which would otherwise be spent on a leisure visit donating work to a good cause overseas. Brands of voluntourism include the "alternative spring break" available to many US and Canadian college students.

8 Tourism

The number of people involved in formally organized exchanges or development-focused projects is, of course, dwarfed by private travel. International tourism – short-term travel and return for leisure purposes – has become a core part of modern life worldwide. Estimates for the size of the tourism sector are impressive: in the vicinity of 1,250,000,000 journeys annually, which averages one trip for every six people on the planet.[52] Despite its size and apparent distance from formal exchange programs, tourism can be included within the brief of public diplomacy in certain circumstances. First, many governments see a tourist's positive experience of a country as part of a location's soft power and therefore seek to promote tourism for political as well as economic reasons through measures ranging from the choice of visa regulations to active courting of visitors through marketing and domestic publicity campaigns to promote hospitality among their home audience. Secondly, governments understand that their own travelers contribute to the country's international image, hence the desire of the British Foreign and Commonwealth Office to rein in the excesses of some of the United Kingdom's visitors overseas. Other countries have attempted to empower their travelers with information and even model answers to use if asked political questions while overseas. The Advertising Council created scripts for American business travelers in the 1950s and, more recently, Israel issued advice for its own travelers on responding effectively to foreigners.[53]

Final thoughts

In an era of international mobility, it is only to be expected that some governments are now questioning the relevance of exchanges designed when global travel was a rarity. Yet global mobility plainly does not necessarily map onto global understanding, and there is still room for exchanges which are engineered specifically to respond to policy needs. Some well-known exchanges have changed to reflect this. Take, for example, the Harkness Fellowship awarded by the Commonwealth Fund of New York. In 1925, the Commonwealth Fund established a scholarship to allow young British scholars and eventually young professionals and scholars from across the British Commonwealth to study in the United States. The concept was one of reciprocating the Rhodes Fellowship. The program flourished for 70 years and nurtured a number of individuals destined to play an important role in promoting mutual Anglo-American understanding, including journalists Alistair Cooke and Harold Evans and historian Hugh Brogan. In 1997, the program abruptly changed tack to focus only on the area of health care, with the understanding that exchange in that area met a greater mutual need than a general academic exchange and was a better fit for the overall agenda of the Commonwealth Fund as a whole.[54] Such evolution makes sense. It is odd to see discussion of fellowships which began with a broad policy purpose and which subsequently acquired social prestige being skewed by the secondary characteristic which they have acquired. This debate is of special significance when public funds are being spent. Such discussion is overdue around many national iterations of the Fulbright Program. That said, it is also important to remember that developing a program to more accurately map to policy goals is not the same thing as politicization.[55]

Deeper questions around contemporary exchanges include their role as potential accelerators of "brain drain" in some portions of the world. Businesses in some areas of the West lobby for expanded international education, not for reasons of global understanding but to ensure a supply of international labor.[56] Then there is the human factor. While the region-building objectives of Europe's ERASMUS program are helped by participants falling in love, marrying, and staying in their exchange location, the policy objectives of many exchanges are undermined by such occurrences. Fulbright has its long-standing obligation to return home for two years before reapplying for a visa to enter the United States. It is only to be expected that transnational education should open a transnational job market to its recipients. Perhaps the danger of brain drain will be mitigated by the development of transnational campuses. The concern has certainly been a driver for some western countries moving away from models of international education requiring travel to the source country. Of course, the real solution to the brain drain is to ensure a circulation of talent and global investment so that personnel are going to regions that can seem like the periphery, rather than just leaving them.

There are questions that emerge from the way we live today. Leisure and education are not the only reasons for citizens to cross borders. International education has yet to catch up with the displacement of populations through war and economic hardship. These populations have immense potential as the connective tissue for global communication and the building of soft power; indeed, they often travel because of the pull of soft power. But conversely they are vulnerable to negative messaging. Displaced persons are an obvious target for those seeking to recruit extremists and are not helped to resist such overtures by negative experiences in their countries of refuge. The current tendency of certain western governments to treat asylum seekers at arm's length is at odds with some cases from the past. During World War II, the British Council saw refugees as an opportunity for cultural relations work and used a "home division" to deliver language and cultural programming to Poles and Czechs in the knowledge that they would one day carry the skills and values learned back home and be part of a special relationship between the United Kingdom and those countries. In a similar vein, the positive treatment of refugees from one Latin American country in another, or indeed in Spain, during respective dictatorships has created a web of positive feelings across that region. Some political exiles from Chile even joke about their time on the road as "the Pinochet scholarship."[57] Attention to and cultivation of transnational populations should be a priority for public diplomacy agencies. Their accounts of kindnesses received or values honored in practice would be a powerful testimony to their social networks at home.

Finally, there are problems within the basic structures of exchange. Exchanges seem to work best between peers and be inhibited by the presence of hierarchy. The teacher–pupil dynamic can be an obstacle when the need is for the teacher to learn from the pupil. In cases of great asymmetry of power, the stronger party tends to forget the mutual learning element and see exchanges as a one-way street. Such attitudes underpin resentment of cultural imperialism. The question of how a culturally powerful people might be stimulated to listen to the culturally disadvantaged remains.

6 International Broadcasting: The Struggle for News

In North Korea, Kim Hyeong-soo was one of the lucky ones. A talented biologist, he worked at an elite research institute. But during the 1990s the institute's projects became increasingly tailored to the bizarre obsessions of one man: the North Korean leader, Kim Jong-il. Research included attempts to match the taste of Rothmans cigarettes using tobacco from Africa; to synthesize a working aphrodisiac using the private parts of lions; and to engineer a super-tender steak, while millions of ordinary North Koreans starved. The professor had one lifeline of sanity: international radio. Around 2003, Kim Hyeong-soo acquired a radio and began tuning in not only to broadcasts from South Korea but also to Korean-language programming on two channels funded by the United States government: Voice of America and Radio Free Asia. For six years he listened in secret, burying himself under bedcovers and drawing the blinds in his home to avoid detection by prying neighbors. He soaked up the news of the outside world like a sponge. Then he heard a story that compelled action. One of the bulletins from the United States reported that Kim Jong-il had chosen his youngest son Kim Jong-un as his successor. Any hope of change in North Korea seemed to evaporate. Although then only in his mid-40s, he saw the regime seeking to perpetuate itself beyond his lifetime. He resolved to defect. After one failure, in February 2009 he obtained fake South Korean documents and successfully crossed into the south. He now works for the NGO Stepping Stones, campaigning for human rights north of the border and for Korean reunification. In February 2018, Kim Hyeong-soo recalled his debt to the radio but urged those who want to change North Korea to study the best methods for reaching the people from high-tech USB sticks to low-tech leaflets and paper flyers.[1]

Every now and again, an element of public diplomacy hits a vein of undisputed effectiveness. Many such moments have been claimed for international broadcasting. Consider the testimony of Mikhail Gorbachev, thanking international broadcasters for keeping him informed during the coup attempt of 1992, or the graffiti spotted on a wall near the Russian parliament at the same time: "Thank you Voice of America for telling the truth."[2] Historically, international broadcasting has been one of the most significant elements of global engagement, but by the same token no element has been as challenged by technological change. This chapter will consider the evolution of international broadcasting and its value today. It will look at various types of international broadcasting, the theoretical foundations, and recent developments. The struggle to get the news to the world remains consistent throughout.

Foundations

International broadcasting grew out of many traditional drivers of foreign public engagement. By the mid-twentieth century, an international broadcasting program in one's own and selected foreign languages seemed as essential to a nation-state as a national airline. It was part of the age-old drive to project an image of the state and its leader. The realization that it could be valuable to distribute news – an ongoing commentary on events – predates the electronic media. It was not unusual for those in power to issue decrees and encyclicals inside their domains and some, like the twelfth-century's Holy Roman Emperor Frederick II, wrote to those beyond. The leaders of the early modern period were often concerned that their theological positions be known overseas. England's King James I was a widely read author beyond his frontiers. The power that flowed from providing the world with news was plain even before the Great War. The US government knew what it was to be outside the cartel of European telegraphic news agencies: Reuters of London, Havas from Paris, and Wolffs Telegraphisches Bureau from Berlin.[3] International broadcasting allowed empires to maintain a relationship with their citizens around the world. Like the early cultural institutes, the broadcasters taught language, carried arts, and worked to diffuse cultural values.

International broadcasting has connections to each of the five elements of global engagement. It has a role in listening. In Britain, the BBC Monitoring Service has been an essential element in the country's global engagement since 1939, and the interactive genres of contemporary international broadcasting take listening to a new level. International broadcasting has a role in advocacy, whether in the entire drive of the station or in one element of content, as with the editorials on Voice of America. International broadcasting has a cultural diplomacy responsibility through its cultural content and has also been connected to exchanges, either as a platform or as a source of suitable candidates for exchanges.

While much international broadcasting positions itself as based on verifiable and balanced journalism it is not immune to cognitive bias. As with all media, it works with the confirmation bias, making material available as swiftly as possible. International broadcasting can work by exploiting emotion, authority, or identifiable victims to establish frames in the same way as any other channel of engagement. It has also exploited similarity. Broadcasters have understood that the voice of a fellow countryman is more impactful than a foreigner when telling the home audience what to think. International broadcasters have been great employers of diasporas. International broadcasting has, however, succeeded in two less predictable ways. The first is the eavesdrop. There is a remarkable history in international broadcasting of audiences tuning into and being influenced by programming which was not meant for them. One of the clearest examples is that of the US Armed Forces Network (AFN) whose signals are available in districts surrounding US bases in places like Western Germany and South Korea. US popular music won a substantial following.[4] The second bias which figures in international broadcasting is that of personal involvement: the so-called IKEA effect. The radio listeners of the past had to work hard to get their signal, building homemade aerials and perhaps retuning the receiver during the broadcast to dodge the jammers. It was an active process, closer to fishing than just turning on a tap. The element of risk compounded the experience. It all added up to a potent experiential cocktail. It was hard for international broadcasters to readjust to a post-Cold War environment in which their signal was one of many and the intimacy of the clandestine no longer applied.

International broadcasters can be segmented by the funding model; there are both state-sponsored stations and non-state/commercial stations (where the corporate parent should be regarded as the actor).[5] They can also be differentiated by content. There are advocacy stations, news stations, and surrogate stations (externally created stations that seek to substitute for domestic broadcasters in a particularly restricted market). A final significant type of broadcaster is the counter-hegemonic station which aims at disrupting the predominant flow of news or culture in the international marketplace.[6] As with the elements of public diplomacy, while each of these may be embodied by an entire network, it could also figure as a single program such as when a cultural station includes a news broadcast or a news station integrates music-based programing. There is also a history of international broadcasting being used for out-and-out distortion when its content is crafted to mislead. Before expanding on these approaches, it is helpful to sketch the evolution of international broadcasting.

The history of international broadcasting

The history of international broadcasting began in 1901 when the Italian-Irish scientist Guglielmo Marconi succeeded in transmitting a transatlantic signal wirelessly. As so often with new media, its earliest role in politics was the reputational boost which accrued to the inventor's country of origin and his backers (Italy and Britain in this case, as Ireland was not yet independent) and to the innovative leaders whose messages were carried in early signals (an exchange of greetings between Britain's King Edward VII and President Theodore Roosevelt in 1903).[7] Actual informational use of Marconi's invention did not arise until 1915, when in the midst of the Great War Germany began issuing regular bulletins of war news in Morse code to circumvent British control of the undersea cable. The Russians developed a similar capacity, using the new medium to announce news of their Brest-Litovsk agreement with Germany in 1918. Almost immediately, the propensity for international disputes to be fought out on the air was clear. In 1919, a radio duel saw rival Morse news releases put out by the United States and the new Bolshevik government in Russia. In 1925, Radio Moscow began regular international broadcasts. In May 1926, Moscow attempted to sway Britain's General Strike, but the British government jammed the signal.[8] As the medium found its feet, the government of the Netherlands resolved to make use of the ability of signals in the shortwave band to bounce off the inside of the earth's ionosphere and be received on the other side of the world. Radio Netherlands' service for the Dutch Empire began in 1927; France launched its Poste Colonial in 1931 and Britain its BBC Empire Service in 1932. Religious organizations did likewise. Marconi partnered with the Jesuit order to launch Radio Vatican in 1931.[9] The first US-based shortwave station, W1XAL (known after 1939 as WRUL), was the product of a single individual working as an international actor, pioneer radio engineer Walter Lemmon. While Lemmon could be loosely considered a religious broadcaster (he was inspired by Christian Science), his multilingual station attracted support from other sponsors, including the Rockefeller Foundation, the State Department, and (quite without its founder's knowledge) Britain's Secret Intelligence Service.[10]

Broadcasting had a key role in the run up to World War II. In 1938, the British government decided to begin broadcasts in Arabic as a way to head off Italian influence in the Middle East. Other languages followed. By the end of 1941, Britain broadcast in more than thirty languages with multiple feeds in some, such as Portuguese. The diplomacy of the era, with its crises and emergency summit meetings, was especially well suited to radio coverage, which was exactly why Adolf Hitler did his best to influence the international system in that direction.

The coming of war in Europe brought not only a clash of ideological positions on the air but also a clash of styles. German broadcasts offered a mix of politically slanted news and commentary aimed at demoralizing foreign listeners into surrender. The best-known exponent was William Joyce, the Irish-born broadcaster nicknamed Lord Haw-Haw who berated British listeners with a cocktail of prophecies of defeat and revelations about the drunkenness of their ruling class. Listeners in the United States were treated to Ferdinand Kuhn who delivered regular "letters" full of anti-British invective to his native Iowa. His approach included that standby of the barroom propagandist, inventing dismissive nicknames to belittle adversaries. Churchill was "Roly-poly Windsy" and his predecessor, Chamberlain, was "Umbrella Man."[11] The BBC's own approach was radically different. Although (or because) the country had a reputation for distortion from the Great War, the British broadcasts in World War II emphasized accuracy above all else. International audiences became used to Britain presenting the bad news as well as the good, correcting German claims upward if necessary and avoiding hyperbole, knowing that if the station was believed when times were bad, its reports of the turn of the tide would also be believed. Goebbels saw the threat and ordered the German press not even to dignify British broadcasts with the term "propaganda," but simply to call them lies.[12] Even before the United States had officially entered World War II, the Roosevelt administration understood that it needed an international radio presence on the British model. Within weeks of joining the war, the United States had an international radio station on the air. The German service of what became known as Voice of America began in early 1942 with the simple pledge, "The news may be good. The news may be bad. We shall tell you the truth." Part of America's special strength was the attractiveness of its popular culture and VOA soon added entertainment to its schedule, drawing listeners as a result.[13]

The years following World War II saw further growth in international broadcasting.[14] Newcomers included Kol Israel (Voice of Israel) which launched a multilingual Kol Zion la'Gola (Voice of Zion to the Diaspora) on shortwave in 1950. Postcolonial states with widely heard signals included Egypt's Radio Cairo. In the United States, broadcasters found themselves in the midst of the emerging Cold War. Voice of America was a favorite whipping boy for the anti-communist witch-hunters. Broadcasting across the international fault line justified a proliferation of foreign-language services. It also brought political pressure to compromise journalistic standards of objectivity. In the United Kingdom, the BBC established a listener-driven approach which focused on the needs of audiences in the eastern bloc, respecting their attachment to their countries and leaders, including Stalin. London avoided invective, name-calling, and mockery and focused criticism instead on the problems implementing communism and the conditions that the system imposed on Soviet citizens.[15] Radio France International took a rigidly neutral line in its Cold War broadcasting at de Gaulle's insistence. As a result, it was never jammed by the Russians.[16]

VOA's struggle to present news in a "full and fair" way was helped by the decision of the CIA to launch its own radio stations – Radio Free Europe and Radio Liberty – staffed by exiles to play propaganda hardball. The Hungarian Uprising of 1956 showed the dangers of this approach. Overenthusiastic broadcasters on Radio Free Hungary encouraged actions on the part of the Hungarian public which the US government could not support. In 1960, the outgoing Eisenhower administration codified VOA objectivity, issuing a presidential charter to present the news in a balanced way. The trials of covering Vietnam and Watergate led to the charter gaining the additional strength of law in 1976.[17]

International broadcasting played a major role in the final phase of the Cold War. The western broadcasters, US, British, West German, and French, were a significant part of life in the communist bloc. An estimated 10 percent of the population listened at least once a week, rising to 80 percent in Poland during particular moments of crisis. The stations helped simply by reminding the East that the western system existed and that its people had not forgotten them. Then there were moments when eastern governments failed to cover an important story and citizens either learned the truth on the rumor "grapevine" or through a western channel. The most significant such story was the nuclear meltdown at Chernobyl in Ukraine in April 1986. Moscow's decision to conceal the story, regardless of health risks for their own people, did immense damage to the credibility of the Kremlin. As reform movements gathered pace, foreign reporting of the actions of one movement worked as a catalyst on another, spurring neighbors in a spiral of protest, concession, and reform.[18] For the US broadcasters, the kudos earned from their role in the denouement of the Cold War allowed them to dodge being downsized as a "peace dividend." Reforms in 1994 gave the US government-sponsored international broadcasters their own home under a federally funded Broadcasting Board of Governors, ensuring that some form of state-sponsored international broadcasting would remain a part of US-post-Cold War public diplomacy. The structure was widely criticized, but the audiences largely continued to listen.[19] In the summer of 2018, following a series of institutional reforms, the agency responsible for overseeing the US government's international broadcasting changed its name to the US Agency for Global Media. The new name reflected the extent to which twenty-first-century international broadcasting focused on providing content rather than a specific technological platform.[20]

Advocacy and international broadcasting

Of the various approaches to international broadcasting, direct advocacy is one of the least appealing. Advocacy stations seek only to sell a political agenda with little regard for the listener's interest or attention, making for very dull listening. Classic examples include communist Albania's Radio Tirana, North Korea's Radio Pyongyang and Mao-era Radio Beijing. These stations were apparently so doctrinaire as not to care about their audience. In the United States, Voice of America was expected by Congress to have an advocacy role. Until the 1970s, this function was fulfilled through the output of commentators and certain feature programs. From 1976, the Voice carried editorials expounding elements of US policy. The editorials were disliked by VOA's journalists and language services, who were known to try to dodge the obligation to use them, broadcasting them after the sign off.[21]

International broadcasting can work in concert with other forms of advocacy to advance particular memes among a foreign audience. Consider wartime BBC's "V for Victory." The symbol began as an initiative of Victor de Laveleye, Belgian politician in exile and head of the BBC's Belgian service. In early 1941, Laveleye urged his listeners in his German-occupied homeland to chalk the letter as a defiant piece of graffiti. The meme was taken up by the assistant news editor Douglas Ritchie who broadcast as "Colonel Britton." He strengthened the "V for Victory" by adding an aural version – the Morse code V (. . . –), which by good fortune was also the famous "fate-knocking" motif from the opening of Beethoven's Fifth Symphony. In an ironic appropriation of Germanic culture, the music became the call sign for London's broadcasts to occupied Europe. Winston Churchill added the final element, taking the two-fingered "V for Victory" as his signature gesture. Evidence of its success may be deduced from German attempts to appropriate the symbol for themselves.[22]

In the post-war period, international broadcasting – like other forms of public diplomacy – became associated with more complex issues than simply advocating for the national interest. There was a double meaning when in 1967 the BBC rebranded its external transmissions as a World Service. International broadcasters have advocated for global causes such as health or climate change.[23]

State-sponsored news

Wise international broadcasters have long understood the power of news to accomplish the purposes of advocacy. John Reith, the founding director general of the BBC argued that news is "the shock troops of propaganda."[24] The theory of state-sponsored news is that benefit accrues to the actor from presenting events to a foreign audience in an objective way; that listeners come to trust the source and appreciate the sponsor and that it helps the sponsor if international audiences view world events according to its frames and priorities rather than those of a strategic rival. The best-known such broadcasters are those attached to the twentieth century's great powers: BBC World Service, Deutsche Welle, Radio France International, and Voice of America. Ideally, these institutions have a mandate from their sponsor to cover world events objectively and a clear firewall to protect the broadcasters from political influence. The BBC director-general at the time of the Iraq war of 2003 – Greg Dyke – not only rejected Tony Blair's request to be more supportive of Britain's role in the invasion but did so with an earthy expletive.[25] While some of the state-sponsored broadcasters have opportunities to be briefed on their government's priorities, distance is the norm. France manages its array of outlets from its Ministry of Culture rather than from Foreign Affairs. The French arrangement implicitly frames objective news as a cultural value.

For all its claims to objectivity, news is inevitably colored by its point of origin. One of the major critiques of state-sponsored news is that it is a vehicle for cultural imperialism and was damaging the global South. The case was powerfully made in 1980 by the famous MacBride Report to UNESCO, which warned: "This situation cannot continue without detriment both to international understanding and to cooperation between nations, without affecting the socio-political and socio-cultural conditions prevailing in different countries and without prejudicing the efforts to satisfy the basic needs, to solve the essential problems of the world's populations and to safeguard world peace."[26]

Responses to the critique have varied. The private news agency Reuters (the international broadcaster of print) launched a journalism education initiative for the developing world. The European broadcasters began to broaden their viewpoint beyond the perspective of any one geographical location, embracing an increasingly floating identity and employing a diverse range of voices to do so. The broadcasters evolved toward being international actors in their own right with reputations distinct from that of their countries of origin. While the output may be stronger, it becomes harder to justify spending taxpayer money on work not immediately serving the ends of national promotion. As of 2014, the BBC World Service no longer receives funding from the Foreign Office budget but is paid for out of the domestic British television license fee.[27] Some governments have cut back dramatically. In 2012, following an 80 percent budget cut, Radio Canada International switched to an internet-only service.[28] Radio Netherlands closed its final broadcast service – shortwave Spanish – in 2014 and now works only by creating shareable media on free-speech issues under the new brand of RNW Media.[29]

Surrogates

The third approach to international broadcasting is that of surrogate broadcasting, a form of broadcasting in which an actor engages a foreign public by creating a locally focused service that serves as a substitute for free media (or media friendly to that actor) in that location. The term was devised by the US government-sponsored broadcasters Radio Free Europe/Radio Liberty at the point in the Cold War when they graduated from secret CIA funds to a Congressional grant. Their motive was to explain the distinctiveness of their work from that of a station focused on global news. It was not a new approach. Some of the earliest surrogates were the BBC services established to reach out to German-occupied areas of Europe during World War II. These services made extensive use of refugees. Their most famous broadcasters were politicians in exile such as Christmas Møller of the Danish service or Victor de Laveleye of the Belgian service, while General de Gaulle's broadcasts to France or King Haakon's address to Norway were vital in maintaining the resistance to German occupation.[30] The West was not the only source of surrogate broadcasting. East Germany sponsored Radio Freedom, the radio propaganda service of South Africa's African National Congress.[31] Radio Moscow regularly relayed the voices of leaders of Third World liberation living in exile and accrued much goodwill as a result. Since the end of the Cold War, the United States has diversified its lineup of surrogates, re-tooling Radio Free Europe and Radio Liberty to focus on Central Asia, and adding Radio Free Asia and the Middle East Broadcasting Network – radio and television aimed at audiences in those regions.

While the achievements of surrogate broadcasters are well known, there are risks. Refugee broadcasters can swiftly become detached from life in their country of origin and sometimes speak with yesterday's accents about out-of-date policies. BBC Russian had to learn this lesson early in the Cold War, but it remains one of the critiques of the US government's surrogate broadcasting to Cuba.[32] Because of their news focus, surrogate broadcasters are reluctant to be considered elements of public diplomacy.

Some surrogate broadcasters reach beyond news to such approaches as satire. A show called *Parazit* (Farsi for static), created by Kambiz Hosseini and Saman Arbabi for VOA's Persian News Network in 2009, soon won substantial audiences in Iran. Its broadcasts were supplemented by Facebook posts, online shares, and bootleg distribution on DVD. The mullahs were incensed but could not block the program. In the end, it was the broadcasters themselves who pulled the plug. *Parazit* fell foul of artistic differences between its creators and went off the air in 2011.[33]

Culture

Culture has historically been an important element of international broadcasting. Radio was used to teach language. The website for Germany's Deutsche Welle still includes access to multiple language-education tools.[34] International broadcasters have always included cultural material, sometimes as a way to reward an audience, a spoonful of cultural sugar to help the advocacy medicine go down. The best-known Cold War examples are Voice of America's phenomenally successful jazz program – *Music USA* – hosted by Willis Conover.[35] RIAS TV, the US-sponsored TV arm of the Radio in the American Sector station in West Berlin, launched youth programming in 1988, including an MTV-inspired show called *High Life*.[36] Contemporary culturally driven operations include the Radio Sawa family through which the US government reaches out to the Middle East and the Horn of Africa with a mix of local and international music and news. BBC services have in their time included children's programs, radio drama, and a lot of sports coverage fitting audience demand (cricket for the Commonwealth; soccer and chess for Russia, and so forth). At its best, the cultural component meets a fundamental cultural need of the audience. The BBC program *Caribbean Voices* (1943–1958) was a launchpad for a generation of West Indian writers, including Derek Walcott and Nobel laureate for literature V.S. Naipaul.[37]

As international broadcasters have diversified into podcasts and shareable media, cultural material has remained significant. Deutsche Welle currently has podcasts dedicated to classical music, "faith matters," climate, health, and European culture among other subjects.[38] VOA's new media success stories include a short video program for sharing on Chinese social media called *OMG! Mieyiu*, in which a bubbly young woman from the United States called Jessica Beinecke introduced contemporary slang terms to

Chinese viewers. Especially popular episodes of the show included "Yucky GUNK" which taught colloquial terms for "all of the icky stuff that comes out of your face." Launched in 2012, she soon racked up more than 15 million views.[39]

Broadcasters have created dramas not only to amuse but also to teach. Following the collapse of the Soviet Union, the BBC sponsored the creation of a Russian radio soap, *Dom 7, Podjezd 4* (*House 7, Entrance 4*) for post-communist Russian listeners which dealt with the trials of setting up a business. In October 1997, Tony Blair visited the studio in Moscow to take a guest role as himself.[40] In Rwanda in 2004, a Dutch NGO launched a conflict-resolution-oriented soap opera called *Musekeweya* (New Dawn) which focused on a Hutu/Tutsi romance. Its producers claimed an audience of around 90 percent of the country.[41] Perhaps the best-known edu-soap is *Naway Kor, Naway Jwand* (New Home, New Life), a family drama created by the BBC Afghan service in 1994 to help development in that country. The BBC partnered with local NGOs and international donors including the UN, EU, and foreign ministries of Switzerland and Belgium to maintain production in both Pashto and Dari. They reached more than a third of Afghan adults though local and BBC broadcasts. Achievements include a major role in raising awareness over unexploded mines after a major character was wounded by a mine. In 2012, the show was transferred to a local Afghan partner and hailed as a job well done.[42]

Interestingly, there is no reason for the cultural content to reflect either the culture of the sponsoring actor or the intended audience. The BBC World Service has responded to the international popularity of both jazz and country and western music with its own shows based on the genres, *Jazz Now and Then* and *Country Style*, harnessing US culture to the cause of British international broadcasting. Religious broadcasting can also be a form of culture-based international broadcasting. Religious content or entire religiously oriented stations have historically served to shore up the moral claims of a regime – as was the case with the religious material on Radio Cairo in the 1950s or with Iranian channels today – or of an outsider to indicate cultural respect and respond to local expectation, as was the case when VOA broadcast readings from the Koran in its Arabic service or Orthodox Christian services in its Russian broadcasts up to 1957.[43]

Commercial

For most of the twentieth century, and so long as it relied on shortwave technology, international broadcasting required levels of investment and promised such limited economic gain that for the most part only governments could, or cared to, use the medium. The advent of satellite television changed this. Satellite signals easily transcend frontiers, including enormous swathes of territory in their "footprint." They also make it possible to transmit a more attractive signal: not the shifting tones of a brittle shortwave radio broadcast but the vivid visuals of a television channel with the power to command sufficient audiences to draw advertising revenue. While there was an early effort by the US government to furnish news programming for international satellite and cable systems with its WORLDNET project in the 1980s, it was the commercial station CNN which became a fixture on international platforms.[44] Others followed. The BBC moved into the satellite news business by developing a commercial subsidiary BBC World to avoid claims of UK taxpayer money subsidizing a commercial enterprise. The advent of the commercial international broadcasters raises the question of who should be considered the actor. CNN, MTV, and their like are not the US government but rather behave as actors in their own right, with their own interests and agendas which may certainly overlap with those of the government of their nation of origin, though this cannot be taken for granted.

The internationalization of commercial channels has had serious consequences for government broadcasters who now face a crowded playing field. Commercial interest has led some content providers to pursue what some saw as appeasement of the more difficult regimes, offering sport, nature documentary, or entertainment to allow access to revenue. Ironically, for all the distance of commercial operators from their countries of origin, they are still regularly assumed to be government mouthpieces by audiences in authoritarian societies.[45] Dismissal is a convenient tactic for those who wish to blunt criticism. The explosion in commercial platforms has opened the space for a wider circulation of commercial content from a variety of sources. Latin American and Indian programming had long commanded international audiences but recent years have seen especial success for drama originating in South Korea and Turkey. Twenty-first-century commercial television is not the soft power tool of one country alone.[46]

Counter-hegemonic

The turn of the millennium brought a range of newcomers to the array of international broadcasters: the counter-hegemonic stations, whose avowed aim was to correct the imbalance of news from the global Northwest. Stations like China's English language CCTV9 (which launched in 2000 and since 2017 has been part of the China Global Television Network, now branded as Voice of China) or Russia's Russia Today (established in 2005 and known since 2009 simply as RT) promised to build soft power overseas. Ironically, given the long heritage of French international media, the launch of France 24 in 2006 was also justified domestically as a counter-hegemonic move to contest the power of the English-language media.

The most innovative counter-hegemonic strategy was that of RT, which with the tagline "Question more" selected its stories to subvert the certainties of western life and politics. The station maintained top-notch production values, fielded conspicuously good-looking presenters, and provided air-time for dissenting voices whose views were unwelcome in their domestic mainstream media. As of 2018, the RT stable includes CIA whistle-blower John Kiriakou, *New York Times* veteran Chris Hedges, and British political mavericks like the former London mayor, Ken Livingstone and Scottish firebrand George Galloway, who was previously a regular contributor to Iran's *Press TV*. RT's editor-in-chief Margarita Simoyan portrays her channel as a surrogate service rather than counter-hegemonic, telling *New York* magazine in 2013 that "The news items that play best in the US are the ones directly touching on critical American issues in public policy and politics and that aren't being seriously explored anywhere else."[47]

While RT and Voice of China are explicitly global, some counter-hegemonic stations, such as Venezuela's TeleSur or Qatar's Al Jazeera, aimed initially for regional markets.[48] Al Jazeera showed the power of the approach. The station launched in 1995 when the emir of Qatar hired a group of Arab-language journalists who had been trained for a cancelled BBC Arabic TV service. The channel struck a chord with a regional audience with its coverage of the Anglo-American bombing of Iraq in 1998, successfully breaking the domination of both state media nationally and western media transnationally. Marc Lynch noted the emergence of a virtual public space for region-wide debate in Arabic. Philip Seib called the phenomenon "the Al Jazeera effect" and correctly predicted seismic changes in Middle Eastern politics.[49] Al Jazeera began English broadcasts in 2006 but found difficulties getting access to cable platforms or regular audiences in the United States.[50] Both RT and Al Jazeera extended their audiences by creating shareable items for social media. Al Jazeera – well aware of the negative connotations of its name in certain markets – developed a sub-brand for this work: AJ+. In 2014, AJ+ debuted as a YouTube channel, taking over the facilities of Current TV in San Francisco, it also launched a dedicated smartphone app. By the end of 2015, the channel had won a Webby award for online news coverage and passed the one-billion-views milestone. The channel has been especially praised for its coverage of US–Mexican border issues.[51]

Interactive broadcasting

Not all the varieties of international broadcasting are expressed at the level of entire stations. Interactive broadcasting works as an element within more general services. The best international broadcasters have always understood that their success hinged on their relevance to their audience. Interactive broadcasting has turned the process of listening and responding into a genre of programming. From their earliest days, international broadcasters solicited and responded to letters from listeners. By the 1990s, this had developed into entire programs based around telephone call-ins. Milestones include the day in June 1990 when the BBC World Service placed Prime Minister Margaret Thatcher herself on the air, fielding calls from listeners worldwide for an hour. The brave studio manager on duty took the liberty of fading out the Iron Lady's final answer to keep the World Service on schedule.[52] The United States developed a strand of programs for WORLDNET whereby satellite links could be used to connect local journalists to political figures in the United States. They found that local channels were more likely to use the interview on air if they included interaction with their own journalists. In the early 2000s, the BBC took interactivity to new levels with their "Have your say" strands at home and abroad. Phone-in/email-in programs like *Africa Have Your Say* not only put local voices on the air but allowed listeners to suggest program topics that London-based producers would not have ordinarily considered, such as the taboo topic of suicide.[53]

Resistance and misdirection

Part of the story of international broadcasting has always been attempts to resist its influence. The best-known technique for this is jamming: the broadcasting of a signal on a frequency used by an opponent to drown them out. While this is illegal under international broadcasting law, it became a major part of the landscape during the Cold War. The first post-war offender was Spain. Radio Madrid began jamming Radio Moscow in 1946. The Soviet Union responded in 1948, attempting to block BBC and VOA Russian-language programming. This was sporadically extended to services aimed at their satellite nations. Jamming is a high-risk strategy. Besides its illegality, it concedes an importance to foreign material and gives it the allure of a forbidden fruit, while costing as much or more than the original broadcasting. The unpopularity of jamming was clear from citizen action. One of the first acts of the Polish unrest of 1956 was an attack on the Posnan jamming station. Other methods to blunt international broadcasting have included campaigns to mock listeners or the stations and laws forbidding listening or the passing on of information heard on the air. The Polish government tried negotiation to persuade the Eisenhower administration to rein in Radio Free Europe. In the last resort, actors have used violence against broadcasters. The best-known example of this is the bomb planted at Radio Free Europe's Munich headquarters in February 1981.[54] Today, the struggle is fought out in cyberspace and there is a cat-and-mouse game between countries who wish to limit their citizens' access to international media by building digital walls and countries who circulate software to circumvent those walls.

The final use of international broadcasting – which lies in the realm of psychological warfare – is its use to misdirect an adversary. History has many examples of so-called black propaganda stations which do not merely conceal their origin but develop an entirely false one. Famous examples include the fake German army stations *Gustav Siegfried Eins* and *Soldatensender Calais* established by Britain's Political Warfare Executive in World War II to sow dissent within German ranks.[55] Today websites and Twitter feeds have moved into this space, leading to the controversy over "fake news." The most comprehensive strategy of misdirection is that associated with media of Russian origin which aim not merely to undermine the reputation of other governments and their institutions but to question the nature of reality. The theory is that when people no longer trust reputations or alliances, they look to the strongest man on the stage: if you work for the strongest man on the stage, why bother with the truth?[56]

Contemporary international information management

The reader who is not in possession of either a state broadcaster or a commercial satellite service might question why it is necessary to include a chapter on international broadcasting. The first response to this, as will be seen in chapter 8, is that for those who lack their own capacity to broadcast, another actor's international broadcaster can be an important collaborator. More than this, contemporary international broadcasting has become a hybrid activity which spills into many areas on engagement. It now needs to be imagined in a wider sense as engagement to promote and defend an international public sphere which the actor sees as contiguous with its ideals and underlying interests. Today's international broadcasters are frequently engaged in capacity building, developing journalism, or broadcasting culture in foreign locations. A prime example is the emergence of the BBC

World Service Trust in 1999, now known as BBC Media Action. Many broadcasters collaborate on programing creating material which mixes the global and the local. Governments may also pursue diplomatic strategies which seek to maximize the prospects for the free exchange of global information as with the discussion around internet governance and the work of the Internet Corporation for Assigned Names and Numbers (ICANN) to maintain a multi-stakeholder approach to the oversight of the internet.

More controversially, contemporary conceptions of international information management include so-called information intervention to inhibit an adversarial actor's ability to engage a foreign public. During the NATO war against Serbia, member states began with an argument by volume: coordinated saturation broadcasting to the enemy's territory in what was called the "ring around Serbia." This escalated into military action to inhibit Serbia's ability to communicate a counter-message to its own public by bombing transmitters and, more controversially, the state TV news headquarters in Belgrade.[57] In the digital realm, states sometimes intervene to inhibit the transmission of messages associated with activity considered criminal, such as the recruitment propaganda of the so-called Islamic State. While states have a legal right to intervene in this way against a non-state actor, it is unclear whether such intervention is wise in the case of jihadi networks, given the value in being able to listen to and learn from their traffic and the astonishing resilience of the networks which renders partial "takedowns" futile.[58] Of course, the state is not the only actor intervening in this way. In 2015, the online collective known as Anonymous intervened against ISIS/Daesh in the digital space.[59]

Impact of new technology

Of all the elements of public diplomacy, international broadcasting has been most affected by changes in technology. Satellite broadcasting and then the rise of the internet led to a decline in shortwave radio use in the developed world and a migration of audiences and programming online in the form of streamed services or shareable individual fragments. Television services have proliferated, with the creation of video material of various kinds to accompany what had previously been sound-only services. Initially, international broadcasters sought out local partners like FM radio stations. However, the tightening of hostile government control of local media in some areas and the decline in FM listening elsewhere has made this also a thing of the past. International broadcasting no longer lines up with neat geographic territories. For more than a decade, the BBC World Service has known that more than 50 percent of the audience for each of its online foreign-language services is located outside the country of origin. BBC Persian is primarily a service for the diaspora.[60] International broadcasters remain relevant to the extent that they are able to reconceptualize their roles as one of transnational content providers able to work with the platforms preferred by the audiences they wish to reach. An example of this was the successful collaboration of the BBC and the WhatsApp mobile device application to communicate to West Africa in 2014 details of how to avoid infection from the Ebola virus. The approach was both authoritative and culturally sensitive.[61] Despite all the dissemination of the internet and cellular technologies in some places, shortwave radio remains an essential method of communication and there is an argument for retaining shortwave capacity for the time being. When in December 2017 a British member of parliament raised concerns that the undersea fiber optic cables on which the internet depends might be vulnerable to snipping, the VOA veteran Kim Andrew Elliott noted wryly on his blog, "Not as easy to snip the ionosphere."[62]

Technology has changed the core orientation of international broadcasting. In the past, broadcasters could count on sustained relationships with audiences. There were so few channels crossing frontiers that even with hostile jamming the great western broadcasters were effectively monopoly suppliers of news from the outside. They were like a city's utility company sending water through pipes to households. Today, they live in a world of competition where broadcasting output is as likely to be transmitted by sharing on a social platform as picked up directly by its end user. International broadcasters are now content creators seeking to share their materials on whichever platforms are used and trusted by their audience. In terms of the water metaphor broadcasters are unable to count on pipes for distribution and are putting their water into shareable bottles which are passed from person to person across a network.[63] The BBC Serbian Service, which relaunched in March 2018, is not only designed for web streaming but also feeds to Facebook and Twitter. Networked audiences have learned that not all information is equal and, just as buyers in the market evaluate bottled water by brand, so in the era of "fake news" the brand attached to a piece of news is becoming increasingly significant. As with a commercial product, it is essential that the quality of a broadcaster's output be maintained. Challenges going forward include budgets. News consumption is a habitual activity and habits must be fed or they will be broken. The relationship of trust between an international broadcaster and its audience is a precious thing, and the withdrawal of a service can be a traumatic event for a community that has relied on that service, more especially if they sense that their need has not diminished. While it is good that BBC Serbian is back, it would have been even better if Britain had not cancelled BBC Serbian in 2011.[64]

For all the technological changes, international broadcasting remains relevant. Many states still use international broadcasting as a mechanism to connect to their diasporas. TV Chile (launched 1986), Italy's RAI Italia (launched 1992), or India's DD India (launched 1995) are just three examples of expatriate-oriented channels now readily available on digital platforms around the world. Other countries are developing services to build influence, including a trend toward South–South connections, as with the Brazilian state's plan to connect to Africa using TV Brasil Internacional. Other states see an English service as a badge of national pride, despite poor ratings, as with South Korea's Arirang or the recently renamed NHKWorld-Japan. The field continues to grow. In 2013, an Israeli businessman, Patrick Drahi, launched i24news, a channel in English, French, and Arabic, explicitly to correct prejudice against Israel with "facts and diversity." A new i24news service aimed at the United States launched in 2017.[65] But the best evidence of the relevance of international broadcasting is the prominence it still has in emergencies. In times of crisis, attention still shifts to the familiar sources of international news, and it is plainly important for these legacy broadcast channels to retain a "surge capacity" for communicating in an emergency.

One issue for the future is the extent to which actors will remain wedded to nation-states. Perhaps transnational actors, like the pan-European cultural channel ARTE, show the way? In an era in which budgets seem likely to remain tight, greater collaboration between international broadcasters is essential. It makes little sense to have multiple services in some languages and none in others. One hopes for a future in which many more actors have an ability to tell their own and others' stories internationally for the purpose of mutual education. Worrying trends toward the repression of free media in many countries have increased the importance of the free exchange of information and the spreading of objective news cultures. As Albert Camus put it in 1955 in a tribute to the great Columbian journalist Eduardo Santos, "A free press can of course be good or bad, but, most certainly, without freedom it will never be anything but bad. . . . Freedom is nothing else but a chance to be better, whereas enslavement is a certainty of the worse."[66]

It is easy to find ways in which our world has been shaped by international broadcasting, but equally important to remember that its absence can be no less significant. Consider the case of Leipzig and Dresden. Leipzig and Dresden, the two great cities of southeastern Germany, share much. Both are located in the province of Saxony; both were part of communist East Germany; both have spectacular cultural histories; they were at opposite ends of Germany's first long-distance railway line in the 1830s and have a long-running friendly rivalry. Yet these two cities have diverged sharply in their political attitudes. Leipzig is a thriving cosmopolitan hub which played a leading role in the movement for political change in 1988. Outward looking, it is now seeking UNESCO recognition for its musical heritage. Dresden is the heartland of the militant anti-immigrant party PEGIDA, Patriotic Europeans Against the Islamisation of the West. Inward looking, it is one of the few cities to lose its UNESCO status after the city government defiantly built a new bridge close to the historic city center. What might account for the divergence? There is one massive difference: a wholly different exposure to international broadcasting during the East German period. While the East German public was officially shut off from outside influences and addressed by a government which relied on heavy use of censorship and propaganda, the regime's media was undercut in most of the country by spillover radio and television signals from West Germany and RIAS in Berlin or the US military's Armed Forces Network broadcasts. But these signals could not reach Dresden because of its location in a valley. The Saxon capital and its surrounding territory duly became known to fellow East Germans as the *Tal der Ahnungslosen,* variously translated as "valley of the clueless," "valley of unknowing," or "valley of the people who know nothing." Its citizens saw no West German prosperity; they heard neither western music nor North American news. The absence of outside media allowed East German propaganda to work unchallenged for decades. Their media diet inside the bubble emphasized a narrow nostalgic parochialism made more potent by the city's special status as a victim because of the damage done by mass Allied bombing of the historic city center in February 1945. Decades as a historic victim seem to have dulled the city's empathy to the suffering of others, if the strength of PEGIDA is any indication. Like a twin study in psychology, the tale of these two cities suggests the value of puncturing a propaganda bubble and the damage that accumulates when it endures for a generation or more. Without news crossing frontiers, we face the prospect of living in a world of many little Dresdens, sealed bubbles of self-pity and mistrust unpricked by empathy or external reality. International broadcasting matters.

7   Nation Brands and Branding: The Metaphor Run Amok

Even having seen survey data on the issue, Ido Aharoni was shocked by what he heard on the tape. The video footage depicted a simple scene: a meeting room in which a cross-section of people sat around taking part in a facilitated conversation. The task in hand was imaginative: if a country was a single house, what would it be like to attend a party there? The answers were initially as he expected. The house of Germany was neat and tidy. The house of Italy was full of conversation, wine, and warmth. The focus group enjoyed imagining being there. Then the facilitator asked about the house of Israel. The answers were stark. The house was dangerous. They imagined concrete walls and security fences. They imagined tension and people worried for their future. They imagined being uncomfortable. The team ran the exercise over and over with different groups. The answer remained the same. In 2004, whether rich or poor, black or white, Jewish or Gentile, sympathetic or not, in London, Paris, New York, and elsewhere in the United States, the focus groups associated Israel primarily with conflict and crisis. Aharoni's task was to look for ways to change that image and somehow align international impressions of Israel with domestic impressions of the country, which matched the image that focus groups had for Italy. Undeterred, he began to strategize about parts of Israel's story that might begin to change this impression: the energy of the Israeli tech sector; the fun of the Tel Aviv night scene; the pluralism of so much Israeli life. He knew it would be an uphill task, but he understood its value. Like a community of communicators around the world at the turn of the millennium, Aharoni conceptualized this task as "nation branding."[1]

Of all the ideas to animate the practice of public diplomacy in the last twenty years, only one approaches soft power in its international traction and that is the term devised in the United Kingdom in the mid-1990s by British analyst and policy advisor Simon Anholt: the nation brand. Like Frankenstein's monster, it was built of components that had had a previous existence, and its life swiftly outstripped the intent of its creator. At its worst, nation and place branding unleashed an orgy of high-priced experts shaking down naive governments from modest cities to the mightiest nation-states with promises of miraculous results from a mix of corporate slogans, logos, mission statements, and mega events, informed by research of varying degrees of scientific reliability. Some slogans have become almost proverbial through repetition: "Incredible India" and "Malaysia, Truly Asia" have endured, but those are the exceptions. Changes of government or the willingness to believe the next consultant to buttonhole the crown prince at Davos led to rapid transitions from one approach to another or countries running divergent campaigns to promote inward investment and tourism at the same time. It was no wonder that soon Anholt was working to distance himself from the creature he had unleashed. He moved to establish a more solid foundation for the future of what he preferred to conceptualize as competitive identity: working to build better national images not through corporate-style communication strategies but through better national realities. The excesses of application of nation branding should not however erase the underlying value of Anholt's initial formulation. Countries and other places can function as brands in the perception of publics, and understanding the prevailing meaning of a place in the mind of an audience is of immense value to a public diplomat. The problem comes with the shift from research to practice and the extension of the understanding of a nation or place brand into the practice of nation or place branding.

Hard on the heels of its emergence as a field of practice, nation and place branding also became a field of study. Much of the writing was by scholars/practitioners looking to sharpen the debates in the field. As well as Anholt's own writing, there were important contributions from Keith Dinnie and Robert Govers. Others questioned the field as symptomatic of a postmodern commodification of life, and its practitioners as what Melissa Aronczyk termed the "transnational promotional class." Still others found the concept a helpful mechanism for decoding behavior, as with Jian Wang's work on expo pavilions in Shanghai 2010 as "branded spaces." Nation branding is used as a component of soft power studies and has produced perceptive single-country readings. The German scholar Jessica Geinow-Hecht has sought to apply it as a frame for historical analysis.[2] Yet the relationship of national brands and branding to the practice of public diplomacy is often unclear. A sustained analysis dispels some of the mystery and leaves an indication both of the true costs of an emphasis on the brand and of a constructive way forward.

Foundations: the brand

Despite the tendency of the public to use the term "brand" as a synonym for a trademark and/or logo, a brand is a complex cluster of elements. It includes designed aspects and both primary and secondary characteristics.

The design elements are the product name, the logo, and any slogans or taglines attached to the product. The primary product elements are the ingredients and features of the product itself. The secondary element is the behavior of the corporate entity associated with the product. For Coca-Cola, the design elements are: the product name, including its calligraphy and "dynamic ribbon" pattern on the can or bottle label; the curved Coke bottle; and the advertising tag, which since January 2016 has been the global slogan, "Taste the feeling."[3] The primary product elements include the flavor and fizzy nature of the drink (as for all the variations within the brand, it is hard to imagine a "Coke Still" line). The secondary product elements incorporate the events which the company chooses to sponsor, which include European soccer championships and FIFA World Cups, and the behaviors of the company, such as its care and concern for its workers, its suppliers, and its environmental footprint (especially its water policy and attitude to recycling). The same matrix can loosely be applied to a nation-state. Brazil, for example, has its design elements: its green and yellow national colors date from the era of the monarchy; its republican flag kept the colors but added a blue disk with southern hemisphere stars and the motto *Ordem e Progresso* (Portuguese for the positivist motto "order and progress").[4] The primary elements of Brazil, which every government is largely stuck with, are its geography and core culture, including such selling points as music and carnival spirit. The secondary elements are the government's record at home and abroad, which includes good things such as foreign aid policy or problems such as political corruption scandals.

While the brand is made of disparate components, the essence of the brand exists in a very concrete place; it in not in a consultant's guidelines or stashed in a safe in a president's office or anywhere in the country represented but dispersed in the minds of the global audience. Simon Anholt has observed that if "the brand image exists in a remote, secure, distributed location," it follows that "talk about 'building' and 'managing' the brand image sound[s] very much like wishful thinking: companies can tinker with the brand identity as much as they like, but whether this affects the brand image is another matter."[5] What is clear is that the strength of a brand is determined by the level of admiration which its audience feels and the ability of the brand to maintain the qualities on which that admiration is based. For a corporation or for a country, quality control is essential to its reputation's health and longevity.

The English word "brand" references symbols indicating origin or ownership which from ancient times were burnt into a surface of a barrel or the skin of a farm animal. While the practice of applying an origin mark likely began as a way to avoid theft, when products of a particular origin began to be recognized as of special quality, the brand took on added meaning. It became a mark of trust, guiding a consumer's choices. Origin could also be indicated through distinctive package shape; archeologists have noted regional styles of amphora around the Mediterranean. Products would build the reputation of a place. While wise leaders worked to improve the reputations of their regions through a better reality – Bias of Priene reportedly wrote 2,000 lines of verse on ways in which his native Ionia could build its prosperity[6] – others throughout history have attempted to short-circuit this process. They named places they built or discovered so as to associate them with positive qualities and thereby encourage people to invest in the place themselves. Examples include the renegade Viking, Eric the Red, who named the northern territory he "discovered" Greenland, hoping to promote its settlement. In medieval England of the 1140s, when the Knights Templar returned from the Crusades and decided to found a new market town north of London, they named it Baldock in tribute to Baghdad (known as *Baldac* in Old French) whose commercial prominence they (rather fancifully) hoped to emulate. The place names of the Colonial Americas are often easily legible in terms of the desire to relocate old-world prestige in the new – New York, New Jersey, and so forth – or to depict the region as a source of wealth with such aspirational place names like Rio Plata/River of Silver, Argentina/Country of Money, and various places named for Eldorado, evoking the legendary kingdom ruled by "the Golden One."

A more complex association of place and image happened in the Netherlands following their breach with the Spanish Empire. One of the country's secret weapons was the fact that its leader – William the Silent – happened to be from a branch of the House of Nassau, which had through marriage merged with the district of Burgundy called Orange. Originally, the Dutch state had looked to a predictable range of symbols inherited from ancient Roman Republicanism (liberty caps, liberty trees, and so forth) but the pun on the name of their prince's house with the name of the fruit and the associated vibrant blend of red and yellow gave but the opportunity for something really powerful. They were able to associate the political quali-ties of a place with a symbolic color. Orange came to embody a fusion of Protestant religion and civic bourgeois capitalism, as well as the place of the Netherlands. The symbol was so powerful that it figured elsewhere, looming large in national and sectional identity politics and political branding in locations as diverse as Ireland, Scotland, and Maritime Canada through the institution of Orange Orders and in South Africa through the incorpora-tion of Dutch iconography into Afrikaner nationalism.

As had been noted already, it is in the nature of revolutionary states that they should work to establish a rapid impression of their values. This process has often included articulating new symbols to mark the rejection or surpassing of the previous state. The leaders of the French Revolution of 1789 sought to articulate an image of their new country through a set of cultural elements, including national symbols, music, and even a calendar. The American Revolutionary state was no different, mixing design elements like flags, slogans, songs, and pageantry with existing folk culture to articulate a distinctly American whole. But the markers of identity are only part of the story. A brand must necessarily reference a set of qualities in the imagination of the audience. The connection between place and quality had been understood for some time through the operation of what was termed the "country-of-origin effect."

Country-of-origin effect

Consumers have long understood that particular countries are associated with excellence of particular products: French wine, German cars, Swiss watches, and so forth. The country-of-origin mechanism is more complex than simply an inventory of desirable products or services originating from a particular location. It operates through the establishment of an association between a place and an abstract quality, which is assumed to be embedded in the product. Germany is associated with precision engineering, and products that benefit from that geographical origin include automobiles. France is associated with elegance and style, and products benefiting from that association include fashion houses, although the reputation extends to enhance other products too. The United Kingdom has a long-standing association for many consumers with ideas of social class and heritage, which helps brands like Burberry or Rolls Royce. The United States, in contrast, has spent two centuries building an association between the country and ideas of freedom, and this rubs off on its products. From a Marlborough cigarette to an iPhone, choosing a product from the United States plays out for many consumers around the world like a small declaration of independence. But the country-of-origin effect is not always a boost. It can place a burden on some countries, making it hard to enter fields with which they are not associated. The best-known example of this is the so-called "Korea discount" which means that electronic products made in Korea retail for some 25 percent less than a product of equivalent quality made in Japan. Korean stocks trade for well below what would be the case for a company with similar earnings elsewhere in East Asia.[7]

Faux brands

It is an irony of the country-of-origin effect that its power is most readily observed through attempts to manipulate it by associating a product with a country image other than one's own, building a faux brand.[8] There is a long history of governments attempting to police origin markings and of manufacturers attempting to fly below the radar. British government missions overseas long ago learned to keep an eye open for spurious Scottish-sounding names on bottles of whiskey distilled far from the "bonnie glens." Similarly, the French have fought battles over exactly what can be described as champagne. The problem grew with trade. In 1883, the French government convened an international conference in Paris to discuss what had become an epidemic of patent violation and false claims of origin. The countries represented agreed to the Paris Convention for the Protection of Industrial Property, Article 10 of which forbade false claims of origin. Eleven nations signed: France, Belgium, Netherlands, Spain, Portugal, Switzerland, Italy, Serbia and, from the other side of the Atlantic, Guatemala, El Salvador, and Brazil. The United Kingdom acceded in 1884. A further meeting in Rome in 1886 strengthened requirements, only to see the conditions unratified by major offenders. Frustrated, the British government passed its landmark Merchandise Marks Act of 1887 requiring country-of-origin markings and warning that products falsely claiming to be made in Britain would be impounded at their port of entry.[9]

The convention, the British law, and their adoption elsewhere did not prevent attempts to find wiggle room. In the aftermath of World War II, Japanese companies felt they had little to gain from stressing their products' origin and even tried to make their own consumers presume products were made elsewhere. Akio Morita, the founder of Sony, picked his company's name because it had a foreign sound evoking both the Latin *sonus* and the English vernacular "Sonny boy," picked up from GIs during the Occupation. He also insisted in rendering the brand in Roman letters rather than Japanese *kanji* as was usual at the time. In the early days of Sony exports to the West, the corporation made its origin labels as small as possible.[10] There are examples of businesses which not only play down their origin but explicitly take on an entirely spurious national identity to take advantage of someone else's country-of-origin effect. The toiletry company Crabtree and Evelyn was founded in Boston in the United States and cultivated a colonial-era image but in time opted to embrace full British identity. The "old world" feel evoked by the product packaging and name prompted the company to expand into the UK retail sector and develop the

British roots that its American customers had assumed it already had. The company has long since passed into East Asian ownership, but the English country-town brand identity remains. In a similar vein, the lingerie retailer Victoria's Secret not only hinted at Britishness in its store decor, packaging, and name (the Victoria was inspired by Queen Victoria) but for many years printed a phony British address on its catalogues.[11] In reality the company originated in Palo Alto, California and was run from a headquarters in Ohio, USA.

While some British goods might play well when in categories helpfully associated with heritage, British tech companies have faced an uphill battle. The master of British faux branding has been the camera and electronics retailer Dixons. In the 1950s, when precision consumer goods were still associated with Germany or Switzerland, Dixons commissioned products from Japan and sold them under a pseudo-German brand name "Prinz" (German for prince). By the 1980s, the Japanese had moved from being the down-market suppliers to the upmarket rivals. Noting that British consumers now actively sought out Japanese-origin electronics, in 1982 Dixons launched the faux Japanese brand Saisho. In 1985, Dixons doubled down on the strategy and rolled out a new line of household electronics for their Currys stores. Named Matsui, the accompanying design materials included a rising sun logo and the tagline "Japanese technology made perfect." Matsui televisions contained components from a number of countries but not so much as a diode from Japan, a fact which ran foul of the United Kingdom's trading standards officials and the law courts, which imposed a fine and enforced an end to the slogan. The Matsui name endured but had its own problems. It wasn't merely a Japanese surname, it was recognizable to many as the name of the man who led the Nanjing Massacre in 1937 and was executed after the Tokyo war crimes trials of 1946. It was as if one of the ailing British car companies of the 1980s had tried to borrow some wind from Germany by launching a new line called the Eichmann. War veterans groups were not amused.[12] In time, Dixons retired the Matsui brand and sold off Saisho, but others have subsequently recognized the value of being mistaken as Japanese. In 1994, an Indian company registered the name Masui Electronics to a corporate office address in Mumbai.[13]

Most faux brands are simply attempts to ride the wave of a reputation and to take advantage of past efforts of the claimed origin country to build positive associations. An additional problem arises when the company trades on an image which the claimed origin country no longer wishes to emphasize. A case in point is the US "casual dining" restaurant chain Outback Steakhouse, which presents itself as Australian. The restaurants began in Tampa, Florida in 1988 in the wake of the success of the hit

Australian comedy *Crocodile Dundee* (1986) and a series of beer commercials featuring that film's star, Paul Hogan. The founders promised "no rules, just right" and have grown by emphasizing a laid-back image with jingle lyrics such as "Life will still be there tomorrow . . . Let's go Outback tonight."[14] The problem from the point of view of the Australian government is that this association of the country with leisure and license now undercuts the country's attempts to emphasize Australian scientific and intellectual capital. Education is a much more significant part of Australia's economy than beer, but Outback does not help that image in the United States or in the more than twenty countries in which it operates. There is no legal recourse for the Australian government. Outback merely claims to be "Australian inspired."[15]

With such currents in play, it was perhaps only to be expected that those directing nation-states and other places would attempt to systematically understand and shape the relationship between identity and place. This is exactly what happened in the 1990s.

The emergence of nation branding

The terminology of nation and place branding emerged in the United Kingdom in the 1990s. The idea was one of many ways in which the Thatcher-era notion that the private/commercial sector had key lessons for the public sector continued to shape British life after she left office. It met the manifest need of governments to respond to the communications revolution, as well as answering the quest for overarching narratives in the post-Cold War world. What were western industrial nation-states about if the existential struggle that had preoccupied two generations had ended? Finally, the idea spoke to a particular moment in British culture. The United Kingdom was in the midst of an identity crisis. In 1993, the then prime minister John Major spoke of Britain as "a country of long shadows on county grounds, warm beer, invincible green suburbs, dog lovers and pools fillers and, as George Orwell said, 'Old maids bicycling to Holy Communion through the morning mist.'"[16] There was an obvious mismatch between such images of tradition and the diverse country of entrepreneurs like Richard Branson, fashion designers like Vivian Westwood, irrepressible entertainers such as the Spice Girls, and the vibrant British creative sector that many not only perceived but also preferred.[17]

The formative insight came from the British policy analyst Simon Anholt, who in 1996 began to speak of the benefits that might accrue to a nation if its government understood the parallels between that nation's image and the reputation of a corporation. He placed particular emphasis on the responsibility to continue to deliver consistent quality. His thinking coalesced in a seminal 1998 article in the *Journal of Brand Management*.[18] Anholt's insight struck a chord with work in progress in policy circles. In August 1997, just a few months after the landslide election of Tony Blair, a twenty-something researcher at the Demos think tank named Mark Leonard published a widely read booklet entitled *Britain TM*, arguing that the time had come for the government to actively manage Britain's identity. Leonard's argument included reference to the success of other countries in apparently repositioning or reinvigorating their "brand" image around the world. He pointed specifically to post-Franco Spain, post-Pinochet Chile, and the newly minted "Celtic Tiger" the Republic of Ireland.[19] Others joining the conversation included Wally Olins of the Wolff–Olins brand consultancy who was especially well placed to leverage the concept in the marketplace. He found eager customers in the Polish government especially. The practice of nation branding – the attempt to shift the perceived meaning of a place for a foreign audience to political or economic gain – had arrived.[20]

The nation-brand seed initially sprouted close to the tree. Mark Leonard's argument for rethinking Britain's image was eagerly taken up by the Blair government. Blair emphasized Britain's contribution to the global knowledge economy, pointing out genuine achievement in such fields as fashion, "Britpop" music, and art. Blair's embracing of resurgent British creativity was soon linked by the media to an existing portmanteau term, borrowed from a Ben and Jerry's ice-cream flavor: Cool Britannia. Cool Britannia was never a formal policy of the Blair government. Some elements, such as hosting young celebrities at 10 Downing Street where they mixed with balding, paunchy politicians, struck a false note at home, but the government had come to an important realization. As the approach matured, Leonard refined his ideas and, from the vantage point of the Foreign Policy Centre, argued for public diplomacy to be more structured.[21] As the notion of soft power was also added to the mix, and the terrorist attacks of September 11, 2001 provided fresh urgency, the British government convened a Public Diplomacy Advisory Board. The structure included Anholt as a member (pro bono) and aimed to coordinate Britain's assets in the international image: the British Council, Visit Britain, and the BBC. Serious and aligned thinking about Britain's image was thus established as a central feature of the country's approach to foreign policy in the twenty-first century.[22]

The British case played out in a more restrained way than excursions into nation branding elsewhere. National image shifted from being measurable and manageable to being magically mutable. It was especially appealing to the countries of the former eastern bloc who were struggling to market

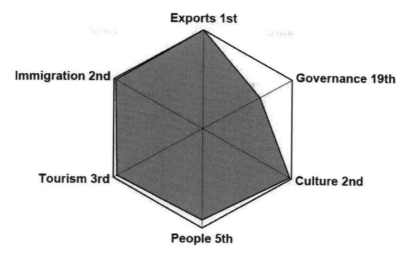

Figure 7.1 Anholt's hexagon for the United States as created from data collected during the 2016 US presidential election. Reproduced by kind permission of Simon Anholt.

themselves as part of the process of accession to the European Union and perhaps had yet to develop the skepticism to the marketer's smooth talk that one found in existing EU members. The project of nation branding attracted no shortage of criticism. The launch of design elements of a country brand could be sure to elicit both anger over the aesthetic aspects and resentment over the emphases on the country's perceived best qualities and inevitable exclusions from such lists. Finally, there would always be a body of opinion denouncing the corporate sector and the vulgarity of applying a process developed for soap powder to the most treasured element in many people's identity: nation.[23]

Anholt focused on communicating the range of factors contributing to a nation's image, developing his hexagon diagram as a way of showing the comparative strength of six core components of international reputation. These were: people; tourism; exports; investment and immigration; foreign and domestic policy; and heritage/culture. The shape of each hexagon revealed the unique footprint of a particular nation.[24]

Anholt realized that a more sustained and general analysis would help, and in 2005 he unveiled the first of what would become an annual survey, the Nation Brands Index, now known as the Anholt-*GfK* Nation Brands Index. The NBI considered the reputation of 50 "brand" countries by carrying out research across twenty national publics, conducting 1,000 online interviews in each. Now into its second decade, the index has a special credibility based on both the breadth of its research in each year and its value as a data series. Ironically, its most striking finding is that its findings are not in themselves striking. When he first embarked on the NBI, Anholt assumed that the data would be as volatile as the stock market and that national reputations would spike or dip based on the tides of scandal or planned set-piece events like the hosting of the Olympics. He initially conducted the survey four times a year. He found the opposite. National reputations are surprisingly – almost frustratingly – stable. He came to joke that he had created the world's most boring data set. Australia, Switzerland, and Sweden seem permanently to be in the eighth, ninth, and tenth brand places. Britain is in recent years stable at number three. Even hosting the Olympics in 2012 couldn't bump the country up. While British politicians who had invested in a substantial project known as the GREAT campaign were disappointed with the NBI result, Anholt was not surprised, understanding that a country like the United Kingdom needs to host the Olympics or make world-class television shows every now and again simply to stay put in the index, as if paying rent on their position. He felt that advertising "greatness" was a waste of taxpayer money.[25]

A second key finding in Anholt's research was that whatever governments might hope, most people did not spend a great deal of their lives thinking about foreign countries. They had views on the historical superpowers: United States, Russia and China; they had an awareness of four or five aspirational destination countries that they hoped to visit one day, and four or five more that were located in their particular neighborhood and had historic resonance for good or ill. Random countries of personal relevance to an individual as the setting for a favorite movie or location of a family member might take the total number up to twenty or so, but that is barely 10 percent of the possible responses. Most countries just weren't on their radar sufficiently to be considered brands. Even if they were aware of them, the locations did not resonate with their aspirations or imagination or occupy mental space to any measurable extent.

Anholt realized that international images were built over a long period of time. It had taken a long time for audiences to learn to see Canada as the "good citizen" country or Ireland as the friendly country. Anholt went so far as to argue that countries are like stars. Their light takes time to travel to us and what we see is how they were, rather than how they are now. It is also obvious from the data that once established ideas about countries are not lightly discarded, a finding that plays to the so-called endowment effect: people get attached to their possessions, whether physical or psychological. There were some events which impacted on positions in the index. The election of Barack Obama prompted a jump for the United States from seventh to first after what seemed like a depression of the country's reputation during the George W. Bush period. Obama was not wholly unshakable. US standing wobbled in 2014, the year of Edward Snowden's revelations, and Merkel's Germany took the top spot again, but the victory of Donald Trump saw the United States fall back. When data were collected halfway through President Trump's first year, the United States had already tumbled to sixth place and Germany had taken the top spot. Another event that brought movement to the index was the so-called Danish Cartoon Crisis of 2005. Anholt's data showed clearly that Denmark dropped in international perception. Many observers plainly disliked the way in which the Danish government had responded to Muslim criticism of the cartoons mocking the prophet Mohammed. Even non-Muslims soured in their view of Denmark, speculating that all categories of foreigner would find Denmark unfriendly. Audiences also displayed a diminished admiration for the Danish countryside, suggesting that unrelated qualities and areas can be affected by a serious crisis in one aspect of the brand, a finding which is consistent with the psychologists' assertion of the halo effect, albeit demonstrating its negative operation. There was one outlier. The Bush-era US public liked Denmark rather more after the cartoon crisis. Anholt suspected they were simply grateful not to be the only nation catching international criticism.[26]

Of course the data show some rising stars. During the first decade of the NBI, the United Arab Emirates, Poland, and Turkey were all rising. Conversely, most (around two-thirds) brands were gradually falling and – in a fascinating finding – converging. Even if Germany and France were at the top and China and Russia in the middle of the index, the measurable difference between those positions was narrowing every year.[27]

The success of the Nation Brands Index sparked a second gold rush toward league tables, many of which were operated by consultancies also offering to sell countries services to improve their standing. Leading contenders included the FutureBrand Country Brand Index (CBI), which debuted in the wake of Anholt's index in 2005 and appeared biannually thereafter. Although the CBI presented assessments of 75 countries, their data led them to question whether any more than 22 of these had reputations strong enough to be considered brands. Their methodology included input from industry professionals giving their view of Country X's image management over the previous year, which added volatility to the findings.[28] Late to the party was EastWest Communications, which launched a "perception index" in 2008. Their index seemed to show amazing volatility but only by ignoring polling and measuring media treatment instead. Their league was the largest, including all members of the United Nations. The first EastWest index had Singapore in the lead, the United Kingdom in tenth place, and the poor old United States, despite being the country most mentioned in the world's media, languishing in 132nd place behind Senegal. Such oddities proved no obstacle to the consultancy, creating further iterations of the index and marketing its services to help improve images around the world or, as the corporate tag put it, "branding countries to compete globally."[29] In similar vein, Bloom Consulting launched a family of indices including both country and city metrics based on search-engine data which they considered was a "clear indicator of country brand or city brand appeal." The rankings provided some surprises. The 2017 version placed the United Kingdom in the top spot and suggested the reputation of Sweden was in 23rd place, behind Russia, Portugal, and Argentina.[30]

A parallel method for evaluating brand strength was the financial/value-focused approach developed by the Brand Finance consultancy in 2006, initially building on Anholt's data set.[31] Their metrics could deliver eye-catching results, such as the revelation in 2009 that the election of Barack Obama added US$2 trillion on to the valuation of the US national brand.[32] Others were also climbing. In 2010, Brand Finance named China as its fourth most-valuable brand. By 2011, it was third. Despite challengers, the United States (home to the world's most powerful commercial brands) has always headed the Brand Finance league and continues to do so, even if the election of President Trump seemed to slow growth in the reputation.[33]

One helpful development came from a new British think tank – the Institute for Government – where an analyst named Jonathan McClory looked to bring together the ranking approach with objective measures to produce a tool to establish the relative soft power of major nations.[34] He hoped that findings might actually help governments in their diplomatic work. The index appeared in 2009 with the media partner *Monocle Magazine*, whose network of foreign correspondents served as a focus group to add to the findings. The *Monocle*/McClory index (officially the Institute of Government's *New Persuaders, I, II and III*) had particular traction in UK political circles most especially when, after placing the United Kingdom second in 2009 and 2011, the index adjudged Britain to be the world's soft power leader in 2013, suggesting that the investment of the London Olympics had paid off.[35] McClory parleyed his *Monocle* experience to develop a role at the Portland Communications consultancy where it was possible to bring poll data into the mix and add analytic material provided (in anonymized form) by Facebook. Today, McClory is the driving force behind the annual *Soft Power Thirty*, a study of 30 countries developing reputations, which continues to act as a bridge between international relations scholarship and the commercial realm of reputation measurement.[36]

But why wait for a favorable index? It was only a matter of time before a country became so irritated with the perceived injustice of the available league tables that they created their own. So it was. In 2009, the newly formed Presidential Council on Nation Branding of South Korea with the help of Samsung analysts unveiled their own index placing South Korea above its level in the Anholt index and in which their country proceeded to rise in subsequent years.[37] But the improvement was not enough to prevent successive South Korean governments from switching to other tacks evolving into a less marketing-focused approach that mixes cultural diplomacy, advocacy as needed, and international development work.

When stripped of its mythology and promises of corporate miracle cures, insights from the nation brand concept may be readily reconciled with the rest of public diplomacy theory and practice. Branding research is a form of listening. It can suggest key themes to be emphasized in advocacy to focus attention on strengths – giving an underlying structure to what would otherwise be isolated stories – or plug gaps in the target audience's perception; it can also determine the content of cultural diplomacy, as culture is a key element in national distinctiveness; it can shape the content and emphasis of exchange programs and international broadcasting, but most importantly of all it can feed into policy and underpin projects not just to say the right thing to foreign audiences, but to be the right thing going forward into the future. In terms of cognitive bias, nation branding can be seen as a mechanism to establish a frame of positive perceptions that can be confirmed by later experiences; it works through the mechanism of the halo, seeking to enhance the entirety of a nation's story through exposure to one or two emblematic components.

Place making

The mechanisms of research-based identity-focused engagement are applied at various levels of place promotion. City branding appears more plausible, given that cities are small enough to actually have meaningful identities based on shared culture and activity and seem less prone to the kinds of political stalemate which are so common at the national level in the twenty-first century. Some apparently successful city cases – such as the now legendary I ❤ NY (1977) or Glasgow's Miles Better (1983) – worked by rallying residents to be their best, as well as reminding outsiders of the value in the city.[38]

The pinnacle of the brander's art is probably the practice of place making, by which previously unconnected places are drawn into a region or even a route is brought to public attention and becomes a part of the collective mental furniture. A successful case is that of Ireland's Wild Atlantic Way. While the west coast of Ireland had a certain presence in the public imagination, it tended to be in terms of individual beauty spots such as the cliffs of Moher, the peak of Croagh Patrick, or the beaches of Connemara. County Kerry had a circuit of lovely views called the Ring, which had become a destination in its own right. In 2014, the Irish tourist board had the insight to label a coastal route "the Wild Atlantic Way" and use the branding of the route as a mechanism to promote businesses along its length, turning a trip from one end to the other into a "thing to do." The inspiration was California's Route One drive from San Francisco to LA, but the Irish equivalent turned out to be longer, with many more points of interest. The boldest attempts at place making, however, have been those seeking to build places that cross national boundaries: transnational regions.[39]

In 2000, a spectacular bridge opened linking the Danish capital Copenhagen with the Swedish city of Malmo across the stretch of water known as the Oresund. The Øresund/Öresund bridge made it possible for citizens of the two cities to share the same international airport and offered the prospect of jointly marketing the shared urban region as a destination for inward investment. The port administrations merged under a single management in 2001, and the two cities resolved to begin branding and promoting the transnational region of Oresund.[40] A shared region needed shared stories, so early projects included the Oresund Film Commission which launched in 2003 to promote joint film and television development. The 2011 hit television series *The Bridge* (*Broen* in Danish and *Bron* in Swedish) was the result. The world watched in fascination as mismatched detectives from the cities at each end of the bridge investigated the mystery behind a body found at its center point. As promotion of the new Oresund transnational region rolled forward, there was only one snag:, while Swedes and Danes all knew where the Oresund was, very few foreigners did. Everything worked well except the name. In the end, the pragmatic Swedes bowed to the inevitable and allowed the region to be rebranded in terms that were recognizable more widely as Greater Copenhagen.[41] Even the storytelling element foundered. The film commission split into separate Danish and Swedish entities.[42] Other experiments with transnational regions include the Anglo-French–Belgian region of Transmanche and the joint Austrian–Slovak region incorporating the Vienna/Bratislava Corridor. There, also, the problem seems to be the foundational knowledge and expectation of the audience. People have been used to thinking in national categories for a long time and old habits die hard.

The case of Germany

Given the current status of Germany at the head of most indexes of comparative brand strength, it makes sense to ask how this happened. Certainly, Germany has a conventional nation-branding campaign. It is the "Germany: Land of Ideas" campaign, launched around the time that Germany hosted the 2006 FIFA World Cup, which includes an eye-catching poster of model Claudia Schiffer wearing only the German flag above text that reads "Interested in a serious relationship?"[43] Yet no one would see Germany's current position as stemming from anything so recent or – with apologies to Ms Schiffer – so relatively forgettable. Germany's strength is based on a reputation for quality exports and engineering which has been built over a century or more. It was not always thus, and the reputation was not acquired by accident. Throughout the German story, individuals and institutions have been active, steering the country forward.

While German lands had a historical reputation for craftsmanship based around their medieval guild system and for trade based on the Hanseatic ports, Germany did not arrive in the nineteenth century at the head of the pack. The country – in the process of its political formation – industrialized late compared to the other European powers and embraced the most obvious gap for its exports at the bottom of the international market. Wake-up calls included the German contribution to the Philadelphia World's Fair of 1876 at which German products were dismissed by American critics as trash.[44] The German government was slow to respond but eventually took steps to protect copyright. From 1891, its products were numbered and stamped with the letters DRGM short for *Deutsches Reichs Gebrauchmuster* (German Imperial Patent). It was a regular feature of tin toys though not necessarily identified with quality. Children in Edwardian Britain said it stood for "dirty rotten German make."[45]

The road back began with listening or, more precisely, observation. The observer concerned was an architect from Saxony named Herman Muthesius. In 1896, Muthesius took the post of cultural attaché at the German embassy in London. The task of an embassy cultural attaché in the nineteenth century was as much about studying the culture of the country to which they were assigned as it was about promoting their own culture. So it was with Muthesius. During his tenure in London, Muthesius devoted himself to the study of British building and design. He was especially fascinated by the way in which the Arts and Crafts movement of William Morris and his circle had revived British design in the industrial age and he became convinced that the key to advancing Germany's fortunes was to create a similar movement. In 1904, back in Germany, he published the first in a three-volume study of the English house and began lecturing on the need for a comprehensive reexamination of German industrial output and a focus on quality.[46] His words were not universally welcomed. Some felt that his criticism of German products was unpatriotic. However, his message inspired a group of designers and artists to rally to the cause. In 1907 they founded the so called *Werkbund* (work group) to rebuild German's output from a foundation of excellent design. They argued that every aspect of the country could benefit from design; as their famous motto had it, *vom sofak-issen zum städtebau* (from sofa cushions to urban design).[47] The *Werkbund* gave a shape and purpose to existing ideas in German art and industry. It inspired the architects of the Bauhaus. It served as both an institutional incubator and a narrative linking other aspects of German life and history. It could draw on the heritage of the craftsman and the storied German scientific and university tradition with a measure of Protestant work ethic. The work of industrial pioneers like Robert Bosch or Carl Benz now existed in a context that related to national identity. With Prussian state sponsorship, excellence in design was officially what Germany was "about."

The outbreak of the Great War did little to interrupt the dawning of German design. The Cologne Fair of 1914 showed the way with sensational objects and a breathtaking bullet-shaped glass pavilion designed by Bruno Taut. There were exhibitions in Switzerland and Copenhagen and even a show of German furniture in wartime London. All of this was valuable ammunition for the post-war task of combatting the image of Germans as uncultured "Huns" bent only on conquest. The key to the transition from the Werkbund emphasis on design as an expression of German identity to a global perception of German efficiency and quality in manufacturing was the ability of Germany to sustain a reality of excellence (or, in the jargon of the brander, to "live the brand").

Perhaps the most notable feature of this perception of German efficiency was the way in which it was so well established by mid-century that even the disasters and atrocities of the Third Reich could be read abroad as affirming it. Hitler was seen as efficiency and design misdirected. This image is so strong in the post-war United States that science fiction fans have noted a genre cliché now dubbed "Godwin's Law of Time Travel" in which the smallest disruption to the earth timeline will result in Hitler, or an analogue, winning World War II.[48] Ray Bradbury's classic story "The Sound of Thunder" describes how the simple act of a time traveler crushing a butterfly in the Jurassic period result in a Hitler-type regime ruling the world. A memorable episode of the TV show *Star Trek* depicts an earth historian's attempt to accelerate a planet's evolution by recreating a Nazi-style regime on the grounds that Nazi Germany was "the most efficient state Earth ever knew. . . ." The attempt is a disaster, but the ever logical Mr Spock has no trouble endorsing the underlying historical argument. Raising an eyebrow, he assures Captain Kirk, "Quite true, Captain. A tiny country, beaten, bankrupt, defeated, rose in a few years to stand only one step away from global domination . . ."[49] No serious historian of the Hitler period would make such a claim.[50] It is all symptomatic of the extent to which, for better or worse, German efficiency, design, and capability undoubtedly occupies a unique place in the collective imagination. With this foundation, the "Germany: Land of Ideas" campaign was more a reminder of things that audiences already knew than news. It is an enviable position for a nation.

Whatever the world perceives, it is to Germany's credit that it is prepared to include its efforts at reconciliation with its past in spaces that for other countries would be purely promotional. The German pavilion at the Shanghai Expo of 2010, while full of splendid examples of German industry, included a small exhibit of the *Stolpersteine*, stumble stones, engraved brass cobbles which were set into the surface of German streets to deliberately interrupt passing feet and mark a spot where something horrible happened in the time of Hitler. Launched in 1992 by the artist Gunter Demnig, *Stolpersteine* were by 2010 also taking off as a mechanism for remembering Nazi atrocities beyond the boundaries of Germany. It was brave to include *Stolpersteine* within the pavilion, though they too – when all is said and done – were a remarkable piece of design.[51]

Applying nation branding

The application of nation branding is necessarily limited. It is restricted by the limits of the audience's mind, the ideas, values and impressions already there, and the sad fact that manifestly not many countries actually matter to most people. A branding campaign can structure positive stories but it certainly can't work miracles. Some elements of brand thinking can direct attention to undervalued strengths, such as the potential locked in the reputation of a city or region. Brand analysis can also reveal snags, such as the contradiction between the preferred image of the Ministry of Tourism and that of the Ministry of Trade and Industry. Mexico is the poster child for this kind of clash. The twenty-first century has added new elements to a country's portfolio, such as the impact of a country's behavior online and its e-image, which has been a success for Brazil and Estonia, but a negative for Russia and Macedonia. Diaspora has also gained importance. This was a worry for Romania (whose image was already rocky, given that its best-known citizen was the fictional vampire Count Dracula) when the country became identified with the small number of Roma gypsies involved in street crime in European tourist spots. The bottom line for any image must be the question of how to ensure that its citizens deliver and "live the brand."

A word of warning

The consequences for violating a brand image can be considerable. In 2004, the image of the United States took a tremendous blow around the world. The cause was the revelation of US mistreatment of Iraqi prisoners at the Abu Ghraib jail, evidence of mistreatment at the Guantanamo detention camp and revelations of CIA use of what amounted to torture at special rendition facilities in former Eastern Europe. A decade later, the revelation of the scale of US online surveillance knocked back the image of the Obama administration (albeit not to quite the same extent). To many American observers, the bump seemed unfair, as if the United States was expected to keep different rules to other states. The reason that the world was so angry at these revelations was that over the past century it had absorbed the narrative that the United States was the homeland of freedom, justice, and the rule of law. Torture and surveillance was supposed to be what the United States was against. Some nation-states were understood to "play rough" with their own people and foreigners and could do so without dramatic damage to their international standing, but the United States was not considered one of those. By moving into that territory so unapologetically, the US government had reached into the minds of everyone around the world who felt they knew the country and dented one of the pillars upon which the positive image of the country rested. But it is not all bad news for the United States. Some events which appall Americans and trigger a tsunami of domestic self-doubt seem to already be factored into global assessments of the country. Foreigners know that some Wall Street tycoons are thieves, some Hollywood producers are sexual predators, that ready access to high-powered weapons enables mass shootings in schools, and that US democracy sometimes places eccentric people in high office, but they admire the country anyway. They see underlying good.

Being good

Anholt's research showed that while global audiences give a certain admiration to wealth and to strength, the quality that contributes most to positive reputation is being seen to be good. This suggests that the best way to cultivate a reputation for being a good country is to actually seek to do good in ways that are relevant to the global audience and to ensure that the world notices. Rather than focus on perception, Anholt chose to readjust his focus and develop a parallel tool for measuring the "good" that each country does relative to its size and wealth. The result was the so-called Good Country Index. While conceptions of good vary around the world, the seven categories measured in the index represent a cross-section of ways in which nations serve the benefit of humanity as a whole: science and technology; culture; international peace and security; world order; planet/climate; prosperity and equality; health/wellbeing. While there is an impressive 80 percent correlation between the objectively measured "good countries" and the reputations reflected in the NBI (suggesting global publics are perceptive in their views), the focus on good reveals some mismatches in its allocation of the laurels. The first iteration had Ireland contributing most to global good relative to the size of its economy, while the 2017 version showed the Netherlands in first place, whereas both rank outside the top ten in the Nation Brands Index. The 2017 Good Country index ranks Switzerland (the NBI's #8) second and Denmark (the NBI's #15) third. The United States' global contribution is not especially impressive. In 2017 it ranked 25th in its adjusted contribution to global good relative to comparative GDP, down from 21st in the initial version of the figures.[52] The project is deliberately provocative but it represents an undoubted breath of fresh air and a challenge for countries to focus on what is really important in the long term: a better reality, and a reality which is relevant to global audiences. It is a form of public diplomacy in its own right – index diplomacy, perhaps – but on behalf of everyone rather than a single country.

Whether or not the government of a nation or other place formally attempts to study how it is perceived, images of the place will be formed. It makes sense to differentiate oneself from rivals and neighbors. The process of place image management offers some opportunity to take a measure of control, even if many elements remain beyond any hope of redirection. A brand identity – like Britain's "Great" campaign – can structure such good news as comes along. Of course, there is a law of unintended consequences; a reputation for sound welfare policies can be read as a welcome mat for migrants. States must remember to beware of the gap between reputation and reality, bearing in mind that global publics feel a sense of ownership over such impressions of countries as they have accumulated and will over-react to violations of those impressions. Finally, states should remember that a focus on the reputation of the country can become an obstacle in other aspects of diplomacy. The true cost of nation branding may not be paid in fees to a consultant but in opportunities lost to work in a way which increasingly defines success on the international stage: partnership and collaboration.

8   Partnership: The Emerging Paradigm

British Robinson faced a formidable foe on a daunting battlefield. As a senior administrator of the US President's Emergency Plan for AIDS Relief (PEPFAR) at the Department of State, her task was to mobilize against HIV/AIDS in the region where its ravages were worst: Africa. Her specific role was that of Deputy Coordinator/Director of Private Sector Engagement. Fortunately, she soon found allies. While the challenge at first seemed overwhelming, she and her partners understood the value of acting from a foundation of research. They knew that AIDS in Africa was driven by a complex set of medical, economic, and social factors. They also understood that given the necessity of targeting their response, it made most sense to focus on young people and women. PEPFAR had been established by the George W. Bush administration in 2004. It provided a structure for coordinating the efforts of the US government (USAID, Health, Center for Disease Control, Labor, Commerce, Defense, and even Peace Corps were all included), but more importantly it was a trusted convener for effective partnerships linking the public and private sectors. Robinson joined PEPFAR in 2006. One of the best ideas of 2009 was to reach out to young women on their own terms through the creation of a television soap opera. The idea was that of the Norwegian government and UNICEF, and it found an eager partner at MTV who saw the program as ideal for the MTV Base (Africa) music channel that they had launched in 2005. Robinson was glad to bring PEPFAR's resources to the project, but she soon realized that the show would require careful handling. All needed to be honest about why their high-profile commercial partners were helping: they had corporate social responsibility programs and hence would expect to publicize their good works. The project had to have artistic as well as instructional merit and it required a degree of political courage. A drama with messages about HIV/AIDS would have to treat sex in an explicit way and that could mean controversy in both the United States and the project country of Kenya. The show found its writer, a dynamic young South African named Amanda Lane, its title – *Shuga* – and its star, a then-unknown American-trained actress of Kenyan origin named Lupita Nyong'o who took the title role. The rest is history. Though the first season of *Shuga* comprised of just three shows, it was a sensational success. It proved so popular that it lived on for many more seasons, relocating to Nigeria and then South Africa as it acquired a life of its own. More importantly, Robinson saw that it broke new ground in communicating core messages around HIV transmission. It was something the US government could never have hoped to do alone. It showed the power of partnership.

Partnership has become central to public diplomacy. While classic practices of public diplomacy – listening, advocacy, cultural diplomacy, exchanges, and international broadcasting – developed in a world built of nation-states and in which it was possible for nation-states to act alone, this is no longer the case. This chapter will consider the reasons that collaboration has become so important to public diplomacy; it will consider both good and bad practice and examine some successful cases of partnership around global public engagement. The conclusion will pull together some elements of good practice which can be applied in the field.

The case for partnerships

The most potent argument in favor of partnership is the increase in problems beyond the ability of a lone nation-state to solve. The world is full of what the former UN Secretary-General Kofi Annan called "problems without passports": climate change, epidemics, terrorism, and so on.[1] While these problems existed in the past, the nation-state, global institutions, and the global communications network have evolved to a point where a collective response is possible in a way it was not when the world of kings and castles faced the Black Death. Nations may collaborate more effectively than they did when their muskets and messengers faced Napoleonic France. While we might debate whether the problems on the agenda have really grown, the resources available to any one actor have certainly diminished. Collaboration provides a mechanism to maximize resources to engage around an issue. It should also be said – given the shifting landscape of credibility – that partnerships are essential to reach a diverse public. No actor is universally credible. All actors could gain from working with a partner. Finally, it should also be acknowledged that working with a partner or partners can be an intrinsically rewarding process, stimulating new ideas and approaches through new mixes, juxtapositions, and connections. Public diplomacy partnerships typically include actors from a wide range of backgrounds, including nongovernmental organizations with issue-specific knowledge and the advantage of limited historical baggage: corporate actors with deep pockets and an eagerness to demonstrate their inherent goodness; regional-, city-, and community-level actors with local knowledge and the ability to mobilize civil society; and international organizations that can rise above national history and legitimately convene collective responses without others wondering about their motives. All such actors have unique strengths to bring to partnerships.

Partnerships and cognitive/social biases

In terms of cognitive and social biases, partnerships provide a mechanism to extend an actor's leverage. Actors can work with partners able to speak with scientific or other authority, who have a similarity to the intended audience through shared region, religion, generation, or gender, or with a halo effect to strengthen the message. The best examples of this are the prominence of celebrities as spokespeople in development and other partnerships.[2] Partners can help deliver messages more swiftly, serve as multipliers to spread messages more widely, and add emotional resonance. Multiple partners can harness the bandwagon effect that flows from a perception that a particular position is widely held. When it comes to cementing relations between partners, the experience of working together is inherently valuable as a force for convergence. British scholar Brian Hocking has spoken of a process of "reconfiguring public diplomacy: from competition to collaboration."[3] US scholars Geoffrey Cowan and Amelia Arsenault have positioned partnership as the third level of public diplomacy: beyond monologue and dialogue.[4]

Models of imperfect partnership

Given the self-evident advantages of partnership, it is perhaps surprising how poorly it has been done. The foreign policy space abounds with stories of unsuccessful collaborations. There are four obvious models of imperfection: the dictators, who insist on controlling the entire process and stifle the creativity of their collaborator (sometimes merely using the term "partner" to spin a relationship which is actually that of an employer and a contractor); the ventriloquists, who value partners only to the extent that they repeat the authorized message; the heroic narcissists, who use up their partners, leaving unpaid bills in their wake, but claim all credit for any success. And finally – on the initiating side of the equation – there are the bus drivers, who work frantically to get to a destination but whose partners are actually just passengers, along for the ride. Examples in practice include: the failure of the BBC Arabic TV channel in the 1990s – when the BBC insisted on editorial independence and declined to be a ventriloquist's dummy for its

Saudi partner Orbit Communications, the deal fell apart; the failure of the State Department to properly pay the unlucky architect who delivered the US pavilion at the Milan Expo of 2015, James Bieber; and – as an institution subject to passengers along for the ride – UNESCO, the perpetual venue for political grandstanding of members which adds little to the realization of its great mission.[5] As with the listening process, the flaws of partnership seem to be endemic and are to be expected, but they can be overcome through design.

Partnership in public diplomacy

Partnership was always a central feature of the internal administration of public diplomacy, with actors routinely seeking to rally assets across government or within their nation to tell a common story. Many of public diplomacy's greatest highlights – the great expos; the United Kingdom's mobilization against American neutrality in the world wars; the transnational campaign against apartheid – were stories of partnerships between actors across sectors. Much of the history of the United States Information Agency has revolved around attempts to rally its own sometimes wayward elements, other branches of the US government, and private sector partners to a common cause.[6] Exchange programs are especially reliant on partnerships, and many, like Brazil's Science without Borders program, the China Education Association for International Exchange, or the German–American Partnership Program, are partnerships to promote partnerships. There are partnerships aimed at diasporas, such as Israel's Partnership2gether program, operated by the Jewish Agency for Israel, or Ireland's Global Irish Network and Global Irish Economic Forum.[7] Bilateral partnership initiatives include that between Canada and Mexico launched in 2004 or that between India and Russia as announced in 2015.[8] International organizations like the United Nations and the European Union generally work as platforms coordinating activity in the foreign policy field rather than as unilateral actors (albeit with a multilateral mandate), and their increasing significance has been one of the drivers in the rise of partnerships. The EU public diplomat David Ringrose (head of Policy Outreach for the European Commission) compares the EU to an iPhone and challenges partners to create the applications to do wonderful things building on the foundation of the platform.[9] New platforms for partnership include multistakeholder international organizations convened to advance the Millennium Development Goals, such as the Global Partnership for Education, launched in 2002 (as the Education for All – Fast Track Initiative).[10]

It is possible to find terrific examples of partnership throughout the history of public diplomacy, sometimes with the national actor in the driving seat, sometimes with nongovernmental actors taking the lead, working across the five core elements of global public engagement.

Partnership in listening: The BBC Monitoring Service and the FBIS

While broadcasting is usually associated with transmission, listening has been a major element in the success of western international broadcasting. Not only have UK and US broadcasters each had access to complex systems of radio monitoring broadcasts from around the world, they have collaborated in the collection of material to maximize coverage and insight. This was of particular value when trying to understand areas of the world otherwise closed to analysis or dialogue. The partnership was a tale of two institutions. The BBC Monitoring Service was established in 1939 to track and transcribe the world's radio broadcasts from a network of listening posts around the world, producing both regular summaries of daily output and on-demand projects of in-depth listening. At moments of crisis, the BBC Monitoring Service became a quoted news source in its own right.[11] On the American side, the equivalent institution was the Foreign Broadcast Monitoring Service (FBMS), set up in 1941 by Franklin Roosevelt to track Axis radio propaganda as the United States drew closer to war. The FBMS became the FBIS, the "I" standing initially for "intelligence" and eventually for "information." The administration of FBIS passed from the Federal Communications Commission to the military and – in 1947 – to the CIA, where it had a unique position as an element which worked with open-source material and readily shared its findings.[12] The creation of Radio Free Europe/Radio Liberty required a specific audience research effort to understand listeners in the eastern bloc. BBC, FBIS, and RFE's own efforts generated a tremendously detailed picture of life in the East which could be plowed into programming. The scale of the joint achievement became clear only after the end of the Cold War. Remarkably, dynamics of opinion tracked remotely by RFE/RL and the BBC match fairly precisely the findings of the KGB and its equivalents when they looked at their own societies.[13]

Partnership in advocacy/cultural diplomacy: *The God that Failed*

The early Cold War also provides an interesting example of partnership in the realm of advocacy which doubles as a piece of cultural diplomacy.

In 1949, a British Labour party member of parliament (and veteran of Eisenhower's wartime psychological warfare team) named Richard Crossman realized that the most powerful weapon against communism for its potential recruits would always be the testimony of those who had once believed but had become disillusioned. He conceived of an anthology of confessional testimony by leading intellectuals from around the world who had once been communists but who had come to realize the error of their ways. The book was called *The God that Failed.* Crossman was able to recruit a glittering array of talent to present its experience, including Germany's Arthur Koestler, Britain's Stephen Spender, France's André Gide (who had just won the Nobel Prize for literature) and, from the United States, Richard Wright, one of the greatest African-American writers of the day. On publication, the book itself became the focus of a second partnership – with the national security apparatus of the United Kingdom and the United States. Its publication in 1949 was boosted both by the covert propaganda arm of the Foreign Office – the Information Research Department – and by the US government, who could see the value in subsidizing translations and cheap editions of the book across the developing world. In the end, all foreign rights were owned by the United States Information Agency, and the book became a staple of its political education work, alongside that other spin-off from the disillusioned British Left, George Orwell's *Animal Farm.*[14]

Partnership in exchanges: the EU's ERASMUS program

For most of the twentieth century, nation-states acted as the gatekeepers for educational exchange programs, and relations were conceived in bilateral terms. This changed in much of Europe in the 1980s when the European Economic Community (predecessor of the European Union) began experimenting with collaborative student exchange at a continental level. In 1987, the EEC launched its grand design: the ERASMUS program. The title was a pun on the name of the great Dutch scholar and a near-acronym of the European Community Action Scheme for the Mobility of University Students. The program allowed students from around the EEC to move freely to other countries in the program, ensuring that credits earned for a semester or year of foreign immersion in one country counted toward a degree in another. It also provided funding for faculty to take part in exchanges. In its first quarter-century of operation, nearly three million students took part in the program.[15] ERASMUS became a part of youth culture within the European Union, not simply promoting a European political perspective but also transnational relationships of a more elemental kind. Soon it acquired the nickname "Orgasmus." The potential for international romance was at the heart of the affectionate Franco-Spanish comedy drama film from 2002 based on the program, *L'Auberge espagnol* (The Spanish Inn). But the interpersonal impact was more than anecdotal. In 2014, the European Commission's *ERASMUS Impact Study* found that 33 percent of ERASMUS alumni chose a life partner from a different nationality (three times the rate for non-mobile European students) and that an impressive 27 percent of ERASMUS alumni had met their current life partner during their stay abroad.[16] While skeptics speculated that the pool of ERASMUS students might be self-selecting, with a predisposition to a cosmopolitan outlook, many saw a genuine mechanism for building a true pan-European consciousness. The EU increased budgets and opened parallel projects, including ERASMUS Mundus, launched in 2009 to support collaborative graduate education programs between EU-based institutions and universities in the wider world and, in 2013, ERASMUS+, a program to establish Europe-wide exchanges at all levels of training, education, and sporting exchange.

Partnership in international broadcasting: Broadcasting for Child Survival

Partnership in international broadcasting can bring spectacular results, opening access to new audiences through the relay or exchange of programming for example, but the case of Broadcasting for Child Survival is especially wide-ranging in its implications. The concept of child survival had emerged as a particular priority in the 1980s during the tenure of James P. Grant as executive director of UNICEF. In 1991, UNICEF had instituted an annual International Children's Day of Broadcasting to increase awareness of the special needs of youngsters, but the problem was immense. By the mid-1990s, an estimated 12 million children under five died from preventable causes each year. Meanwhile, international broadcasting had its own problems. In the wake of the Cold War, international broadcasters had to adapt to remain relevant to governments and audiences alike. They faced new competition from global satellite television but without the Cold War to justify expenditure. Such was the reality when Geoffrey Cowan became director of Voice of America in the first Clinton administration. Cowan was impressed to find that VOA was already developing programs to assist issues like conflict resolution and global health. He brought Greg Pirio, most recently director of VOA English and Portuguese broadcasts to Africa, into his office to develop further VOA work in such areas and pursue external foundation support. Pirio welcomed the opportunity because he had seen firsthand how African audiences had responded to programs aimed at peacebuilding and how, if properly constructed, radio could advance social good without compromising journalistic impartiality. Pirio's first step was to bring the US Agency for International Development on board. It helped that some VOA veterans had moved into USAID projects. Elizabeth Fox became an especially important connection. Together, VOA and USAID mounted a cross-sector two-day conference held in Washington, DC in April 1998.

The VOA/USAID conference brought together delegates from 30 countries, including health professionals, communication scholars, development experts, and representatives from UNICEF, foundations, and the western international broadcasters, to present needs and best practice. Tipper Gore, wife of the vice-president, represented the White House. The conference also included broadcasters from local stations in the developing world who would become retransmitters of key messages. The conference was a triumph. Delegates generated a clear sense of both the challenges and of the capabilities of broadcast information to help. Other international broadcasters, including BBC World Service, Radio France International, Deutsche Welle, and Radio Netherlands, pledged to work together. Twenty-eight local VOA affiliates joined forces to form an Association of Broadcasters for Child Survival to develop joint programming around the theme. The first programing initiative began on September 1, 1998, when VOA began to air public service announcements in all its languages targeting child health issues including nutrition, dehydration, vaccine promotion, and measures to prevent transmission of HIV/AIDS. The Voice and its partners followed up with child health-themed reporting, online journalism training, and a ten-part radio soap opera for Bolivia. VOA created a website of resources for partners to use, including a library of programs. Evaluating the work, USAID attributed millions of extra inoculations to the effectiveness of VOA and its partners. While the Alliance of Broadcasters for Child Survival didn't endure, many long-term initiatives can be traced forward from the 1998 conference. UNICEF itself developed the idea of communication for development as the focus for work in old and new media. VOA and USAID continued to work closely together but focused on specific issues where funding was most readily available, especially polio eradication, HIV/AIDs prevention, and health journalism training. The global trends suggest effectiveness – fewer than six million children under five years old now die annually – though much remains to be done.[17]

While it is possible to find such examples across the history of public diplomacy, the contemporary moment has required a much greater emphasis on collaboration with an increasingly diverse range of partners.

The collaborative turn: the US case

The turn toward collaboration in US diplomacy grew out of practices at USAID where partnership was necessary to get around expenditure restrictions. The World Summit on Sustainable Development (Rio+10) held in Johannesburg in the late summer of 2002, placed partnerships firmly on the agenda by calling for what participants termed Type II partnerships as the way ahead to deliver on the Millennium Development Goals. Type I partnerships were clunky agreements between nation-states but Type II partners were ad hoc voluntary partnerships between a range of actors, including national, subnational, civil society, and corporate, based on specific goals.[18] Even though the United States was imperfectly represented at the summit – President Bush snubbed the event and Secretary Powell appeared only at its end – USAID resolved to take up the models instituted there, appointing its own internal partnership specialists. The State Department was less enthusiastic, and the concept of development partnership spent most of the Bush period with legal advisors, even as the president characterized his "Global War on Terror" as a "coalition of the willing."

The election of Barack Obama in November 2008 opened up new possibilities. Partnerships were particularly appealing to Secretary of State Hillary Clinton, who immediately set up a US Global Partnership Initiative, envisioning the United States acting as convener, catalyst, and collaborator with a range of partners around the world. It was just one part of a strategy that could be called public diplomacy by deed, which she termed "smart power." Early successes included the Global Alliance for Clean Cookstoves. Launched in 2010, the alliance connected donors, researchers, and governments to address the problems of carbon pollution and accidental death which arose from cooking over an open fire or simple brazier. The project had special significance for women, who were disproportionately the victims of open-fire accidents. The Dutch corporation Philips developed an innovative design and the State Department worked with a range of nongovernmental organizations and local governments to get the stoves into use. Remarkably, even the Chinese and Indian governments joined the initiative. The project was so successful that it spun off from the State Department to find a home at the United Nations Foundation.[19] In 2011, Clinton's team launched the International Diaspora Engagement Alliance (IdEA), a range of partnerships between diaspora communities located in the United States and their countries of origin, which aimed to be a mechanism for promoting entrepreneurship, self-help, and development. The program included the promotion of volunteerism, with partners traveling back to their countries of origin and the sending of remittance money to assist. Developments included projects for online mentoring.[20] In 2012, the launch of LIONS@frica (the "backronym" stood for Liberalizing Innovation Opportunity Nations) saw a partnership of tech giants Nokia of Finland and Microsoft of the United States with a range of contributors, including the John Templeton Foundation, NGOs, and USAID, to kick-start technological entrepreneurship on the continent of Africa.[21]

Clinton's successor, Secretary of State John Kerry, tweaked the super-structure of the Department's partnership work, raising the initiative to the level of an *Office* of Global Partnerships (with the designation S/GP). The vision changed slightly to focus on providing an interagency partnership resource to help the entire US government with training and networking around the task of cross-sector international partnerships. Signature projects included the Fishackathon (#codeforfish), which began in 2014 as an annual global multi-city public–private partnership event, in which the Office challenged partners to create apps and designs to support the secretary's Ocean Agenda. Partners included Amazon and the government of Canada.[22] In 2016, the Office launched a pair of initiatives to partner with academia, Diplomacy Lab and Wonk Tank, both of which aimed to bring new ideas from students and faculty. Kerry also introduced the P3 Impact Award to recognize the best international partnerships. Momentum was such that the initiatives continued under the Trump administration.

The collaborative turn: the UK case

The same processes which were driving the transformation of US diplomacy were also at work in the United Kingdom, but in the UK case the focus was more explicitly on public diplomacy. For some practitioners in the early Blair era – including Simon Anholt – the obsession with the narrow promotion of a national brand appeared to be a blind alley. In 2002, a review of the public diplomacy landscape, chaired by the FCO's Chris Wilton, called for a formal structure to improve partnership within British public diplomacy. The FCO created a Public Diplomacy Strategy Board. In 2003, the new board wrote partnership into their definition of public diplomacy as "work which aims at influencing in a positive way, *including through the creation of relationships and partnerships*, the perceptions of individuals and organisations overseas about the UK and their engagement with the UK, in support of HMG's overseas objectives."[23] The wording reflected the existing priorities and approach of the British Council. The leadership of the Foreign and Commonwealth Office began to suspect that deeper changes were needed. The watershed came in 2005 when Lord Carter of Coles presented a full review of British public diplomacy and called for a focus on strategic objectives.[24] The task of applying the idea fell to Lord David Triesman, parliamentary undersecretary of state at the Foreign Office with responsibility for public diplomacy. As he explained to an audience of students at the London School of Economics in April 2007: "We have refocused our effort on talking about the issues we care about directly with the people in the countries we want to influence. And we don't just explain our policy, we debate it, we engage with people who may agree with us or passionately disagree." Lord Triesman even found a quote from Shakespeare to underline the approach: "They that thrive well take counsel of their friends."[25]

The focus of British public diplomacy now fell on four strategic objectives. These were: (1) climate security; (2) countering violent extremism and promoting understanding across cultural lines; (3) promoting the knowledge economy; and (4) the advancing multilateral partnership especially with the European Union.[26] Coordination was overseen by a reconfigured board, chaired by Lord Triesman, consisting of two "independent members" with knowledge of international communication issues (Chris Powell and Simon Anholt), Martin Davidson (director general of the British Council), Lucian Hudson (the FCO's director of communication), and Nigel Chapman (director of the BBC World Service, who sat in as an observer).[27] It was true that much of the old "cool Britannia" agenda fitted within the knowledge economy, but the frames presented were an ideal foundation for collaboration. The repositioning of climate change as "climate security" was a miracle of effective word choice. The FCO sought to promulgate this approach, launching a series of conferences on public diplomacy at Wilton Park and looking to spread a collaborative approach through its partners, advisors, and allies.[28] In 2008, the FCO commissioned an anthology of writing around the subject of the new public diplomacy under the title *Engagement: Public Diplomacy in a Globalised World* and worked to ensure that the volume was available on both sides of the Atlantic.[29]

Seeking to provide an even more effective foundation for collaboration, the FCO commissioned its outgoing director of communications, Lucian Hudson, to write a detailed report on the subject. The result, *The Enabling State: Collaborating for Success*, was a major contribution to understanding the potential and limits of cross-sector partnerships and remains an excellent starting place for those interested in the subject.[30] The final phase of the process came about in 2010 when the FCO revised its overall definition of public diplomacy to focus on partnership: "Public Diplomacy is a process of achieving the UK's international strategic priorities through partnerships with like-minded organizations and individuals in the public arena . . . NGOs, think tanks, opinion formers, young people, businesses and individual citizens."[31]

The collaborative turn in the United Kingdom was interrupted by the general election of May 2010 which brought a Conservative-dominated coalition government to power, led by David Cameron. In 2011, the government launched a soft power initiative known as the "Great" campaign, which seemed in some ways to be a return to a nation-brand-focused approach. Yet for all the flag waving and "backing Britain" ballyhoo behind the scenes, transnational and trans-sector partnerships remained the order of the day. There is no other way to work effectively in the twenty-first century.

Modeling good practice

While the benefits of collaboration are obvious, the methods for creating a partnership are often harder to pin down. Collaboration plainly requires leadership, and there is an element of cheek in intentionally drawing on the resources of others. Any model for facilitating partnerships requires attention to both communication and the establishment of a solid platform around which contributions can be marshaled. One model may be found in the old European fable known as "stone soup" in the west, "nail soup" in the north, and "axe soup" in the east of the continent. It goes like this. In a time of famine a stranger is traveling though unfamiliar country; some say he is a pilgrim, others say he is a soldier returning from war. He comes to a village and finds the doors closed to him. "Don't ask us for food," he is told by a gruff villager. "We have none. Best move on." But the stranger insists he has not come to beg for food but rather to demonstrate a cooking miracle. "I will show you how to make soup using just these stones," he says, holding out three little rocks. "All I need is a cauldron of water and a fire under it." The villager is curious. He fetches a cauldron and sets it up in the center of the village. The stranger drops his three stones into the cauldron and begins to stir the water with a long spoon. As he stirs, he speaks to himself. "Oh, stone soup is so good. . . ." Villagers come out of their homes and drift over to see what is going on. They come closer to hear what he is saying. "Stone soup is so good, but it is even better with just a little salt." One says, "I have a little salt at home. I'll fetch it for you." The salt is added.

The stranger continues stirring and speaking to himself: "Stone soup is so good, but it is even better with a few herbs . . ." Herbs are brought. The stranger continues: "Stone soup is so good, but it is even better with just a few potatoes." Another villager brings a few potatoes. The stranger continues speaking of carrots, beans, even meat, and one by one the villagers volunteer ingredients. By the end of the afternoon, the cauldron is full of a nourishing soup which the stranger proceeds to share with the astonished crowd. When everyone has eaten, he takes his leave and moves on.

The fable is consistent with the model advanced in 2012 by William Bratton and Zachary Tumin in their book *Collaborate or Perish! Reaching Across Boundaries in a Networked World.* They were themselves a cross-boundary collaboration: a former Los Angeles police chief working with a professor from Harvard's Kennedy School of Government. The book presented the requisite cases of unusual partnerships delivering results, but it also built a framework for constructing and managing collaboration. Their nine steps were as follows:

1. Begin with vision: an articulation of the goal that is clear to you, broad and compelling to others too.
2. Know the problem: research the area which you wish to tackle in your collaboration so that you truly understand its nature.
3. "Right-size" the problem: choose which elements can be viably addressed, given the resources available.
4. Build a platform: construct a mechanism through which collaboration can be effectively managed.
5. Locate partners: recruit participants in the project.
6. Sell the win–win: demonstrate to these partners how collaboration is to everyone's benefit.
7. Frame the story: present the collaboration externally in a way which will support its accomplishment.
8. Remember the political realities: understand that your partners have complex contexts of their own and both you and they will be limited in what you can achieve.
9. Accept the limits of the partnership: do not overstate the significance of collaboration or take other parties for granted.

These tasks all draw to a greater or lesser extent on the same skills as public diplomacy: listening, careful framing, and skilled advocacy.[32]

The Bratton–Tumin formula fits the fable of stone soup rather well. The stranger begins with a vision: getting a meal. He knows the problem: famine and the mistrust that comes with a critical scarcity of resources. He "right-sizes" the problem: getting a single meal rather than eating for life.

He builds a platform: setting up a cauldron in the center of the village. He locates partners by tempting them with his comments. He sells the "win–win" by promising that everyone will get to eat. He frames the story as a chance to see a "cooking miracle." He remembers the political realities by managing relations with the crowd gathered around the pot and delivering bowls of soup all round at the end of the day. He accepts the limits of the partnership by moving on at the end of the story. It also fits Bratton's experience running the LAPD.

In 2002, Bratton took office in a city synonymous with riots, gangs, and vindictive, trigger-happy policing. He presented a vision of a safer LA. He immediately set about getting to know the problem of crime in the city through a program of study, data analysis, and intense listening to representatives of LA's diverse communities. The process of "right-sizing" the problem suggested that, rather than attempting to tackle the woes of an entire city of four million people, it would be better to engage crime in five particularly notorious neighborhoods on the understanding that reducing crime in these locations would free resources to improve bordering areas. The theory at work was the same "fixing the broken windows" approach that Bratton had used effectively in New York City in the mid-1990s.[33] The platform that Bratton built was a network of forums for regular engagement with the community. He located partners in community organizations, including community groups and trade unions. The win–win he presented to those groups was community success. His frame followed from this: the common good of all citizens of the city. The political realities which he faced included mixed relations with the mayor and the city council who were not ecstatic about having the chief of police engaging constituents directly. Bratton certainly understood the limits of the partnership: his community partners could not be expected to back him or the LAPD on everything. For example, when, on May 1, 2007, officers of the LAPD used excessive force to disperse demonstrations for immigrant rights held at MacArthur Park, the community was outraged. The Police Union expected the members of Bratton's community groups to side with them over the incident. Bratton took a different view. He not only defended the community's right to disagree, he also personally attended town hall meetings about the incident and pressed for stiff penalties against offending LAPD officers. He demoted the senior officer in charge that day and used the incident as a driver for reorganization of the department.[34] The partnership paid dividends. When Bratton ended his term in 2009, crime had declined for an unprecedented six years in a row and had continued its fall despite the marked downturn in the economy.[35] Bratton believed that his policies in LA were of broader value and even traveled the world during his tenure in LA to speak about his experience. At the end of his tenure, he moved into the private sector and worked to find more general applications. His work with Tumin was an extension of this. His advice was considered sufficiently valuable in the United Kingdom for him to be awarded a medal by the queen and invited to help Britain respond to its own riots of 2011.[36]

The same kind of dynamics may be identified in successful cases of partnership outlined earlier in this chapter.

Analysis: the BBC and the FBIS

For the listening partnership between the BBC and the FBIS, the vision was initially security in an era of war and cold war. "Right-sizing" the problem involved segmenting the challenge into manageable tasks which, for BBC and FBIS monitors, meant tracking particular stations and programs and selecting which to translate. The platform was the procedure for research exchange created between the United States and the United Kingdom early in the war and formally set out in a written agreement of 1947. Partners in the process included smaller Allied countries, like the research conducted by Australia's Office of National Assessments.[37] The win–win in this situation was not hard to find. However, the political reality for all participants was that the significance of their work was often neglected by their own governments. The history of the joint monitoring initiative seems to be a constant round of one or the other side managing budget cuts. With the FBIS now known as the Open Source Center and the BBC MS required to monetize its activity, it is unclear if the listening challenges of the future will be as well met as those of the past.[38]

Analysis: *The God that Failed*

In terms of Bratton and Tumin, the vision of *The God that Failed* was a broad contesting of communism. Crossman certainly knew the problem. In his youth visiting Berlin, he had worked with the key Bolshevik propagandist in Western Europe, Willi Münzenberg.[39] He understood that communism was a threat because it was intellectually compelling. Crossman's "right-sizing" of the problem was to focus on intellectuals and understand that they would be influenced by the experience of other intellectuals. His platform was the literary anthology. The win–win was to both a personal expiation of past errors and a contribution to the collective crusade against communism. The frame for the project was its title: *The*

God that Failed was a precise summation of the level of disappointment and existential alienation which the contributors had felt when their faith in the Soviet approach evaporated. It was positioned as a private statement rather than as a piece of state propaganda, but it was excellent ammunition for the state-backed campaigns. Crossman's approach – partnering with people who are credible to his target audience – is a fine model for the challenges of our own time against violent extremism.

Analysis: ERASMUS

The ERASMUS program is an effective piece of exchange partnership. It is a collaborative platform built by another of the world's most impressive collaborative platforms: the European Union. The underlying vision was of course greater European integration. Knowledge of the problem directed attention to education which for many students presented a strictly national horizon for bureaucratic reasons, whereas with a little prompting they would have embraced a more cosmopolitan perspective. "Right-sizing" the problem meant focusing on university students, facilitating their ability to spend between a semester and a year outside their home country. The platform was the ERASMUS program; the partners were both the individual educational institutions and the students who had to be encouraged to take part. The win–win was the prospect of mutual discovery across the Union. The frame was embedded in the title, associating contemporary exchange with one of the masters of the European renaissance and implying a new opportunity for rebirth and exponential growth. The political realities were the limits that member states initially placed on the program. France, Germany, and the United Kingdom initially resisted the project, worrying that their own well-developed exchange channels would lose out. The idea has grown over time, and it has even become possible to reach beyond the EU's boundaries with ERASMUS MUNDUS.

Analysis: Broadcasting for Child Survival

In the case of the VOA initiative Broadcasting for Child Survival, the vision of director Geoff Cowan and his staffer Greg Pirio was for international broadcasting to make a difference in the developing world. "Knowing the problem" of world health revealed that lack of accurate information was an issue and one which VOA was ideally equipped to correct. The process of "right-sizing" the problem involved focusing on one area where lack of information caused particular damage: the child health agenda advanced by UNICEF. The platform was the conference that VOA and USAID mounted in April 1998. The "win–win" lay in making a significant contribution to the lives of audiences and being seen to deliver on humanitarian aspects of foreign policy. The "frame" of the initiative was expressed in the conference title, Broadcasting for Child Survival, with its focus on reducing critical causes of child mortality rather than simple child wellbeing. Political limits abounded. The idea had emerged under Geoff Cowan but the conference was hosted under his successor Evelyn Lieberman, who had reassigned Pirio by that point. Follow-up fell to Lieberman's successor, Sandford Ungar. All brought their own emphases. The VOA/AID element had to work through the bureaucracy around interagency partnership, and the whole initiative had to adjust to the transition to the George W. Bush administration and the decline in openness to US leadership in many quarters overseas. The transition of important aspects of the project to UNICEF doubtless helped to bring about the involvement of some parties. Despite some concerns, the case shows how the right collaborative platform at the right moment can unlock disproportionate results in a networked world.[40]

Lessons learned: ten secrets of success

In June 2012, the State Department's Office of the Global Partnership Initiatives partnered with the Institute for Corporate Responsibility at the George Washington University School of Business to host a one-day conference to consider the emerging lessons from the range of partnership activity initiated during Hillary Clinton's tenure as secretary of state. The gathering brought together interested scholars, practitioners, and representatives from some of the State Department's prominent partners, including Ford Motors, and such NGOs as Vital Voices, Rainforest Alliance, and World Vision. The title for the day was "Uncommon Alliances: Real Partnerships, Real Experiences, Real Impacts."[41] The final session summarized the lessons generated across the day. Experience tumbled into the room. Sifting through the material, ten secrets of a happy partnership emerged.

1. Agree objectives. It is important that all parties to a partnership have a clear idea of objectives and share a vision for the project.
2. Manage expectations. It is important that all parties understand the limits of the partnership, most especially issues around duration and who else parties might choose to partner.
3. Establish trust. It is important that all parties come to trust one

another. Despite the march of electronic media, the view of practitioners was that there was no substitute for face-to-face meetings when building the kind of trust necessary to run a successful collaboration.

4. Protect trust. It is important that all parties *continue* to trust one another, and the best way to do that is to remain in regular touch.

5. Insist on equality. Practitioners reported that part of the preparation for a successful partnership was to insist that all parties be treated equally and not segmented by rank. Most especially, it was important that the scale of particular financial donations not be disclosed, and that contributions in kind be given equal status.

6. Allow and respect specialism. The extension of the equality principle was to be open to a diversity of expertise and to understand that different partners bring different expertise to the table.

7. Cross boundaries, sectors, and generations. Partnership not only allows but requires boundary crossing and working with people from across divides of professional experience. Barriers need not be geographical.

8. Celebrate the differences. The practitioners reported that diversity within partnerships was actually one of the things that made them fun and that it made sense to explicitly emphasize and direct attention to the range of actors involved.

9. Share the credit. Veterans of partnerships recalled that an otherwise successful instance of cooperation could be tarnished by one partner taking the lion's share of the credit and failing to acknowledge the role of a collaborator.

10. Part before it gets old. The most surprising piece of advice from participants in partnerships was the recognition that the best partnerships had a sunset built in and that parties should not be made to feel that entering into a partnership was an exclusive or indefinite commitment. Combination and recombination of partners in fresh projects kept even familiar issues exciting, continually opening new perspectives.

Collaboration and CVE: defeating ISIS/Daesh

One of the best recent examples of the power of collaboration is the collective effort of public engagement in CVE. In its early stages, CVE in the West was often mired in the difficulty of building partnerships within a single national bureaucracy, let alone attempting to enroll international partners.[42] From 2011, however, the partnership process moved to the international level with the successful creation of the Global Counterterrorism Forum (GCF), co-chaired by the Netherlands and Morocco. The GCF provided a platform for sharing best practices, many of which reflect such markers of effective public diplomacy as focusing on relationships and building evaluation into programs from the concept stage onward.[43] In 2012, the United Arab Emirates took an important step to strengthen content, launching a hub called the Hedayah International Center of Excellence for Countering Violent Extremism, located in Abu Dhabi, to help generate and exchange effective shareable media.[44]

As the challenge of Daesh grew, the Obama White House moved to encourage cooperation, hosting a CVE summit in February 2015. Its approach emphasized international partnership not only with other countries but also with technology companies whose platforms were intrinsic to the transmission of messages for and against jihad. The White House promised "technology camps" to empower young people to speak out for moderation in their localities.[45] Activities included the creation of a Strong Cities Network – built by the US Department of State working with the governments of Norway and Denmark and the UK-based Institute for Strategic Dialogue – to pool the experience of mayors and local governments in their anti-extremism work.[46] The United Nations also moved to develop cooperation with the UN secretary-general's plan to counter violent extremism, presented in January 2016. Such efforts found eager partners in the corporate sector, where players like Google were looking to demonstrate corporate social responsibility through operations like their Google Ideas think tank (now known as Google Jisgsaw). The corporate sector also saw the emergence of specialist contractors looking to partner different levels of government to facilitate the creation of media or harness big data as part of the CVE effort. Examples included Horizon PR, a subsidiary of the British advertising agency M&C Saatchi, created in 2015 specifically for CVE and related faith- and identity-focused projects, or Moonshot CVE, whose tag is "countering violent extremism through data driven innovation."[47]

The UK Foreign Office took a lead in coordinating the effort against Daesh. In the autumn of 2015, the Foreign Office established a coalition communication cell under the leadership of Daniel Chugg. The unit included staff loaned from 11 partner countries. Its core objective was to contest Daesh's own claims and seductive self-aggrandizement. In Chugg's words:

> Our first task was to change the narrative around Daesh from one of success to one of failure. We needed to damage the Daesh brand by showing that, contrary to its own propaganda, Daesh was failing to win battles, failing to provide services to people in the territory under its control, and failing to live up to its promises.[48]

Activities included the creation of a daily update on Daesh's activities, complete with suggested tweets and retweets for 1,000 officials in 60 partner countries; a website and social media feed giving examples of Daesh atrocities and defeats; quarterly meetings with 30 partner countries to develop skills, share material, build common messages, and build in private-sector partners. Evidence of success included the use of anti-Daesh cell material at all levels of partner messaging, including, Chugg was proud to note, statements by the prime ministers of Australia and Spain. The net effect was to make Daesh seem "less cool, less credible and less competent." Consequently, Chugg noted, "they found it more difficult to convince people to join them, both from among the local population in Iraq and from third countries."[49] Military defeat underlined the message.

The collective CVE effort has produced some remarkable examples of persuasion. Some of the most celebrated include the #notanotherbrother campaign, created by British think tank Quilliam in 2015,[50] or the work of the website Open Your Eyes.net, with its short but pointed vox pop videos by British Muslims.[51] But the effort has not been without its critics. Issues have included lack of transparency and the role of contractors in helping to generate anti-extremist material. In 2016, the United Kingdom's *Guardian* newspaper drew attention to the role of a company called Breakthrough Media which, it claimed, had received more than £11 million in UK government funding for CVE communication and had not only fed material to sympathetic media organizations but also when necessary created some, too.[52] Civil Rights activists Ben Hayes and Asim Qureshi, writing on the Open Democracy website, raised concerns over British government-sponsored work being falsely "presented as community-based operations" and noted that the eagerness of the private sector to be involved now constituted a "counter-radicalization industry." They were also puzzled by the eagerness of the government to partner with the so-called "formers" – ex-jihadis – noting, "One of the most astonishing achievements of the counter-radicalisation industry is its burial of the idea that the people best placed to deter individuals from extremism might actually be those who have never engaged in any form of it."[53] Implicit in their account of UK government partnership was the suggestion that some "partners" might not actually be aware that a western government was supporting their activity, and the revelation of such help might damage their credibility or even place them in danger. For his part, Chugg, on the eve of promotion to the post of British Ambassador in Myanmar, also placed a dampener on complacency, noting that for all its success to date the collective communication struggle against Daesh was about to get more difficult. The destruction of the central Daesh communication mechanism has fragmented the organization's messaging into multiple strands which lack a central story and require attention to myriad local narratives, each of which will entail careful listening to understand their specific dynamics. For all the efficacy of the methods adopted thus far, there is still much new work to be done.[54]

Conclusion: reviving collaboration

While collaboration has become a key characteristic of contemporary global public engagement, it is also clear that it is still not always done well. The emphasis of Bratton and Tumin on platforms is well placed. Many contemporary collaborative projects lack clear donor coordination structures, leaving local partners uncertain of when their next injection of funding from the European Union, OESC, or a kindly German *Stiftung* might be due. The uncertainty breeds short-term thinking and is especially damaging to projects in the media development field, where continuity of skilled staff is essential. Collaborative platforms continue to emerge. One of the most exciting is EUNIC – the European Union National Institutes of Culture – a partnership which provides a platform for erstwhile rivals such as the Goethe Institute, Italian Cultural Institute, and the British Council to work together to advance issues of common concern through the arts around the world. EUNIC partnerships are established between cultural diplomacy organizations on a city-by-city basis. Their makeup is strongly influenced by past history, with former colonial powers in a location tending to be less open to joining than countries who are newer to the neighborhood.

In cases where partnership is impossible because of the established foreign policy objectives of potential actors, the difficulty should be read as a strong indication that the objectives are wrong. The need for partnership provides an especially powerful critique of the obsession with national brands. It is better to move against a problem than hold off for want of having one's flag on a project. More than this, being known as a good "team player" or a "facilitator" of partnership will in the long term enhance an international actor's soft power. Conversely, insisting on acting alone or with a personal fanfare will in the long term also be noticed, with negative consequences. Finally, the emerging focus on partnership has implications for the study of public diplomacy. If public diplomacy is a multi-stakeholder, collaborative, relationship-focused activity, it makes little sense to segment its academic study into national cases. Just as practitioners have learned to think in terms of partnership, so must scholars. Only if scholars consider how actors of many kinds have come together through networks to address common problems can scholarship be fully supportive of the next phase in global public engagement.

Conclusion: Public Diplomacy and the Crisis of Our Time

In the winter of 2014, Ukraine reeled from a twin barrage: a physical invasion of foreign military forces and an invasion of distorted information. The Russian government took advantage of the cloud of confusion to present that invasion as a separatist rebellion. In a matter of weeks, Russian troops had occupied Crimea. Foreign observers began to speak of hybrid warfare.[1] For many Ukrainians, it was simply warfare. At Kyiv's Mohyla School of Journalism, academics gathered to consider how they might coordinate a possible communication response as actors in their own right. It was a journalist and recent graduate of the school's Digital Future of Journalism Program called Olga Yurkova who caught the imagination of the meeting. Yurkova proposed a website to expose the fakery. Professor of Communication Yevgeni Fedchenko immediately saw the value in her idea. In March 2014, he led the launch of StopFake as a multilingual fact-checking website offering a resource initially for his Russian-speaking compatriots and for English-speaking international observers of the crisis in Ukraine. Staffed by volunteers from the Ukrainian journalism and media academic communities, StopFake exposed the fabricated stories circulating online: invented atrocities illustrated with repurposed images from completely different conflicts, including Syria and even Mexico, were especially abundant, but other early fakes exposed included a death certificate for Ukraine's ex-president Victor Yanukovych and a report that American mercenaries had been deployed in the troubled Donetsk region. The site was an immediate success. After three months, it was logging moe than 1.5 million unique visitors each month.[2]

StopFake was even-handed. When supporters of the Ukrainian government bent the truth, the site flagged that distortion also. But part of the value of the site was as a living book of record. By logging and flagging fakes as they appeared, it revealed a dramatic geography of deception. StopFake was part of the process of sounding the alarm in a Europe with little desire to see a return to cold war. Western NGOs and sympathetic governments began to support StopFake as a resource in the struggle to defend the media. They understood that in the new digital world it was better to approach a communication issue with the attitude "Who can I empower?", rather than the old-school question of "What can I say?" By the end of 2016, StopFake materials were not only available in ten languages, but StopFake veterans were also traveling to provide training to media communities elsewhere in the post-Soviet world, helping journalists and politicians in Armenia, Azerbaijan, Georgia, and Kazakhstan understand and respond appropriately to the challenge of Kremlin-sponsored media.[3] It was one example of how motivated individuals can partner with external actors to make a real difference.

The present crisis is deeper than the need to respond to a single rogue state disrupting international media, or even that of multiple states seeking to assert themselves through aggressive use of media, recently dubbed "sharp power."[4] The crisis is a symptom as much as a disease in its own right; it speaks of a world in which many states are using foreign policy as a mechanism to rally domestic support and demonize their neighbors. Many leaders are promising to make their countries great again, to withdraw from old alliances, rebuild walls, and settle old scores. Some nations have embraced the tools (if not the spirit) of public diplomacy as a mechanism for projecting their national image and agenda. But the reality is that the problems we face are too great for any one country. The time of asserting independence has passed. The world needs to acknowledge its interdependence and see what can be learned across national boundaries to address our collective challenges. The crisis of our time demands specific responses, but before addressing those it is important not to lose sight of the underlying lessons of public diplomacy practice thus far, which have been outlined by the discussion in this book and should be kept in mind as international actors consider the way forward.[5]

Lesson 1: public diplomacy begins with listening

Global public engagement must begin with listening: systematically collecting and analyzing the opinions of foreign publics. Listening must be seen to be done and should be open-ended and unhindered by preconceived categories. New technology has made listening easier, inasmuch as software can monitor blogs and Twitter feeds in real time, but the practitioner must remember that technology may also place new distance between them and their audience. In public diplomacy, relationships remain paramount.

Lesson 2: public diplomacy must be connected to policy

The golden rule of public diplomacy is that what counts is not what you say but what you do. There is no substitute for sound policy, and an actor with a reputation for sound policy will find their power in the world enhanced. By extension, the most important link in any public engagement structure is that which connects "listening" to policy making and ensures that foreign opinion is weighed in the foreign policy process. Once sound policies have been identified, they should be publicized by or coordinated with public diplomacy. There is, in addition, a need to coordinate with those partners whose role could be considered "engagement by deed." Conversely, actors should remember that in the wired world a major policy error is seen globally.

Lesson 3: public diplomacy is not a performance for domestic consumption

One of the major problems facing public diplomats today is the tendency of some governments to conceive of their work not as a means to engage international publics but rather as a mechanism to impress domestic audiences. These governments are keen to show their own people all that is being done to educate the world or to correct the misperceptions of "ignorant foreigners." They conduct public diplomacy overseas for the purposes of propaganda at home, hoping to give their own people the gift of the world's admiration. Today, the political context of much foreign public engagement requires that it yield measurable results, which in turn threatens to create a bias toward those elements of public diplomacy that can most easily show short-term effectiveness. This bias has placed culture and exchange – with their longer horizons – at a disadvantage. If public diplomacy is to retain a mission beyond winning short-term political gain, it will require restraint and vision on the part of leaders.

Lesson 4: effective public diplomacy requires credibility

The value of credibility has been proverbial since the day Aesop's shepherd boy first cried "Wolf." The problem is that the ways of achieving credibility differ from one element of public diplomacy to another and are harmed if too closely associated. There is a clear advantage to the Anglo-German model of separating elements of public engagement into firewalled units, coordinated at the highest level, rather than corralling them all within a foreign ministry. Credibility remains the foundation of all effective public diplomacy, and social networks provide even greater scope for that credibility to resonate. As the volume of information available over the internet grows, the provenance of that information becomes ever more significant.

Public diplomacy has its own brands, and information provided under those brands can have special authority and is more likely to be voluntarily passed on by one internet user to a peer, so long as the credibility of those brands is upheld.

Lesson 5: sometimes the most credible voice is not your own

The desire to be seen to be effective has been one of the factors that have historically pushed actors to place themselves center stage in their public diplomacy, regardless of whether their voice is best suited to advance the cause they wish to help. Some of the most effective cases of foreign public engagement have occurred when actors have empowered others to tell their story. National public diplomacy does well to privilege voices from its regions and minorities. All actors do well to seek out partners who are credible to their audiences. In the era of peer-to-peer technology, the ultimate credibility rests with similarity. This means that effective public diplomacy will be that which enrolls "people like me" and provides them with information that they can pass to their peers. The corresponding conceptualization of engagement is that of a mechanism not for making single communications to a target audience but for introducing a reproducible idea into a network so that it can be passed among a target group.

Lesson 6: public diplomacy is not always "about you"

Public diplomacy is about advancing foreign policy, and that foreign policy may not necessarily concern the image of an actor: it may be directed at engineering an improvement of the international environment, or empowering local voices within a target state or states. Once liberated from a narrow obsession with national image, foreign public engagement holds the potential to address a wide range of global issues. It is one of the few tools available to an international actor wishing to engage the international public that holds the fate of the earth in its hands as never before. More than this, with public diplomacy now aimed at shared issues and using networks, old models of success are redundant. Some governments still have a narrow idea of success in international affairs. They understand the value of networks and relationships but look for a unilateral advantage at the end of the process. This is untenable. One cannot "win" one's relationships. Relationships have to be based on mutual interest. The desire to win one's relationships is a symptom of psychosis.

Lesson 7: public diplomacy is everyone's business

It is tempting to compartmentalize foreign public engagement as the exclusive preserve of those who draw salaries for working in the field; but this is to ignore both the contribution of "citizen diplomats" and the "people-to-people" public diplomacy, carried out through formal work like town twinning and myriad positive connections across frontiers. Arguably, the greatest achievement of public diplomacy in the last half-century is the reconciliation between Germany and France, a process in which the local town-to-town exchanges preceded the nationally organized schemes by 15 years. No less significantly, the citizen plays a role in promoting the message or image which the public diplomat is seeking to project to the world. Just as public diplomacy is vulnerable to bad policy, so is it vulnerable to bad people. If a nation fails to uphold its "brand," any messaging will be undermined. A small number of people can cause a great deal of damage. Sometimes, the key battle in engaging a foreign public is persuading the population at home to live up to a positive reputation.

Today, government-sponsored messages are only one mechanism by which we communicate across frontiers. Opinion is also formed via its interchange between individuals meeting directly. A country's image can be shaped as much by the experience of a returning migrant or the fate of an asylum seeker as by the words of its highest-ranking officials. Images will always be judged against experience. Citizens of diasporas are a resource for public diplomacy partnerships for their countries of origin as well as for their countries of residence. They are also an important audience. For a society to prosper in the international marketplace of ideas, it is necessary not only to strive to say the right thing but, in the concluding words of Maya Angelou's *I Know Why the Caged Bird Sings*, to "be the right thing inside" or, as Simon Anholt puts it, work to be a "good country."

Beyond these seven lessons are four needs which have emerged from the present international difficulties.

Need 1: to build reputational security

The crisis of our moment raises serious issues about the international order. If parts of Ukraine can be swallowed by a neighbor with relative impunity, who is safe? The fate of Ukraine raises the possibility that public diplomacy, soft power, and nation branding may have been conceptualized in the wrong way. These concepts are often seen as luxuries of the wealthiest and best-known countries. The reality is that at the other end of the spectrum smaller or newer countries need to engage to establish reputational security. Reputational security is a place on the high ground of the global imagination. Once established, it means that when a challenge comes – whether from a neighbor contesting sovereignty, internal secession, or a natural threat like rising sea levels – the world cares. Ukraine plainly lacked reputational security. It was simply not understood by international audiences as sufficiently distinct from Russia to provoke the same kind of reaction as, for example, the threat to Polish sovereignty which the West read into the declaration of martial law in Poland in 1981.

The quest for reputational security helps to explain the national branding efforts of Kosovo – its attempts to win diplomatic recognition and work to be present on such international cultural platforms as the Venice Biennales. Reputational security concerns also seem to be drivers of Taiwan's engagement with foreign publics. Nation branding is simply too relaxed a frame for the reality of the goal. Similarly, Kazakhstan's hard work to build a reputation in its first 30 years are not solely about attracting investment, but reflects a deeper need to be relevant beyond its borders. Hence the government of President Nazarbayev hosted the expo of 2017, initiated a cycle of interfaith conferences, launched the Astana film festival, and invested in an externally oriented university sector. The model is that of Singapore rather than Dubai. The hope is to be both relevant and better connected. Aids to this connectivity include use of English as the language of instruction for all STEM education and the decision to abandon the Cyrillic alphabet of the Soviet era and adopt the Latin alphabet going forward. The desire to be known is such that even virtual slanders like the 2006 comedy film *Borat: Cultural Learnings of America for Make Benefit Glorious Nation of Kazakhstan* are understood as gifts by some Kazakh officials. Knowing that Kazakhstan is the "Borat country" gives it a place on the mental map of western audiences which Tajikistan, Uzbekistan, Turkmenistan, and Kyrgyzstan lack. It is a starting point on which more accurate knowledge and an awareness of the country's relevance can be built. Without meaning something to the world, there is much less at stake should a rapacious neighbor decide to compromise Kazakh sovereignty. Foreign public engagement is one way to build reputational security.

Need 2: to contest disinformation

The surge in disinformation requires a response. While it is tempting to respond to fake news in kind, NATO's collective response to the crisis has avoided compromising established news values. Western media should be careful not to demonize the Russian people while attacking their leaders and might do well to adopt the same strategy as the BBC in the 1950s and focus criticism on issues rather than personalities. Certainly, western countries should be careful not to conform to the stereotypes promulgated by their enemies. Thus far, the western allies have worked to *expose* disinformation and distortion where it is happening: support for StopFake and other activities like the European Union's External Action Service Disinformation Review is part of this.[6] But this is not enough. It is also crucial that the western allies *engage* audiences under pressure from disinformation and hybrid threats through the established channels of public diplomacy, including cultural relations, exchange, and international broadcasting. to assist in the construction of resilient societies better able to cope with such threats. In addition, there is a need to *enhance* indigenous media – a public diplomacy of empowerment to support the local creation of reliable news depicting the world authoritatively from the location under threat. In a city like Narva, the Russian-speaking border town in Estonia, the answer to a "one-size-fits-all" message from Moscow is not a "one-size-fits-all" message from Washington, DC but work to provide media which fit the complexities of that community, which seeks to be simultaneously Russian-speaking, Estonian, and European. Finally, it is worth remembering that the answer to a communication problem may not necessarily lie in the field of communication. Perhaps weaponized information needs an information disarmament process; certainly, that was part of the solution to the media challenge of the Cold War in the late 1980s.[7]

Need 3: to counter victim narratives

In the marketplace of ideas, the meme of the victim narrative has become the fat little cuckoo chick pushing other ideas out of the nest. The victim narrative is an ideal message to resonate in social media. It tells the audience that its community has a special story of suffering and needs to be attended to before the needs of others can be considered. Such narratives kept communities apart in the 1990s and – with symmetrical embrace – fueled the decade's ugliest disputes including Israel/Palestine and the breakup of Yugoslavia. In the first decade of the twenty-first century, they drove recruitment to the global jihad. In the second decade, they are fueling the new populism. Public diplomacy needs to consider how victim narratives of the past have been diffused and look for ways to overcome them using the kind of resources that were devoted to countering violent extremism in recent years. We have been here before. Victim narratives and mutual fear were part of the antipathy underpinning the great struggles of the twentieth century. These struggles were not simply overcome by force of arms but by communication of a vision. The challenge for our generation is to achieve the same result without the trial by fire.

Need 4: to articulate a vision of the future

As the portions of this book dealing with psychology have indicated, the cognitive biases shared by all people make it hard to shift a fixed idea once established. Beyond the power of the confirmation bias that supports the first presentation of an argument, an idea is defended by a variety of the endowment effect. Overcoming negative and divisive messaging requires a compelling alternative. In the case of international relations, that must be a vision of the future.

Consider the tightrope walker. Tightrope walkers have a simple secret. In order to stay stable on the high wire, they fix their eyes on their destination: the far end of the wire. If they cannot see the end, they are equally well served by turning around and focusing on their point of origin. If they are looking at neither, they wobble and will fall. Much the same is true for nations. Stability requires either a clear sense of a future destination or a vision of the past. The crisis of our moment is based on so many leaders around the world drawing their stability from visions of their past. Beyond simply trying to correct the mutually antithetical visions of the past, our collective public diplomacy should also consider ways to turn the tightrope walker around and articulate compelling visions of the future. The history of public diplomacy suggests that such turnarounds are possible; indeed, they are the chief way in which the great international crises of the past were solved. Consider the Great War; World War II; the Cold War. The road beyond these conflicts required the articulation of a vision of the future so attractive that not only allies found it compelling but adversaries also. US presidents were essential to this process. Woodrow Wilson, Franklin Roosevelt, John F. Kennedy, and Ronald Reagan were all masters of presenting positive visions of the future. But they did not speak alone. Their messages were carried by the public diplomacy apparatus of their respective era, and participants shaped the presentation. The greatest communicators of the era were part of the process. In the Great War, for example, when the British government realized that it needed to present a vision of the future to the German public, they hired the man best known for his writing about the subject: H. G. Wells.[8] The problem was not the lack of the vision's plausibility but the failure of the post-war settlement to live up to wartime promises.

Despite the current obsession with hurts and glories of the past, there are some public diplomacy actors who are already articulating visions of the future. The UN, for example, has rallied member states behind 17 sustainable development goals (SDGs) to be achieved by 2030.[9] Positive visions of the future were part of the Astana Expo in 2017 and underpin plans for the Dubai Expo in 2020. Other projects focusing on the future include a remarkable project by the city of Oslo to demonstrate its commitment to the future by building a library of the future. Designed by Scottish artist Katie Paterson, this is not simply an eco-friendly new space but a collection of books commissioned from and delivered by one major author each year which will not be published until 2114. Participating writers announced so far include Canadian Nobel laureate Margaret Atwood and *Cloud Atlas* author David Mitchell. The library has also planted a forest of a thousand trees to provide the paper for the pages when the time comes.[10] In a similar vein, a team affiliated with the Hebrew University in Jerusalem has chosen to mark the centenary of Einstein's theory of relativity not by looking back or reiterating his achievement but by seeking out a hundred visions from visionary thinkers in our own time and anthologizing them to inspire the next generation in the way that Einstein fired up our parents and grandparents.[11]

The era of social media has opened up fresh possibilities, but it has not erased the relevance of the history of public diplomacy. On the contrary, the lessons of the past seem even more relevant in an age in which communications play an unprecedented role. Whether the communications travel electronically at the speed of light or in hand-delivered notes written with quills, the underlying foundations remain as valid today as they were when the term "public diplomacy" was coined in the 1960s or, when in previous centuries, generations practiced the art oblivious to its name. At the dawn of a systematic approach to human government, Bias of Priene was asked a simple question about the nature of human endeavor: "What is sweet to men?" He answered with typical clarity: "Hope."[12] Two-and-a-half thousand years later, we still need hope. Public diplomacy can be the mechanism for communicating that hope but, still more importantly, given the right vision and the right interconnection, it can be part of the process by which the publics themselves become the hope.

Notes

Chapter 1 Diplomacy through Foreign Public Engagement: Core Terminology and History

1 http://www.nytimes.com/2012/02/16/world/asia/xi-jinping-of-china-makes-a-return-trip-to-iowa.html?_r=0. The visit, the Dvorchaks, and its resonance today are featured in the forthcoming documentary film on Sino-American relations: *Better Angels* (dir., Malcolm Clarke, 2018).

2 Eytan Gilboa, "Searching for a Theory of Public Diplomacy," *ANNALS of the American Academy of Political and Social Science* 616(1) (2008): 5–757, part of a special issue which provides multiple perspectives. See also Kathy Fitzpatrick, "Advancing the New Public Diplomacy: A Public Relations Perspective," *The Hague Journal of Diplomacy* 2(3) (2007): 187–211; and Nancy Snow and Nicholas J. Cull, *The Routledge Handbook of Public Diplomacy*, 2nd edn, Abingdon: Routledge, 2019.

3 Institutions using the term "public diplomacy" include the Public Diplomacy Council in Washington, DC, the journal *Place Branding and Public Diplomacy*, the Center on Public Diplomacy at USC, the Center for the Study of Public Diplomacy at Ilmenau in Germany, the Center on Public Diplomacy at Beijing Foreign Studies University, the Public Diplomacy interest group of the International Communication Association (established in 2016) and the degree programs in public diplomacy offered by the University of Southern California, Syracuse and Beijing Foreign Studies University.

4 The formulation of "diplomacy as ways in which an international actor seeks to manage the international environment" comes from Harold Nicolson, though he sees negotiation as the mechanism of diplomacy and sets all propaganda activity outside of the definition; see *Diplomacy*, 2nd edn, Oxford: Oxford University Press, 1950, p. i.

5 The motto is quoted in Diogenes Laertius' "Life of Bias," paragraph v, in *The Lives and Opinions of the Eminent Philosophers*, trans. C. D. Yonge, London: Henry G. Bohn, 1853, pp. 38–40.

6 See, for example, Sun Tzu, *The Art of War* (trans. Samuel B. Griffith), Oxford: Oxford University Press, 1963 (ch. XIII, v. 4), p. 145.

7 Herodotus, 7, 150: see A. D. Godley, trans., *Herodotus*, Vol. III, London: Heinemann, 1919, pp. 459, 461.

8 The best articulation of this process remains Dimitri Obolensky, *The Byzantine Commonwealth: Eastern Europe, 500–1453*, London: Weidenfeld and Nicolson, 1971.

9 For a convenient survey of the practice focusing on Viking Iceland, see Jenny Jochens, "Fosterage," in Margaret Schaus, *Women and Gender in Medieval Europe: An Encyclopedia*, New York: Taylor and Francis, 2006, pp. 296–7.

10 Frederick II wanted to transform the sixth crusade into a negotiated settlement. His approach is well described in David Abulafia, *Frederick II: A Medieval Emperor*, Oxford: Oxford University Press, 1988, pp. 290–321. For an example of a letter to Henry III from 1229, see https://legacy.fordham.edu/Halsall/source/fred2cdelets.asp

11 The present author makes this argument at length in his essay "New Tricks or New Dogs? How Propaganda became Public Diplomacy, then morphed into Public Diplomacy 2.0," in Jonathan Auerbach and Russ Castronovo (eds), *The Oxford Handbook of Propaganda Studies*, Oxford: Oxford University Press, 2013, pp. 131–46.

12 Daryl Copeland in Nicholas J. Cull and Michael Hawes (eds), *Canadian Public Diplomacy*, New York: Palgrave, 2019.

13 This formulation borrows from the famous dictum of the Romanian historian of religion Micea Eliade regarding the relationship between the sacred and consciousness.

14 The siege story is in paragraph II of Diogenes' "Life of Bias." For an English version, see Diogenes Laertius, *The Lives and Opinions of the Eminent Philosophers*, trans. C. D. Yonge, London: Henry G. Bohn, 1853, pp. 38–40.

15 Kautilya's *Arthashastra*, Book X, Relating to War, ch. I, encampment.

16 The standard work on the image of Alexander is Andrew F. Stewart, *Faces of Power: Alexander's Image and Hellenistic Politics*. Oakland, CA: University of California Press, 1993.

17 The text is included in Ignatius of Loyola, *The Constitutions of the Society of Jesus*, trans. George E. Ganss, S.J., St Louis, MO: Institute of Jesuit Sources, 1970, item [3] on p. 66. While the word "propagate" and its derivatives have an agricultural origin, their use in an ideological context was part of their classical origin. Cicero's treatise "On Divination" includes the observation in book 2, section 149, "*Quam ob rem, ut religio propaganda etiam est, quae est inucta cum cognitione naturae, sic superstitionis stirpes omnes eiiciendae*" (Wherefore, as this religion which is united with the knowledge of nature is to be propagated, so also are all the roots of superstition to be destroyed). The translation is from Cicero (trans./ed. C. D. Yonge), *The Treatise of M. T. Cicero*, London: Henry G. Bohn, 1852, p. 262.

18 On the need to study rhetoric, see Loyola, ibid. [351 & 352] pp. 187–8; on preaching, see [402–5], pp. 201–2. For commentary on early Jesuit preaching, see John M. McManamon, S. J., *The Texts and Contexts of Ignatius Loyola's "Autobiography,"* New York: Fordham University Press, 2013, pp. 79–80.

19 On the foundation of the Sacred Congregation for *Propaganda Fide*, see Peter Guilday, "The Sacred Congregation de Propaganda Fide (1622–1922)," *The Catholic Historical Review* 6, 1922: 478–94. The early entry of the bias against

propaganda is noted by Garth S. Jowett and Victoria O'Donnell, *Propaganda and Persuasion*, Thousand Oaks, CA: Sage, 2014, p. 82.

20 Jonathan Israel, *The Dutch Republic: Its Rise, Greatness and Fall, 1477–1806*, Oxford: Oxford University Press, 1995; Pierre Loyseleur (ed.), *The Apologie of William of Orange against the proclamation of the King of Spaine*, Ann Arbor, MI: ProQuest/EEBO, 2010. English precursors include Henry VIII's decision in 1522 to publicize his split with the church internationally, "to the intent that the falsehood, iniquity, malice and injustice of the bishop of Rome may thereby appear to all the world." See Geoffrey de C. Parmiter, *The King's Great Matter: A Study of Anglo-Papal Relations, 1527–1534*. London: Longmans, 1967, pp. 259–62, 268–70.

21 Robert Thomas Fallon, *Milton in Government*. University Park: Pennsylvania State University Press, 1993; Dora Neill Raymond, *Oliver's Secretary: John Milton in an Era of Revolt,*. New York: Minton, Balch and Co., 1932.

22 On the international impact of the Declaration of Independence, see David Armitage, *The Declaration of Independence: A Global History*, Cambridge: Harvard University Press, 2007.

23 The story is told in Harry Ammon, *The Genet Mission*, New York: Norton, 1973.

24 Selim Deringel, *The Well Protected Domains: Ideology and the Legitimation of Power in the Ottoman Empire, 1876–1909*, London: I. B. Tauris, 1998.

25 On Great War propaganda, see Michael L. Sanders and Philip M. Taylor, *British Propaganda during the First World War, 1914–18*, London: Macmillan, 1982.

26 I addressed this story in detail in Nicholas J. Cull, *The Cold War and the United States Information Agency: American Propaganda and Public Diplomacy, 1945–1989*. Cambridge: Cambridge University Press; see esp. ch. 2.

27 Robert F. Delaney and John S. Gibson (eds), *American Public Diplomacy: The Perspective of Fifty Years*, Medford, MA: The Edward R. Murrow Center of Public Diplomacy, Fletcher School of Law and Diplomacy/Lincoln Filene Center for Citizenship and Public Affairs, 1967, p. 31, as cited in John Brown, "The Anti-Propaganda Tradition in the United States," *Bulletin Board for Peace,* 29 June 2003, posted at http://www.publicdiplomacy.org/19.htm

28 Cull, *The Cold War and the United States Information Agency*, esp. pp. 259–61.

29 Frank Ninkovich, *The Diplomacy of Ideas: U.S. Foreign Policy and Cultural Relations, 1938–1950*, New York: Cambridge University Press, 1981.

30 For discussion, see Tim Rivera, *Distinguishing Cultural Relations from Cultural Diplomacy: The British Council's Relationship With Her Majesty's Government*, Los Angeles: CPD Perspectives of Public Diplomacy, 2015.

31 Kathy R. Fitzpatrick, *The Collapse of American Public Diplomacy: What Diplomatic Experts Say about Rebuilding America's Image in the World – A View from the Trenches*, Hamden, CT: USIA Alumni Assoc./Qunnipiac University, 2008: http://www.publicdiplomacy.org/Fitzpatrick2008.pdf, esp. p. 9. "Good

relationships" were rated sixth in both time periods, and "respect" was rated ninth in the Cold War and eighth for the present day.

32 This story is told in Nicholas J. Cull, *The Decline and Fall of the United States Information Agency: American Public Diplomacy, 1989–2001*, New York: Palgrave, 2012.

33 Jan Melissen (ed.), *The New Public Diplomacy: Soft Power in International Relations*, New York: Palgrave, 2005; James Pamment, *New Public Diplomacy: A Comparative Study of Policy and Practice*, Abingdon: Routledge, 2013; R.S. Zaharna, Amelia Arsenault, Ali Fisher (eds), *Relational, Networked and Collaborative Approaches to Public Diplomacy: The Connective Mindshift*, Abingdon: Routledge, 2014.

34 On varieties of actors, see Ellen Huijgh, "The Public Diplomacy of Federated Entities: Examining the Quebec Model," in David Criekemans (ed.), *Regional Sub-State Diplomacy Today*, Leiden: Martinus Nijhoff, 2010, pp. 125–50; Rodrigo Tavares, *Paradiplomacy: Cities and States as Global Players*, Oxford: Oxford University Press, 2016. On the European Union, see Mai'a K. Davis Cross and Teresa La Porte, "The European Union and Image Resilience during Times of Crisis: The Role of Public Diplomacy," *The Hague Journal of Diplomacy* 12 (2016): 1–26; Steffen B. Rasmussen, "The Messages and Practices of the European Union's Public Diplomacy," *The Hague Journal of Diplomacy* 5(1) (2010): 121–3.

35 Isaiah 40, v. 5: "And the glory of the Lord shall be revealed, and all flesh shall see it together."

36 Manuel Castells, *The Rise of the Network Society: The Information Age, Society and Culture*, New York: John Wiley & Sons, 2012.

37 For comment, see Peter Ford, "Europe Cringes at Bush 'Crusade' against Terrorists," *Christian Science Monitor,* September 19, 1991; also Paul Vallely, "The Fifth Crusade: George Bush and the Christianisation of the War in Iraq," in Alastair Crooke et al., *Re-Imagining Security*, London: British Council/Counterpoint, 2004, pp. 42–68.

38 This has been a particular concern in US public diplomacy since the so-called "Cairo tweet" of September 2012. S Max Fisher, "Worldviews: US Embassy in Cairo's Controversial Twitter Feed Deleted after One Too Many Public Spats," *Washington Post*, April 3, 2013.

39 This argument is developed in Cull, "The 2008 Olympics and the Rise of Chinese Soft Power," in Monroe Price and Daniel Dayan (eds), *Owning the Olympics: Narratives of the New China*, Ann Arbor: University of Michigan Press, 2008.

40 Philion is now general director for international media relations at the Office of the President, Mexico City. He shared this anecdote at an Anglo-Mexican conference, "Maximizing Soft Power Assets: Toward Prosperity," held May 19–21, 2014 at the Hacienda Cantalagua, Mexico, in cooperation with the UK Foreign and Commonwealth Office conference center: Wilton Park. It is repeated here with his permission.

41 On soft power, see Joseph Nye, *Soft Power: The Means to Success in World Politics*, New York: Public Affairs, 2004; and Joseph Nye, *The Future of Power*, New York, PublicAffairs, 2011.

42 For multiple uses in a speech by President Xi from October 2017, see http://www.chinadaily.com.cn/china/19thcpcnationalcongress/2017-11/04/content_34115212.htm.

43 "Thailand's gastro diplomacy," *The Economist*, February 21, 2002.

44 A key moment for the articulation of smart power was the release of Richard Armitage and Joseph Nye (co-chairs), *CSIS Commission on Smart Power: A Smarter More Secure America*, CSIS: Washington, DC, 2009. See also Massimo Calabresi, "Hillary Clinton and the Rise of Smart Power," *Time,* November 7, 2011, pp. 26–33.

45 Daya Kishan Thussu, *Communicating India's Soft Power: Buddha to Bollywood*, New York: Palgrave, 2013; David Shambaugh, "China's Soft-Power Push: The Search for Respect," *Foreign Affairs*, July/August, 2015, pp. 99–107; Senem Çevik and Philip Seib (eds), *Turkey's Public Diplomacy*, New York: Palgrave, 2015. For multi-country comparisons, see Craig Hayden, *The Rhetoric of Soft Power: Public Diplomacy in Global Contexts*, Lanham, MD: Lexington, 2012; and Efe Sevin, *Public Diplomacy and the Implementation of Foreign Policy in the US, Sweden and Turkey*, New York: Palgrave, 2017. Work on Russian soft power includes Sinikukka Saari, "Russia's Post-Orange Revolution Strategies to Increase Its Influence in Former Soviet Republics: Public Diplomacy *po russkii*," *Europe-Asia Studies* 66(1), January 2014: 50–66. On the Asia Pacific, include Caitlin Byrne (ed.), "Recasting Soft Power for the Asia Pacific," a special issue of *Politics and Policy* 45(5) (2017).

46 For a video of Anholt's remarks, see https://www.youtube.com/watch?v=zbKW7RDvz5s

47 James Pamment, *British Public Diplomacy and Soft Power: Diplomatic Influence and the Digital Revolution*, Abingdon: Routledge, 2015, p. 2.

48 Peter Pomeranzev and Michael Weis, *The Menace of Unreality: How the Kremlin Weaponizes Information, Culture and Money.* New York: Institute of Modern Russia, 2014.

Chapter 2 Listening: The Foundational Skill

1 Author conversations with PRS staff in 2007, Johannes Matyassy, Seraina Flury Schmid, and Mirjam Matti.

2 Andrew Dobson, *Listening for Democracy: Recognition, Representation, Reconciliation*, Oxford: Oxford University Press, 2014.

3 See, for example, Sun Tzu, *The Art of War* (trans. Lionel Giles), ch. XIII ,"On Spies."

4 http://news.bbc.co.uk/1/hi/world/middle_east/1465114.stm

5 As of 2018, the show has been adapted into seventeen local versions around the world with more in the pipeline, making it one of the most successful TV formats ever. The show is a property of Studio Lambert.

6 Sun Tzu (trans. Lionel Giles), *Art of War*, ch. VII, "Maneuvering," v. 29.

7 From Patricia Buckley Ebrey (ed.), *Chinese Civilization: A Sourcebook*, 2nd edn, New York: Free Press, 1993, pp. 112–15.

8 *Foreign Relations of the United States*, Vol. I, Washington, DC: US Government Printing Office, 1862; for a good example, see Adams to Seward, October 10, 1862, p. 92.

9 Cull, *The Cold War and the United States Information Agency*; on Gallup and Benton, see pp. 24–5, 139.

10 For a case, see Erika Yepsen, *Practicing Successful Twitter Diplomacy: A Model and Case Study of US Efforts in Venezuela*. Los Angeles: CPD Perspectives on Public Diplomacy/Center on Public Diplomacy, 2012.

11 Dobson, *Listening for Democracy*, pp. 181–2. Keynote listening is explored in Jonathan Gosling et al., "Keynote Listening: Turning the Tables on the Sage on the Stage," *Business Review* 9(1) (2012): 1–9.

12 Stacy Schiff, *A Great Improvisation: Franklin, France, and the Birth of America*, New York: Holt, 2005, p. 42.

13 The current author has discussed this campaign at length in his book, *Selling War: The British Propaganda Campaign Against American "Neutrality" in World War II*, Oxford: Oxford University Press, 1994. Some of Berlin's reports were anthologized and published as H. G. Nicholas (ed.)/Isaiah Berlin, (intro.), *Washington Despatches, 1941–1945: Weekly Political Reports from the British Embassy*, London: Weidenfeld and Nicolson, 1981.

14 On Crespi, see http://www.washingtonpost.com/wp-dyn/content/article/2008/07/16/AR2008071602876.html. Crespi's private papers survive at his alma mater, Princeton.

15 On this period in US public diplomacy, see Cull, *The Cold War and the United States Information Agency*, pp. 181–3; Mark Haefele, "John F. Kennedy, USIA, and World Public Opinion," *Diplomatic History* 25(1) (2001): 63–84.

16 For a point of entry, see Robert Banks, *A Resource Guide to Public Diplomacy Evaluation*, Los Angeles: CPD/Perspectives, 2011.

17 Gregory M. Tomlin, *Murrow's Cold War: Public Diplomacy for the Kennedy Administration*. Lincoln: University of Nebraska Press, 2016, p. 250.

18 The present author has assisted in the evaluation of British public diplomacy as an external consultant.

19 Mark Haefele, "John F. Kennedy, USIA, and World Public Opinion," *Diplomatic History*, 25(1) (2001): 63–84.

20 The case is discussed in Robert Albro, "The Disjunction of Image and Word in US and Chinese Soft Power Projection," *International Journal of Cultural Policy* 21(4) (2015): 382–99.

21 For a summary of her tour, see Tom Regan, "US State Department 'Charm Offensive' Hits Bumps," *Christian Science Monitor*, October 24, 2005; on Hughes learning, see Steve Inskeep, "Hughes: No Short-Term Fix for US Image Abroad," *NPR Morning Edition*, March 28, 2006, http://www.npr.org/templates/story/story.php?storyId=5304491.

22 Speech to Conservative Party Conference, October 10, 1980.

23 The study and cataloguing of cognitive and social biases has a wide following as a meeting point for social scientists, psychologists, behavioral economists, marketers, and even some hobbyists. A convenient point of entry is Daniel Kahneman, *Thinking, Fast and Slow*, New York: Farah, Straus and Giroux, 2011. Other helpful starting points include the diagram of biases created by Buster Benson: https://betterhumans.coach.me/cognitive-bias-cheat-sheet-55a472476b18 and the Wikipedia page: https://en.wikipedia.org/wiki/List_of_cognitive_biases. Curiosities in the study of bias include the CIA's text-book, Richards J. Heuer, Jr., *Psychology of Intelligence Analysis*, Langley, VA: Center for the Study of Intelligence, 1986. The chapters dealing with cognitive bias begin at https://www.cia.gov/library/center-for-the-study-of-intelligence/csi-publications/books-and-monographs/psychology-of-intelligence-analysis/art12.html

24 In Latin: *Quis, quid, quando, ubi, cur, quem ad modum, quibus adminiculis*, following a formulation by Hermagoras of Temnos in Augustine's *De Retoricia* but popularized for Britain in the verse Rudyard Kipling appended to his story "The Elephant's Child":

> I keep six honest serving-men/(They taught me all I knew);
> Their names are What and Why and When/And How and Where and Who.]

25 A more nuanced approach focuses on the "belief bias," whereby a statement is judged on the plausibility of the conclusion rather than the merits of the argument; for discussion; see Robert J. Sternberg and Jacqueline P. Leighton, *The Nature of Reasoning*, Cambridge: Cambridge University Press, 2004, p. 300.

26 The revelation is in William M. Hammond's official history: *Public Affairs, The Military and the Media, 1968–1973*, Washington, DC: US GPO, 1996, pp. 223–4.

27 I owe this reference to Ole Brage of the Danish Film Institute.

28 For a point of entry into the literature, see Susan T. Fiske, "Stereotyping, Prejudice, and Discrimination at the Seam between the Centuries: Evolution, Culture, Mind, and Brain." *European Journal of Social Psychology* 30(2) (2000): 299–322.

29 For research on the role of the halo in elections, see Brad Verhulst, Milton Lodge, and Howard Lavine, "The Attractiveness Halo: Why Some Candidates are Perceived More Favorably than Others," *Journal of Nonverbal Behavior* 34(2) (2010): 111–17.

30 On first occurrence bias, see Richard A. Clarke and R. P. Eddy, *Warnings: Finding Cassandras to Stop Catastrophes*, New York: HarperCollins, 2017.

31 Deborah E. Lipstadt, *Beyond Belief: The American Press and the Coming of the Holocaust, 1933–1945*. New York: Touchstone, 1983.

32 The problem of normalcy is outlined in Clarke and Eddy, *Warnings*. For the problem as it relates to natural disasters, see Amanda Ripley, *The Unthinkable: Who Survives When Disaster Strikes and Why*. New York: Crown, 2008.

33 The idea of an availability heuristic was first put forward in Amos Tversky and Daniel Kahneman, "Availability: A Heuristic for Judging Frequency and Probability," *Cognitive Psychology* 5(2) (1973): 207–32. The availability cascade was outlined in Timur Kuran and Cass R. Sunstein, "Availability Cascades and Risk Regulation," *Stanford Law Review* 51(4) (1999): 683–768.

34 On the endowment effect, see Kahneman, *Thinking, Fast and Slow*, pp. 293–99.

35 For an overview of priming, see Evan Weingarten et al., "From Primed Concepts to Action: A Meta-analysis of the Behavioral Effects of Incidentally Presented Words," *Psychological Bulletin* 142(5) (May 2016): 472–97.

36 See Amos Tversky and Daniel Kahneman, "Judgment under Uncertainty: Heuristics and Biases," *Science* 185(4157) (1974): 1124–31.

37 For an interesting experiment showing the strength of the bias, see Elaine Walster and Leon Festinger, "The Effectiveness of Overheard Persuasive Communications," *Journal of Abnormal and Social Psychology* 65(6) (1962): 395–402, finding that Stanford students who overheard warnings against smoking were more influenced by them than students who were warned directly.

38 See David Mauer, *The Big Con: The Story of the Confidence Man*, Indianapolis: Bobbs-Merrill, 1940.

39 I owe this insight to Soumi Chatterjee. British examples include John Major's "bastards" gaffe in 1993 and Gordon Brown's "bigoted woman" gaffe from 2010. US foreign policy examples include Ronald Reagan's "Bomb Russia" gaffe from 1983 and Barack Obama's overheard remarks to Dimitri Medvedev in 2012.

40 For a convenient primer on the issue, see Glenn Kessler, "Fact Checker: The Pre-War Intelligence on Iraq: Wrong or Hyped by the Bush White House?" *Washington Post*, December 13, 2016.

41 For discussion of this oversight from the UK point of view, see Anthony Parsons, *They Say the Lion: Britain's Legacy to the Arabs, A Personal Point of View*, London: Jonathan Cape, 1986.

42 For foundational work on congruence, see Peter C. Wason, "On the Failure to Eliminate Hypotheses in a Conceptual Task," *Quarterly Journal of Experimental Psychology* 12(3) (1960): 129–40.

43 On the bias blind spot, see Emily Pronin, Daniel Lin, and Lee Ross, "The Bias Blind Spot: Perceptions of Bias in Self Versus Others," *Personality and Social Psychology Bulletin* 28(2) (2002): 369–81.

44 This saying is the starting point for Joe Lurie, *Perception and Deception: A Mind Opening Journey across Cultures*, Berkeley: Cultural Detective, 2015.

45 The story is told in H. M. Durand, *The Life of Major-General Sir Henry Marion Durand*. London: W. H. Allen, 1883.

46 I owe the comment on the golder plover to Arnar Gudmundsson. For a sustained argument, see Michael Shermer, *Why People Believe Weird Things*, New York: Henry Holt and Co., 1997. The quote is from a book review by him in the *Washington Post* from November 21, 1999.

47 Kahneman: *Thinking, Fast and Slow.* especially pp. 222–33.

48 I owe this observation to pilot and trainer, Captain Paul Ambrose of British Airways.

49 The office is discussed in Yosef Kuperwasser, "Lessons from Israel's Intelligence Reforms," Brookings Institution Saban Center, ANALYSIS PAPER, #14, October 2007. For online discussion, see https://www.quora.com/World-War-Z-2013-movie-Do-the-Israelis-really-have-a-10th-man-doctrine

50 https://www.gchq.gov.uk/features/daring-think-differently-and-be-different. GCHQ has had in-house neurodiversity support since the 1990s. https://www.gchq.gov.uk/news-article/gchq-becomes-stonewall-top-100-lgbt-employer. This is, of course, a contrast to the historical mistreatment of gay people within the British security state, as documented by the case of Alan Turing.

51 See Leonard Waks, "Listening and Questioning: The Apophatic/Cataphatic Distinction Revisited," *Learning Inquiry* 1(2) (2007): 153–61; and Leonard Waks, "Two Types of Interpersonal Listening,W *Teachers College Record* 112(11) (2010): 2743–62. On clinical best practice, see Sheila Shipley, "Listening: A Concept Analysis," *Nursing Forum* 45(2), (2010): 2833–49. These approaches are noted by Andrew Dobson. Print versions of the police beating story include Jason Epstein, "The CIA and the Intellectuals," *New York Review of Books*, April 20, 1967.

52 For an example, see the case of the BBC and Radio Free Europe dividing listening tasks during the Cold War, discussed in chapter 8.

53 Reporting is also an eligible element in the Award for Excellence in International Security Affairs, see https://fam.state.gov/searchapps/viewer?format=html&query=award%20reporting&links=AWARD,REPORT&url=/FAM/03FAM/03FAM4830.html#M4832_9_1

54 For the official website, see https://unglobalpulse.org. Uganda work is noted at https://radio.unglobalpulse.net/uganda/. On Indonesia, see https://www.unglobalpulse.org/blog/haze-gazer-crisis-analysis-tool and http://hazegazer.org/

Chapter 3 Advocacy: The Cutting Edge

1 I owe this story to Navdeep Suri and Riva Ganguli Das. Inspiration for the original challenge was a US State Department competition to submit short films entitled "Democracy Is . . ."

2 For first use, see the Djerejian commission report: Ambassador Edward Djerejian (chair), *Changing Minds, Winning Peace: A New Strategic Direction for US Public Diplomacy in the Arab and Muslim World*, Washington, DC: Department of State, 2004, pp. 16, 66. The phrase was coined by commission member (and later Undersecretary of State) James K. Glassman.

3 Ignatius of Loyola, *The Constitutions of the Society of Jesus,* trans. George E. Ganss, S. J.,. St Louis, MO: Institute of Jesuit Sources, 1970, p. 275. The relevant instruction is [622 d & e].

4 Ali Fisher and Aurélie Bröckerhoff, *Options for Influence: Global Campaigns*

of Persuasion in the New Worlds of Public Diplomacy, London: British Council Counterpoint, 2008, p. 25.

5 Andrew Cooper, *Celebrity Diplomacy*, Abingdon: Routledge, 2008.

6 The successor to this work is the website https://travelaware.campaign.gov.uk/.

7 On the power of frames, see Robert M. Entman, "Framing: Toward Clarification of a Fractured Paradigm," *Journal of Communication* 43(4) (1993): 51–8; Robert M. Entman, *Projections of Power: Framing News, Public Opinion, and US Foreign Policy*, Chicago: The University of Chicago Press, 2004.

8 This aphorism is noted by the Belgian author Fernand van Langenhove at the opening of his study of German rumors at the beginning of World War I: *Comment naît un cycle de legends*, Paris: Payot, 1916, p. 1.

9 This saying was told me by the Catalan scholar of propaganda, Marc Argemí Ballbè.

10 The campaign is discussed at https://www.telegraph.co.uk/news/5836455/Foreign-Office-defends-lewd-language-in-Dont-be-a-Dick-holiday-campaign.html.

11 Evangelina Cosio was an imprisoned Cuban dissident, freed after the Hearst press arranged a raid on her prison in 1897; Clemencia Arango was a young woman searched by Spanish authorities on the US-bound ship *Olivette* and reported in a salacious way also by the Hearst press in February 1897.

12 This point is made in writer/producer/director Andrew Niccol in an NPR interview at: https://www.scpr.org/programs/the-frame/2015/05/15/42893/andrew-niccol-s-good-kill-looks-at-the-lives-of-dr/. The British film on the same theme, *Eye in the Sky* (2015), opted for a higher resolution without ill effect; in that latter case, it was the plot that lacked credibility.

13 For analysis of AQ messaging, see Jeffrey Halverson, H. L. Goodall, Jr, and Steven R. Corman, *The Master Narratives of Islamic Extremism*, New York: Palgrave, 2011.

14 For a complete history, see Barbara Tuchman, *The Zimmerman Telegram*, New York: Viking Press, 1958.

15 https://secure.avaaz.org/page/en/about/.

16 Michael Norton, Daniel Mochon, and Dan Ariely, "The IKEA effect: When Labor Leads to Love," *Journal of Consumer Psychology* 22(3) (2011): 453–60.

17 On some occasions, I have called the Crowding the Space approach "Stacking the Deck" – I am not doing so here to avoid confusion with the classic list of propaganda tactics drawn up by the Institute of Propaganda Analysis in 1937, which used the term "Stacking the Deck" to refer to a tactic of presenting one or two of an opponent's arguments to establish an impression of balance and then overwhelming them with multiple refuting arguments of one's own.

18 The Confederates had their own press agents and, interestingly, scored some successes by embedding European war correspondents with their forces. The journalists who were personally present with the Confederates wildly overes-

timated the strength of the rebel states. It was an early example of the value in empowering another to tell one's story.

19 This case is based on the author's interviews with David Abshire and Walter Raymond.

20 The 4° map remains live and can be accessed at https://www.metoffice.gov.uk/ climate-guide/climate-change/impacts/four-degree-rise/map.

21 The Stern review can be accessed at: http://webarchive.nationalarchives.gov.uk/ 20100407172811/http://www.hm-treasury.gov.uk/stern_review_report.htm. For a full treatment of the review as public diplomacy, see James Pamment, *British Public Diplomacy and Soft Power Diplomatic Influence and the Digital Revolution*, Abingdon: Routledge, 2015, pp. 123–30.

22 This paragraph is a summary of the current author's ongoing research.

23 This case is based on Cull, *Selling War: The British Propaganda Campaign Against American "Neutrality" in World War II*, Oxford: Oxford University Press, 1994.

24 Joseph A. Fry, *Henry S. Sanford: Diplomacy and Business in Nineteenth-Century America*, Reno: University of Nevada Press, 1982.

25 The allegation is noted in Graham Fairclough, "The Cold War in Context," in John Scofield and Wayne Cocroft (eds), *A Fearsome Heritage: Diverse Legacies of the Cold War*, Walnut Creek, CA: Left Coast Press, 2007, p. 28.

26 Cull, *Selling War*, pp. 169–75, 189–90.

27 The official UK government inquiry into this incident may be found here: https://www.gov.uk/government/uploads/system/uploads/attachment_data/ file/228975/7934.pdf.

28 Richard Dawkins, *The Selfish Gene*, 2nd edn, Oxford: Oxford University Press, 1989, p. 192.

29 Chip Heath and Dan Heath, *Made to Stick: Why Some Ideas Survive and Others Die*, New York: Random House, 2007.

30 For an extended visual discussion of this, see *The Power of Nightmares*, a documentary by Adam Curtis (BBC, 2004).

31 The chart appears in the original version of TV miniseries *Roots* (1977) and is consulted by the slave traders played by Edward Asner and Vic Morrow.

32 For background, see http://time.com/3878665/cecil-beaton-portrait-of-eileen-dunne-1940-london-blitz/; see also Cull, *Selling War*, p. 107.

33 I owe this case to Evan Potter.

34 For a comprehensive presentation of the approach, see Alister Miskimmon, Ben O'Loughlin, and Laura Roselle (eds), *Forging the World: Strategic Narratives and International Relations*, Ann Arbor: University of Michigan Press, 2017.

35 The figures come from the annual Twiplomacy study conducted by PR film company Burson Marsteller: http://twiplomacy.com/blog/twiplomacy-study-2017/

36 Noam Coen, "The Toughest Qs Answered in the Briefest Tweets," *New York Times*, January 4, 2009, p. WK4. The tweet translates as "We are pro negotiation. Currently talks are held with the Palestinian Authority plus talks

on the two-state solution. We talk only with people who accept our right to live."

37 For works midway in the evolution of digital engagement, see Amelia Arsenault, "Public Diplomacy 2.0," in Philip Seib (ed.), *Toward a New Public Diplomacy: Redirecting US Foreign Policy*, New York: Palgrave Macmillan, 2009, pp. 135–53; and Lina Khatib, William Dutton, and Michael Thelwall. "Public Diplomacy 2.0: A Case Study of the US Digital Outreach Team," *Middle East Journal* 66(3) (2012): 453–72.

38 Corneliu Bjola and Marcus Holmes (eds), *Digital Diplomacy: Theory and Practice*, Abingdon: Routledge, 2015; Romit Kampf, Ilan Manor, and Elad Segev, "Digital Diplomacy 2.0? A Cross-national Comparison of Public Engagement in Facebook and Twitter," *The Hague Journal of Diplomacy* 10(4) (2015): 331–62. See also Brian Hocking and Jan Melissen, *Diplomacy in the Digital Age*, Clingendael Report, Netherlands Institute of International Relations, July 2015.

39 On Love Army, see https://www.lovearmy.org/.

40 Jian Wang, "Case: Advertising China," in Keith Dinnie, *Nation Branding: Concepts, Issues, Practice*, 2nd edn, Abingdon: Routledge, 2016, pp. 80–3.

41 https://www.climaterealityproject.org/.

42 https://www.propublica.org/article/from-russia-with-pr-ketchum-cnbc.

43 The ISD was founded by the publisher Lord Weidenfeld in 2006. Its declared mission is "powering new generations against extremism"; for homepage, see https://www.isdglobal.org/

44 The manual is at http://www.isdglobal.org/wp-content/uploads/2016/06/Counter-narrative-Handbook_1.pdf.

45 https://obamawhitehouse.archives.gov/the-press-office/2015/02/18/fact-sheet-white-house-summit-countering-violent-extremism.

46 http://www.abdullahx.com/ Abdullah X's media coverage was not helpful to his credibility and raised issues around the ethics of the presumed sponsorship of his activity. For a discussion of this issue, see https://www.opendemocracy.net/ben-hayes-asim-qureshi/going-global-uk-government-s-propaganda-and-censorship-silicon-valley-and-cve.

47 Halverson, Goodall, and Corman, *The Master Narratives of Islamic Extremism*.

48 Brendan Nyhan and Jason Reifler, "When Corrections Fail: The Persistence of Political Misconceptions," *Political Behavior* 32(2) (June 2010): 303–30.

Chapter 4 Culture: The Friendly Persuader

1 This case in based on a conversation with Alicia Adams, for background see Nelson Pressley, "The Kennedy Center's Alicia Adams brings the world to D.C. stages," *Washington Post*, February 27, 2011; Jeremy D. Birch, "Kennedy Center: ARABESQUE – Arts of the Arab World," Playbill, February 23, 2009: http://www.playbill.com/article/kennedy-center-arabesque-arts-of-the-arab-world; for details of design elements, see https://www.studiogardere.com/en/projects/exhibition/arabesque/.

2 For a survey of the field, see Patricia Goff, "Cultural Diplomacy," in Andrew F. Cooper, Jorge Heine, and Ramesh Thakur (eds), *The Oxford Handbook of Modern Diplomacy*, Oxford: Oxford University Press, 2013, pp. 419–35.

3 This argument has been well made by Mexican scholar Cesar Villanueva Rivas. For work setting cultural diplomacy outside of public diplomacy, see Harvey B. Feigenbaum, "Globalization and Cultural Diplomacy," Center for Arts and Culture, 2001 at http://www.culturalpolicy.org/pdf/globalization.pdf.

4 Edward Corse, *A Battle for Neutral Europe: British Cultural Propaganda during the Second World War*, London: Bloomsbury, 2013, p. 147.

5 Frank Trommler, *Kulturmacht ohne Kompass: Deutsche auswärtige Kulturbeziehungen im 20. Jahrhundert*, Köln: Böhlau-Verlag Gmbh, 2013.

6 A search of works digitized on Google Books reveals usage including: Georg Eltzschig, "Kulturdiplomatie," in Heinrich Ritter von Frauendorfer and Edgar Jaffé (eds), *Europäische staats-und wirtschafts-zeitung* 6 (1921): 33, 38, 39; a piece discussing Japan in *China Weekly Review* 77 (1936) by Yen Ying Lu entitled "Cultural Diplomacy," pp. 188–9; and a Japanese journal published by the Nippon Cultural Federation also from 1936 – *Cultural Nippon* – which includes an essay by Chikao Fujisawa (vols 4 and 5) which notes that for Japan: "Fujiyama and Geishagirl diplomacy is now giving way to a much more sober type of *cultural diplomacy* which stresses the intrinsic value of our culture from a world point of view," p. 513.

7 For a text from this period, see Anthony Haigh, *Cultural Diplomacy in Europe*, Strasbourg: Council of Europe, 1974, archived online at https://files.eric. ed.gov/fulltext/ED102067.pdf.

8 French rulers also had to contend with the regional sister languages to French (the *langues d'oïl*, or languages in which the word for yes is "*oïl/oui*") like Norman, Picard, Burgundian, and so forth.

9 J. H. Robinson (ed.), *Readings in European History*, Vol. 2, Boston: Ginn, 1906, pp. 271–2.

10 The ordinance of 1539 was known as *Ordonnance de Villers-Cotterêts*. The most accessible English language source on the interface between the French language and nationalism is Eric Hobsbawm, *Nations and Nationalism since 1780: Programme, Myth, Reality*, Cambridge: Cambridge University Press, 1990.

11 Matthew Arnold, *Literature and Dogma: An Essay Toward the Better Appreciation for the Bible*, New York: Macmillan, 1873, p. 13.

12 Jessica Geinow-Hecht, *Sound Diplomacy: Music and Emotions in Transatlantic Relations, 1850–1920*, Chicago: University of Chicago Press, 2006.

13 For a centenary history, see Maurice Bruézière, *L'Alliance Française: Histoire d'une Institution 1883–1983*, Paris: Librairie Hachette, 1983.

14 R. E. McMurray and M. Lee, *The Cultural Approach: Another Way in International Relations*, Chapel Hill: University of North Carolina Press, 1947, pp. 9–15, 43. Philip M. Taylor, *The Projection of Britain: British Overseas Publicity and Propaganda, 1919–1939*, Cambridge: Cambridge University

Press, 1981, pp. 126–7. On VDA, see http://www.vda-kultur.de/de/ueber_uns/ueber-uns.php.

15 This story is told in Michael Llewellyn Smith, *Olympics in Athens 1896: The Invention of the Modern Olympic Games*, London: Profile Books, 2004.

16 For a sustained treatment of this impulse, see David W. Ellwood, *The Shock of America: Europe and the Challenge of the Century*, Oxford: Oxford University Press, 2012.

17 Peter Buitenhuis, *The Great War of Words: British, American and Canadian Propaganda and Fiction, 1914–1933*, Vancouver: University of British Columbia, 1987.

18 For a survey of this work, see George Creel, *How We Advertised America*, New York: Harper & Bros., 1920, esp. pp. 117–32.

19 Gregory Paschalidis, "Exporting National Culture: Histories of Cultural Institutes Abroad," *International Journal of Cultural Policy* 15(3) (2009): 275–89.

20 Richard T. Arndt, *The First Resort of Kings: American Cultural Diplomacy in the Twentieth Century*, Dulles, VA: Potomac Books, 2005; Edward Corse, *A Battle for Neutral Europe*, p. 83.

21 Tony Shaw, "Nightmare on Nevsky Prospekt: *The Blue Bird* as a Curious Instance of US–Soviet Film Collaboration during the Cold War," *Journal of Cold War Studies* 14(1) (Winter 2012): 3–33.

22 Samuel P. Huntington, "The Clash of Civilizations?" *Foreign Affairs* 72(3) (Summer 1993): 22–49.

23 https://www.britishcouncil.org/organisation/policy-insight-research/research/trust-pays.

24; https://www.britishcouncil.org/sites/default/files/3418_bc_edinburgh_university_soft_power_report_03b.pdf

25 Eidgenössisches Departement für Auswärtige Angelegenheiten. Politische Abteilung V, Sektion Kultur und UNESCO.

26 For the ifa's mission statement, see http://www.ifa.de/en/about-us/mission-objectives.html

27 On Venice, see Enzo di Martino, *The History of the Venice Biennale: 1895–2007*, Venice: Papiro Arte, 2007. For a treatment of the cultural diplomacy of cities, see Mariano Martín Zamorano and Arturo Rodríguez Morató. "The Cultural Paradiplomacy of Barcelona since the 1980s: Understanding Transformations in Local Cultural Paradiplomacy," *International Journal of Cultural Policy* 21(5) (October 2015): 554–76.

28 Graham Carr, "'No Political Significance of Any Kind': Glenn Gould's Tour of the Soviet Union and the Culture of the Cold War," *Canadian Historical Review* 95(1) (2014): 1–29.

29 Yudhishthir Raj Isar, "'Culture in EU External Relations': An Idea Whose Time Has Come?, *International Journal of Cultural Policy* 21(4) (2015): 494–508. For quote, see https://eeas.europa.eu/headquarters/headquarters-homepage/

4038/mogherini-and-commission-aim-put-culture-heart-eu-international-relations_en

30 Membership currently stands at 57 states, including the Canadian provinces of Quebec and New Brunswick and non-colonial countries with a strong tradition of French language like Albania and Bulgaria.

31 J. P. Singh, *United Nations Educational, Scientific and Cultural Organization (UNESCO): Creating Norms for a Complex World*, New York: Routledge, 2011.

32 For details, see http://www.iccn.or.kr/.

33 For details, see https://exchanges.state.gov/us/program/german-american-partnership-program and http://www.gmfus.org/.

34 For details, see http://culcon.jusfc.gov/.

35 The network as of the 1990s is documented in an archived USIA website at: http://dosfan.lib.uic.edu/usia/E-USIA/education/engteaching/eal-elp1.htm#Ind

36 https://artsbeat.blogs.nytimes.com/2011/11/18/lil-buck-jooks-his-way-through-beijing-with-yo-yo-ma-and-meryl-streep/.

37 http://cubaskate.com/.

38 On this case, see Sarah E. K. Smith's essay in Nicholas Cull and Michael Hawes (eds), *Canadian Public Diplomacy*, New York: Palgrave, forthcoming.

39 Steve Crawshaw, "Shakespeare Goes to Serbia; Two Years Ago Britain Bombed Belgrave. Now the National Theatre has Sent its Hamlet as a Gesture of Peace," *The Independent*, February 18, 2001, pp. 1, 2; Dan De Luce in Tehran and Jeevan Vasagar, "Curtain Up, Veils Down: Bard Builds a Bridge with Iran, *Winter's Tale* Blazes Trail with Iranians Starved of Culture," *The Guardian*, January 22, 2003.

40 Tony Howard, "Blood on the Bright Young Things: Shakespeare in the 1930s," in Clive Barker and Maggie B. Gale (eds), *British Theatre Between the Wars*, Cambridge: Cambridge University Press, 2000, pp. 155–6.

41 David Monod, "'He is a cripple an' needs my love': *Porgy and Bess* as Cold War Propaganda," in Giles Scott-Smith and Hans Krabbendam (eds), *The Cultural Cold War in Western Europe: 1945–1960*, London: Frank Cass, 2003, pp. 300–12.

42 For the NFB/ONF platform for aboriginal film, see https://www.nfb.ca/indigenous-cinema/?&film_lang=en&sort=year:desc,title&year=1917..201.

43 On the play – entitled *Shopping and Fucking* – see Lorna Duckworth, "Blunkett Attack on Rent Boy Play Cash," *Mail on Sunday*, March 22, 1998, p. 18; Martin Bright, Richard Brooks, and Roger Tredre, "Blunkett Slams Grant for 'Foul' drama," *The Observer*, March 22, 1998, p. 3; John Mckie, "How Mark Went Shopping for a Worldwide Hit," *Evening Standard*, January 19, 1998, p. 52.

44 Falk Hartig, *Chinese Public Diplomacy: the rise of the Confucius Institute*, Abingdon: Routledge, 2016.

45 The partnership is even recalled in the brief online history of the theater at http://elteatrocampesino.com/our-history/.

46 I owe this reference to Simon Gammell of the British Council, which supported the project as a junior partner.

47 On West Heavens, see http://westheavens.net/en/aboutusen. The film was Huo Jianqi (dir.), *Xuanzang* (China Film/Eros International, 2016).

48 For the website, see http://can4culture.ca/.

49 See US Department of State, Bureau of Educational and Cultural Affairs, Cultural Programs Division, Grants Awarded 2006 at: http://exchanges.state.gov/education/citizens/culture/grants/awarded.htm.

50 For example, the Council's 2010 project to bring the play *The Great Game* to the United States included a 48-page anthology of essays edited by Christopher Merrill: *Trust Me, I'm an Expert: Talking Culture from Inside and Out*: http://www.britishcouncil.org/trust_me__i_m_an_expert.pdf

51 George Bruce, *Festival in the North: The Story of the Edinburgh Festival*, London: Robert Hale & Co., 1975, pp. 17–24.

52 For a range of sport cases, see Stuart Murray (guest ed.), "Sports Diplomacy," *The Hague Journal of Diplomacy* 8(3–4) (2013).

53 Byblos, in contrast, was excavated by the French. Interestingly, these contributions are memorialized, suggesting an interest in drawing value from past contributions also. Personal site visits, 2008.

54 For a study of this approach, see Christina Luke and Morgan M. Kersel, *US Cultural Diplomacy and Archeology: Soft Power, Hard Heritage*, New York: Routledge, 2013.

55 For a convenient introduction to gastro-diplomacy, see the winter 2014 issue of *Public Diplomacy Magazine* at: http://publicdiplomacymagazine.com/tag/gastrodiplomacy/.

56 As of 2018, these higher budgets are slated to be dramatically cut. See https://www.state.gov/documents/organization/277155.pdf.

57 See Barry Sanders, *American Avatar: The United States in the Global Imagination*, Dulles, VA: Potomac Books, 2011; and, for wider discussion of the challenge of America's cultural footprint, see Nathan Gardels and Mike Medavoy, *American Idol after Iraq: Competing for Hearts and Minds in the Global Media Age*, Malden, MA: Wiley-Blackwell, 2009; and Martha Bayles, *Through A Screen Darkly: Popular Culture, Public Diplomacy, and America's Image Abroad*, New Haven: Yale University Press, 2014.

58 https://www.teachingenglish.org.uk/overview/promoting-21st-century-skills.

59 Michael Krenn, *Fall-Out Shelters for the Human Spirit: American Art and the Cold War*, Chapel Hill: University of North Carolina Press, 2006, pp. 230–1.

60 http://www.bosch-stiftung.de/en/story/film-prize-international-cooperation.

Chapter 5 Exchange and Education: The Soul of Public Diplomacy

1 I owe this story to Sharon Harroun, chair of the CFPNI. For a full account, see Sharon Harroun, "How a Youth Program can Promote Peace, Reconciliation, and New Leadership," in Joseph L. Popiolkowski and Nicholas J. Cull (eds.) *Public Diplomacy, Cultural Interventions & the Peace Process in Northern Ireland:*

Track Two to Peace? Los Angeles: Center on Public Diplomacy, 2009, pp. 83–8 (available online at: https://uscpublicdiplomacy.org/sites/uscpublicdiplomacy. org/files/legacy/media/Track%20Two%20to%20Peace%20FINAL). The notoriety of the murder was such that Mrs McMullin remains a semi-public figure in Northern Ireland, voicing concern over leniency of the prison sentence for her husband's killer and the release of a documentary dealing with the hunger strike of 1981 which was part of the backdrop to the Proctor murder.

2 http://oig.state.gov/documents/organization/186048.pdf. Reports on the government-wide use of exchanges may be found at: http://www.iawg.gov. At the time of writing, the budget for exchanges is a subject of dispute between the White House and the Department of State and its supporters on Capitol Hill.

3 On UK relationships, see http://www.nicaraguasc.org.uk/solidarity/twin-towns/. US cities with civic links to Nicaragua included the author's hometown in the late 1980s and early 1990s, Princeton, New Jersey.

4 Eiichi Kiyooka (trans.), *The Autobiography of Yukichi Fukuzawa*, New York: Columbia University Press, 2007.

5 For a biography in English, see Francis G. Crowley, *Domingo Faustino Sarmiento*, New York: Twayne, 1972. I owe this reference to my colleague, Robert Banks.

6 Giles Scott-Smith, *Networks of Empire: The US State Department's Foreign Leader Program in the Netherlands, France, and Britain, 1950–70*, Brussels: Peter Lang, 2008.

7 Manuel Castells, *Communication Power*, New York: Oxford University Press, 2010. pp. 20–6.

8 The story is in paragraph I of Diogenes' "Life of Bias." For an English version, see Diogenes Laertius, *The Lives and Opinions of the Eminent Philosophers*, trans. C. D. Yonge, London: Henry G. Bohn, 1853, pp. 38–40.

9 David Braud, *Rome and the Friendly King: The Character of the Client Kingship*, London: Routledge, 1983.

10 The early medieval moment is sketched in David G. Mandelbaum, "Comments," pp. 45–6, in "Attitudes and Adjustment in Cross-Cultural Contact: Recent Studies of Foreign Students," *Journal of Social Issues* 12(1), 1956, pp. 1–7. For more recent work, see Peter Stein, *Roman Law in European History*, Cambridge University Press, Cambridge, 1999; Hugh Goddard, *A History of Christian–Muslim Relations*, Edinburgh: Edinburgh University Press, 2000, p. 99; Amalananda Ghosh, *A Guide to Nalanda*, New Delhi: Archeological Survey of India, 1965, p. 9.

11 Helen Waddell, *The Wandering Scholars of the Middle Ages*, London: Constable, 1927.

12 Peter Parkes, "Celtic Fosterage: Adoptive Kinship and Clientage in Northwest Europe," *Society for Comparative Study of Society and History* 48(2) (2006): 359–95.

13 Jean Lelièvre and Maurice Balavoine, *Le Mans-Paderborn 836–1994: Une amitié séculaire un sillage delumière*, Le Mans: Martin, 1994.

14 Tsar Peter's residence in Zaandam, the Netherlands, may still be visited.

15 David E. Mungello, *Curious Land: Jesuit Accommodation and the Origins of Sinology*, Honolulu: University of Hawaii Press, 1989.

16 Stephen K. Batalden, Kathleen Cann, and John Dean, *Sowing the Word: The Cultural Impact of the British and Foreign Bible Society, 1804–2004*. Sheffield: Sheffield Phoenix Press, 2004.

17 For contemporary Indian criticism of Macauley, see Kapil Kapoor, http://veda.wikidot.com/article:decolonizing-the-indian-mind.

18 On Carlsberg, see Kristof Glamann, *Jacobsen of Carlsberg: Brewer and Philanthropist*, Copenhagen: Gyldendal, 1991. On the Danish Cultural Institute, see https://www.danishculture.com/history/.

19 For recent discussion of this, see Charlotte Lerg, "Uses and Abuses of the First German–American Professorial Exchange 1905–1914," in Anne Overbeck and Jürgen Overhoff (eds), *German–American Educational History: Topics, Trends, Fields of Research*, Heilbrunn: Klinkhardt Verlag, 2017, pp. 63–70; Anja Werner, *The Transatlantic World of Higher Education: Americans at German Universities, 1776–1914*, New York: Berghahn, 2013; and Adam Nelson, "The Emergence of the American University: An International Perspective," *History of Education Quarterly* 45(3) (2005): 427–37. Nelson argues that the foreign experiences did not build an international perspective but rather were an incubator of nationalism.

20 Renate Simpson, *How the PhD Came to Britain: A Century of Struggle for Postgraduate Education*, Guildford: Society for Research into Higher Education, 1983.

21 Philip Ziegler, *Cecil Rhodes, the Rhodes Trust and Rhodes Scholarships*, New Haven: Yale University Press, 2008.

22 Weili Ye, *Seeking Modernity in China's Name: Chinese Students in the United States*, Palo Alto: Stanford University Press, 2001.

23 The story is well documented in the classic study by Frank Ninkovich, *The Diplomacy of Ideas: US Foreign Policy and Cultural Relations, 1938–1950*, New York: Cambridge University Press, 1981. On the ALA, see Michael Krenn, *The History of United States Cultural Diplomacy: 1770 to the Present Day*, London: Bloomsbury, 2017, p. 55.

24 I owe this account of Fulbright's motivation to a discussion with his widow, Harriet Fulbright. The original act may be accessed at https://www.loc.gov/law/help/statutes-at-large/79th-congress/session-2/c79s2ch723.pdf.

25 Christopher Shulgan, *The Soviet Ambassador: The Making of the Radical Behind Perestroika*, Toronto: McClelland and Stewart, 2008.

26 Yale Richmond, *Cultural Exchange and the Cold War: Raising the Iron Curtain*, University Park, PA: Penn State University Press, 2003; Robert English, *Russia and the Idea of the West: Gorbachev, Intellectuals and the End of the Cold War*, New York: Columbia University Press, 2000.

27 Ulrich Krotz, *The Ties that Bind: The Parapublic Underpinnings of Franco-German Relations as Construction of International Value*, Cambridge, MA:

Minda de Gunzburg Center for European Studies, Harvard, October 2002; also, Antoine Vion, "Europe from the Bottom Up: Town Twinning in France during the Cold War," *Contemporary European History* 11(4) (2002): 623–40.

28 Barak Kushner, "Cannibalizing the Japanese Media," *The Journal of Popular Culture* 31(3) (1997): 55–68.

29 The emphasis on the welfare of the fostered child seemed odd to societies without the practice. English observers regularly identified Irish and Welsh fosterage as examples of barbarism and exploitation of poor parents by parasitic wealthier families farming out offspring. This is discussed in Peter Parkes, "Fosterage, Kinship and Legend: When Milk was Thicker than Blood," *Comparative Studies in Society and History* 46(3) (July 2004): 587–615.

30 On Australia's approach, see David Lowe, "Australia's Colombo Plans, Old and New: International Students as Foreign Relations," *International Journal of Cultural Policy* 21(4) (2015): 448–62. The film was *Crook* (2010).

31 For an account of Qtub's sojourn, see David Von Drehle, "A Lesson in Hate: How an Egyptian Student Came to Study 1950s America and Left Determined to Wage Holy War," *Smithsonian Magazine*, February 2006.

32 Terry McDermott, *Perfect Soldiers: The 9/11 Hijackers: Who They Were, Why They Did It*, New York: HarperCollins, 2005.

33 The W curve was originally proposed by John T. Gullhorn and Jeane E. Gullhorn, "An Extension of the U-Curve Hypothesis," *Journal of Social Issues* 19(3) (July 1963): 33–47. For recent research on culture shock, see Alfred Presbitero, "Culture Shock and Reverse Culture Shock: The Moderating Role of Cultural Intelligence in International Students' Adaptation," *International Journal of Intercultural Relations* 53 (July 2016): 28–38.

34 Alexey Fominykh, "Russia's Public Diplomacy in Central Asia and the Caucasus: The Role of the Universities," *The Hague Journal of Diplomacy* 12(1) (2017): 56–85.

35 Cynthia Miller-Idriss and Elizabeth Hanauer, "Transnational Higher Education: Offshore Campuses in the Middle East," *Comparative Education* 47(2) (2011): 181–207.

36 J. Manuel Espinosa, *Inter-American Beginnings of US Cultural Diplomacy, 1936–1948*, Washington, DC: Department of State, 1976, pp. 8–12.

37 Cull, *The Cold War and the United States Information Agency*, pp. 50–1.

38 http://www.senado.cl/distinguen-trayectoria-y-el-aporte-del-programa-de-intercambio-cultural-mas-importante-de-estados-unidos/prontus_senado/2015-08-05/211346.html#vtxt_cuerpo_T0; see also https://alumni.state.gov/highlight/chilean-senate-pays-homage-international-visitor-leadership-program.

39 On the EU exchange, see Giles Scott-Smith, "Mending the 'Unhinged Alliance' in the 1970s: Transatlantic Relations, Public Diplomacy, and the Origins of the European Union Visitors Program," *Diplomacy & Statecraft* 16(4) (2006): 749–78.

40 Carol Atkinson has pointed out that 10 percent of the graduates of the Carlyle army education program head their military; see Carol Atkinson, *Military Soft Power: Public Diplomacy through Military Educational Exchanges*, Lanham MD: Rowman & Littlefield Publishers, 2014.

41 http://exchanges.state.gov/non-us/program/techwomen.

42 https://exchanges.state.gov/non-us/iwp; https://iwp.uiowa.edu/residency.

43 John Wallach, *The Enemy Has a Face: The Seeds of Peace Experience*, Washington, DC: United States Institute of Peace, 2000.

44 Richard Mayne, *In Victory, Magnanimity, in Peace, Goodwill: A History of Wilton Park*, London: Frank Cass, 2004.

45 http://exchanges.state.gov/non-us/program/techgirls

46 On Greek diaspora, see https://p.widencdn.net/0kxflz/IIE-2016-Annual-Report; on Palestinians, see https://www.thedailybeast.com/a-palestinian-birthright-trip.

47 Nicholas J. Cull, "The Long Road to Public Diplomacy 2.0: The Internet in US Public Diplomacy," *International Studies Review* 15(1) (March 2013): 123–39.

48 On YALI network, see https://yali.state.gov/network/.

49 https://www.haaretz.com/1.5128004.

50 Emily T. Metzgar, *The JET Program and the US–Japan Relationship: Goodwill Goldmine*, Lanham, MD: Lexington Books, 2017.

51 http://en.ceaie.edu.cn/. The CEAIE also runs a program for voluntary teachers of English, in partnership with the UK charity Project Trust.

52 The statistic comes from https://www.statista.com/statistics/209334/total-number-of-international-tourist-arrivals/, accessed in March 2018, and represents a doubling on the figure from 1996.

53 Cull, *The Cold War and the United States Information Agency*, p. 138; Israel's efforts to enlist outgoing tourists are noted in Max Blumenthal, "Israel Cranks the PR Machine," *The Nation*, October 16, 2013.

54 The present author was a Harkness Fellow at Princeton from 1988 to 1990 and an active alumnus at the time of the change.

55 Molly Bettie, "Ambassadors Unaware: The Fulbright Program and American Public Diplomacy," *Journal of Transatlantic Studies* 13(4) (2015): 358–72.

56 This issue was raised in the United States during the debate over the H1B visa in the final years of the Obama presidency.

57 I owe this reference to Daniel Aguirre Azócar.

Chapter 6 International Broadcasting: The Struggle for News

1 On Kim Hyeong-soo's story, see Sophia Cai, "Human Rights 'desert': An Interview with North Korean Defector Kim Hyeong Soo," Asian Correspondent.Com, February 21, 2018; Elizabeth Shim, "North Korea Defector: News of Kim Jong Un Made Me Leave," *UPI*, November 30, 2017; Emma Batha, "North Korea Defector Reveals Late Leader's Fears over Libido and Diabetes," *Reuters*, March 11, 2016.

2 Cull, *The Decline and Fall of the United States Information Agency: American Public Diplomacy, 1989–2001*, New York: Palgrave, 2012.

3 I owe this observation to Matthew Armstrong.

4 For a German language study acknowledging the role of AFN, see Stephanie Graeber, *Der amerikanische Einfluss auf die Rolle des Radios in Nachkriegsbayern*, München: Grin Verlag, 2010.

5 For exploration of this role, see Amelia Arsenault and Manuel Castells, "Switching Power: Rupert Murdoch and the Global Business of Media Politics: A Sociological Analysis," *International Sociology* 23(4) (2008): 488–513.

6 For a case study of the counter-hegemonic approach, see James Painter, *Counter-Hegemonic News: A Case Study of Al-Jazeera English and Telesur*, Oxford: Reuters Institute for the Study of Journalism, 2008.

7 For an up-to-date biography, see Marc Raboy, *Marconi: The Man Who Networked the World*, Oxford: Oxford University Press, 2016, claiming Marconi was a priority for Italian dictator Benito Mussolini. Marconi received multiple honors, including a peerage from the regime and reciprocated with endorsements of Mussolini's politics.

8 Philip M. Taylor, *Munitions of the Mind: A History of Propaganda*, 3rd edn, Manchester: Manchester University Press, 2003, p. 205.

9 Marilyn J. Matelski, *Vatican Radio: Propagation by the Airwaves*, Westport, CT: Praeger, 1995.

10 The link between WRUL and British intelligence is noted in Cull, *Selling War: The British Propaganda Campaign Against American "Neutrality" in World War II*, Oxford: Oxford University Press, 1994, p. 133. For a contemporaneous account of the station's origins, see Robert J. Clements, "Foreign Language Broadcasting of 'Radio Boston,'" *The Modern Language Journal* 27(3) (March 1943): 175–9.

11 Horst J. P. Bergmeier and Rainer E. Lotz, *Hitler's Airwaves: The Inside Story of Nazi Radio and Propaganda Swing*, New Haven: Yale University Press, 1997; Clayton D. Laurie, "Goebbels's Iowan: Frederick W. Kaltenbach and Nazi Short-Wave Radio Broadcasts to America, 1939–1945," *Annals of Iowa* 53(3) (Summer 1994): 219–45.

12 On British wartime broadcasting, see Asa Briggs, *History of Broadcasting in the United Kingdom: Volume III: The War of Words*, Oxford: Oxford University Press, 1995; and Michael Stenton, *Radio London and Resistance in Occupied Europe: British Political Warfare, 1939–1943*, Oxford: Oxford University Press, 2000. Goebbels's reaction is noted in James Wood, *History of International Broadcasting, Vol. 2*, Stevenage: IET, 1992, p. 24.

13 Cull, *The Cold War and the United States Information Agency*, p. 14.

14 For a convenient comparative table of outputs from 1950 through to the end of the Cold War, see Wood, *History of International Broadcasting*, p. 20.

15 Alban Webb, *London Calling: Britain, the BBC World Service and the Cold War*, London: Bloomsbury, 2012, pp. 60, 130.

16 Wood, *History of International Broadcasting, Vol. 2*, 1992, p. 63.

17 The evolution of the VOA is well drawn in Alan Heil, *Voice of America: A History*, New York: Columbia University Press, 2003.

18 The best overview of the role of broadcasting in the Cold War is Michael Nelson, *War of the Black Heavens: The Battles of Western Broadcasting in the Cold War*, Syracuse: Syracuse University Press, 1997.

19 For a critique of the BBG structure, see Emily Metzgar, *Considering the "Illogical Patchwork": The Broadcasting Board of Governors and US International Broadcasting*, Los Angeles: CPD Perspectives, 2013.

20 For official statement see https://www.usagm.gov/2018/08/22/statement-from-ceo-john-f-lansing-on-agency-rebrand/

21 Until now, editorials have been created by a special office of political appointees within VOA who adapted their arguments from the wider output of the Department of State, White House, and other elements of government. At the time of writing, there is a plan for editorials to be replaced by online links to official statements.

22 Stenton, *Radio London and Resistance in Occupied Europe,* p. 385.

23 A case of broadcasting for development will be considered in detail in chapter 8.

24 John Reith, *Into the Wind*, London: Hodder & Stoughton, 1949, p. 341.

25 Greg Dyke, conversation with author, 2004.

26 http://unesdoc.unesco.org/images/0004/000400/040066eb.pdf. The quote is from p. 37.

27 http://www.bbc.co.uk/bbctrust/news/press_releases/2014/world_service.

28 http://www.cbc.ca/news/canada/new-brunswick/rci-ends-shortwave-broad cast-1.1148370.

29 https://www.rnw.org/.

30 Stenton, *Radio London and Resistance in Occupied Europe.*

31 Lebona Mosia, Charles Riddle, and Jim Zaffiro, "From Revolutionary to Regime Radio: Three Decades of Nationalist Broadcasting in Southern Africa," *Africa Media Review* 8(1) (1994): 1–24.

32 On broadcasting to Cuba, see Daniel C. Walsh, *An Air War with Cuba: The United States Radio Campaign against Castro*, Jefferson, NC: MacFarland, 2012.

33 Tara Bahrampour, "'Expats' *Daily Show*-style VOA Program Enthralls Iranians, Irks their Government," *Washington Post*, December 31, 2010; Elizabeth Flock, "Staffers: Voice Of America Left Lawmakers in the Dark about Loss of Prominent Show *Parazit*," *US News and World Report*, August 23, 2012.

34 http://www.dw.com/en/learn-german/s-2469.

35 For a biography of Conover, see Terrence Ripmaster, *Willis Conover: Broadcasting Jazz to the World*, Lincoln, NE: iUniverse, 2007.

36 A ten-minute promo for the *High Life* program has been preserved on YouTube at https://www.youtube.com/watch?v=ystNNQg0o2U.

37 Philip Nanton and Anne Walmsley, "Henry Swanzy: Pioneering BBC Producer

whose Literary Programmes Launched a Generation of Caribbean Writers," *The Guardian*, March 20, 2004.

38 http://www.dw.com/en/media-center/podcasts/s-100977.

39 https://www.npr.org/2012/11/28/166082428/from-jk-to-eye-gunk-taking-u-s-slang-to-china; Tara Bahrampour, "'OMG Meiyu,' a Breakout Hit Web Show, Schools Chinese in American Slang," *Washington Post*, September 14, 2012. For sample see https://www.youtube.com/watch?v=UhUQMrOLyVU.

40 https://www.independent.co.uk/news/an-everyday-story-of-russian-working-folk-starring-tony-blair-1233970.html.

41 For coverage, see http://www.labenevolencija.org/rwanda/radio-soap/; http://www.loveradio-rwanda.org/episode/1/onair/intro; and https://www.npr.org/2018/04/16/602872309/romeo-juliet-in-kigali-how-a-soap-opera-sought-to-change-behavior-in-rwanda.

42 http://www.unesco.org/education/lwf/doc/portfolio/case3.htm; http://www.bbc.co.uk/mediaaction/where-we-work/asia/afghanistan/aepo; Simon Usborne, "The Afghan Archers: How a Radio Soap Opera Won Hearts and Minds in Afghanistan," *Independent*, October 6, 2014; Andrew Skuse, "Communication for Development and Public Diplomacy: Insights from an Afghan Radio Drama," in Marie Gillespie and Alban Webb (eds), *Diasporas and Diplomacy: Cosmopolitan Contact Zones at the BBC World Service (1932–2012)*, Abingdon: Routledge, 2012, pp. 193–210.

43 On Radio Cairo, see Douglas A. Boyd, "Development of Egypt's Radio: Voice of Arabs under Nasser," *Journalism Quarterly* 52(4) (Winter 1975): 643–53. On the end of VOA's religious content, see Cull, *The Cold War and the United States Information Agency*, p. 136.

44 On WORLDNET, see Alvin Snyder, *Warriors of Disinformation: How Lies, Videotape, and the USIA Won the Cold War: An Insider's Account*, Washington, DC: Arcade, 1995.

45 For example, the president of Serbia, Alexander Vucic, has referred to the local CNN affiliate N1 as "CIA TV."

46 On the soft power of Turkish soap opera, see Senem Çevik, "Turkish Soap Opera Diplomacy: A Western Projection by a Muslim Source,'" *Exchange: The Journal of Public Diplomacy* 5(1) (2014): https://surface.syr.edu/exchange/vol5/iss1/6.

47 Joe Pompeo, "Russia Goes Viral," *New York Magazine*, September 20, 2013: http://nymag.com/daily/intelligencer/2013/09/how-the-rt-network-built-a-us-audience.html.

48 On Telesur, see Craig Hayden, *The Rhetoric of Soft Power: Public Diplomacy in Global Contexts*, Lanham, MD: Lexington, 2012, pp. 131–67.

49 Marc Lynch, *Voices of the New Arab Public: Iraq, al-Jazeera, and Middle East Politics Today*, New York: Columbia University Press, 2007; Philip Seib, *The Al Jazeera Effect: How the New Global Media are Reshaping World Politics*, Washington, DC: Potomac Books, 2008.

50 William Lafi Youmans, *An Unlikely Audience: Al Jazeera's Struggle in America*,

Oxford: Oxford University Press, 2017; also Philip Seib (ed.), *Al Jazeera English: Global News in a Changing World*, New York: Palgrave, 2012.

51 http://www.ajplus.net/english/.

52 Roger Wilmut, in Hamid Ismailov, Marie Gillespie, and Anna Aslanyan (eds), *Tales from Bush House*, Hatfield: Hertfordshire Press, 2012, pp. 108–9.

53 For case studies, see David Herbert and Tracey Black, "What Kind of Global Conversation? Participation, Democratic Deepening and Public Diplomacy through BBC World Service Online Forums: An Examination of Mediated Global Talk about Religion and Politics"; and Jingrong Tong and Hugh Mackay, 'Discussions on BBC Chinese *Have Your Say* Forums: National Identity and International Broadcasting in the Interactive Media Era,' in Marie Gillespie and Alban Webb (eds), *Diasporas and Diplomacy*.

54 For a detailed treatment of the Polish case, see Pawel Machcewicz, *Poland's War on Radio Free Europe, 1950–1989*, Palo Alto: Stanford University Press, 2014. The diplomatic overture is on pp. 86–7. See also Richard Cummings, *Cold War Radio: The Dangerous History of American Broadcasting in Europe, 1950–1989*, Jefferson, NC: McFarland, 2009.

55 David Garnett, *The Secret History of PWE: Political Warfare Executive 1939–1945*, London: St. Ermin's Press, 2002.

56 The landscape of Russian broadcasting at home and abroad is well sketched by Peter Pomerantsev, *Nothing is True and Everything is Possible: Adventures in the New Russia*, London: Faber and Faber, 2015. See also Ilya Yablokov, "Conspiracy Theories as a Russian Public Diplomacy Tool: The Case of Russia Today (RT)," *Politics* 35(3–4) (November 2015): 301–15.

57 On information intervention, see Monroe Price and Mark Thompson (eds), *Forging Peace: Intervention, Human Rights and the Management of Media Space*, Manchester: Manchester University Press, 2002.

58 Ali Fisher, "Swarmcast: How Jihadist Networks Maintain a Persistent Online Presence," *Perspectives on Terrorism* 9(3) (2015): 3–20.

59 Katie Rogers, "Anonymous Hackers Fight ISIS but Reactions are Mixed," *New York Times*, November 25, 2015.

60 Matilda Andersson, Marie Gillespie and Hugh Mackay, "Mapping Digital Diasporas @ BBC World Service: Users and Uses of the Persian and Arabic Websites,"*Middle East Journal of Culture and Communication* 3 (2010): 256–78; the statistic is on p. 261.

61 http://www.adweek.com/digital/bbc-launches-whatsapp-ebola-lifeline-service-in-west-africa/; http://kimelli.nfshost.com/index.php?id=14370.

62 http://kimelli.nfshost.com/, December 12, 2017 commenting on http://www.miamiherald.com/news/nation-world/national/article189222514.html.

63 The intermediate stage in this process at VOA is sketched in Nicholas J. Cull, "New Technology and the Future of International Broadcasting," in Alan Heil (ed.), *US Overseas Networks: Visions for America's Dialogue with the World*, Washington, DC: Public Diplomacy Council, 2008, pp. 99–106.

64 http://www.bbc.co.uk/mediacentre/latestnews/2018/bbc-news-serbian-digital-service-goes-live.

65 Dana Harman, "Move Over Al Jazeera, Israel's Own 24-hour TV News Station is about to Go Live," *Haaretz*, June 26, 2013; https://www.i24news.tv/en.

66 Albert Camus, *Resistance, Rebellion and Death*, New York: Alfred A. Knopf, 1961, p. 104.

Chapter 7 Nation Brands and Branding: The Metaphor Run Amok

1 The "House Party Model" was developed by Boaz Mourad for the Brand Israel Group, a team of experts convened by Ido Aharoni in 2002. The study took place in 2004–5.

2 Robert Govers, "Why Place Branding is Not about Logos and Slogans," *Place Branding and Public Diplomacy* 9(2) (2013): 71–5; Keith Dinnie, *Nation Branding: Concepts, Issues, Practice*, 2nd edn, Abingdon: Routledge, 2016; Melissa Aronczyk, *Branding the Nation: The Global Business of National Identity*, New York: Oxford University Press, 2013; Jian Wang, *Shaping China's Global Image: Branding Nations at the World Expo*, New York: Palgrave, 2013; Carolin Viktorin, Jessica Gienow-Hecht, Annika Estner, and Marcel Will, *Nation Branding in Modern History*, New York: Berghahn Books, 2018. Case studies are a regular feature of the journal *Place Branding and Public Diplomacy*, founded by Anholt and currently edited by Govers and myself.

3 http://www.coca-colacompany.com/stories/taste-the-feeling-launch.

4 The happy juxtaposition of yellow and green may evoke golden beach sand and lush vegetation to foreigners, but it began as a representation of the rather unhappy marriage of the royal houses of its first monarch Pedro I "the liberator" and his first consort Maria Leopoldine of Austria.

5 For the quote and the preceding idea of dispersed image, see Simon Anholt, *Competitive Identity: The New Brand Management for Nations, Cities and Regions*, Basingstoke: Palgrave, 2007, pp. 4–5.

6 The story is in paragraph III of Diogenes' "Life of Bias." For an English version, see Diogenes Laertius, *The Lives and Opinions of the Eminent Philosophers*, trans. C. D. Yonge, London: Henry G. Bohn, 1853, pp. 38–40. Ironically, of course, Bias himself became his city's brand, as his epitaph had it: "Here Bias of Priene lies, whose name / Brought to his home and all Ionia fame."

7 For a survey of the concept, see Keith Dinnie, "Country-of-Origin 1965–2004: A Literature Review," *Journal of Customer Behaviour* 3(2) (2004): 165–213. The Korean Discount was explained to the author by members of the Korean "Presidential Council on Nation Branding" in 2009.

8 These brands have been variously identified by previous writers. Simon Anholt called them cuckoo brands; however, this frames the issue in terms not just of a stolen advantage but a zero sum in which the authentic "chick" in the national nest is killed and the parent state/bird exploited. Another possibility is "false flag" brands, but this implies not only a deceit but intent to undermine a reputation by creating a bad product rather than just a cheap product. Some writers

have referred to "stealth brands"; however, this name has come to be used to refer to brands which are prestigious without being famous and are recognized as such by consumers "in the know." To avoid confusion, the present author has fixed on *faux brand* as a preferred alternative. I appreciate the help of my colleague David Craig in suggesting this term. For Anholt's discussion, see Simon Anholt, *Brand New Justice: How Branding Places and Products Can Help the Developing Works,* 2nd edn, Abingdon: Routledge, 2005, p. 123.

9 For text, see Howard Payn, *The Merchandise Marks Act, 1887,* London: Stevens and Sons, 1888, a volume which includes notes and copies of the earlier conventions. Available in digital form from https://archive.org/stream/merchandisemark00payngoog#page/n5/mode/2up. The Paris convention remains in force and is today administered by the World Intellectual Property Organization, a UN agency established in Geneva in 1967.

10 John Nathan, *Sony: The Private Life.* New York: Houghton Mifflin, 1999, p. 72.

11 This practice is noted in Susan Faludi, *Backlash: The Undeclared War Against American Women*, New York: Random House, 2006, p. 201.

12 The Matsui affair was reported as far away as the United States. See Steve Lohr, "'Made in Japan' or Not? That is the Question," *New York Times*, April 3, 1988. For Anholt's treatment, see *Brand New Justice*, 2nd edn, p. 123. Anholt also gives the example of the Italian-sounding Thai brand Bossini: "The existence of such 'cuckoo brands', as I call them, also serves to emphasize the enormous power of language in the context of building international brands."

13 https://www.zaubacorp.com/company/MATSUI-ELECTRONICS-PRIVATE-LIMITED/U32109MH1994PTC080513.

14 https://www.outback.com/about-us.

15 Interestingly, perhaps, the company makes the limits of its Australianness clear and in terms of corporate social responsibility Outback emphasizes US patriotic causes, aligning itself with the welfare of US armed forces.

16 John Major's speech to the Conservative Group for Europe, April 22, 1993, archived online at http://www.johnmajor.co.uk/page1086.html. For non-English readers, "county grounds" are where cricket is played and "pools fillers" are people who gamble by predicting weekly football results.

17 The starting gun for an appreciation of this was a *Newsweek* cover story: Stryker McGuire, "London Reigns," *Newsweek*, November 4, 1997.

18 Simon Anholt, "Nation-Brands of the Twenty-First Century," *Journal of Brand Management* 5(6) (1998): 395–406.

19 Mark Leonard, *Britain TM: Renewing Our Identity*, London: Demos, 1997, available online at: https://www.demos.co.uk/files/britaintm.pdf.

20 For Olins's own account of this work, see http://nation-branding.info/2006/06/14/wally-olins-branding-poland/.

21 Leonard's output included Mark Leonard and Vidhya Alakeson, *Going Public: Diplomacy for the Information Society*, London: Foreign Policy Center, 2000;

and Mark Leonard, Catherine Stead, and Conrad Smewing, *Public Diplomacy*, London: Foreign Policy Center, 2002.

22 For a detailed account of this process, see James Pamment, *British Public Diplomacy and Soft Power* for new insight into the early Blair period: James Pamment, "Foresight Revisited: Visions of Twenty-First Century Diplomacy," *Place Branding and Public Diplomacy* 14(1) (2018): 47–54.

23 Many of these points are made in Aronczyk, *Branding the Nation.*

24 Anholt launched his hexagon in the second edition of *Brand New Justice* in 2005. The 2003 version had been a pentagon and lacked the dimension of "people." See also Simon Anholt and Jeremy Hildreth, *Brand America*, New York: Cyan, 2005, p. 15.

25 Anholt to author.

26 Anholt to author. Norway also suffered a downturn in its image, owing to the tendency of people to confuse the two Nordic countries with each other.

27 Anholt to author.

28 https://www.futurebrand.com/country-brand-index.

29 The 2008 results are at http://www.eastwestcoms.com/global_annual_2008. htm.

30 https://www.bloom-consulting.com/en/country-brand-ranking.

31 Brand Finance evaluates nations using what it terms "the royalty relief mechanism employed to value the world's largest companies." It segments its analysis to consider the contribution of particular sectors, including tourism.

32 Simon Anholt, "The $2 Trillion Man: How Obama Saved Brand America," *Foreign Policy,* December 19, 2009: http://foreignpolicy.com/2009/12/17/the-2-trillion-man/.

33 For early data, see http://brandfinance.com/images/upload/bfnb_100_2011_web_sp.pdf; for the post-Trump valuation, see: http://brandfinance.com/images/upload/bf_nation_brands_2017.pdf. From 2016 to 2017, the value of the US brand increased by 2 percent ($481 billion) but the value of China (in second place) increased by 44 percent. The US brand is rated as twice as valuable as that of China.

34 For example, his measure of cultural strength in the first index was based on tourism-per-thousand of the population, Olympic medals, the number of foreign correspondents, state-sponsored media-reach, and use of the native language. See Jonathan McClory, *The New Persuaders,* London: Institute of Government, 2009: https://www.instituteforgovernment.org.uk/sites/default/files/publications/The%20new%20persuaders_0.pdf, p. 9.

35 See Jonathan McClory, *The New Persuaders III*, London: Institute of Government, 2013: https://www.instituteforgovernment.org.uk/sites/default/files/publications/The%20new%20persuaders%20III_0.pdf. See also Jonathan McClory, *The New Persuaders II*, London: Institute of Government, 2011: https://www.instituteforgovernment.org.uk/sites/default/files/publications/The%20New%20PersuadersII_0.pdf.

36 https://softpower30.com/ McClory to author.

37 The present author was witness to the meeting in South Korea at which this new index was unveiled.

38 On I ❤ NY, see Alastair Sooke, "Milton Glaser: His Heart was in the Right Place," *Daily Telegraph*, February 7, 2011. On Glasgow's Miles Better, see "John Struthers: Advertising Man Credited with Devising the Famous Glasgow's Miles Better," (Glasgow) *Sunday Herald,* October 2, 2001.

39 http://www.failteireland.ie/Footer/Media-Centre/Minister-Ring-officially-launches-Wild-Atlantic-Wa.aspx; for the associated website, see https://www.wildatlanticway.com/home.

40 Søren Buhl Pedersen, "Place Branding: Giving the Region of Øresund a Competitive Edge," *Journal of Urban Technology* 11(1) (2010): 77–95; Søren Buhl Hornsko, "On the Management of Authenticity: Culture in the Place Branding of Øresund," *Place Branding and Public Diplomacy* 3(3) (2007): 17–331.

41 Jesper Falkheimer, "Place Branding in the Øresund Region: From a Transnational Region to a Bi-national City-Region," *Place Branding and Public Diplomacy* 12(2–3) (2016): 160–71.

42 http://cphfilmfund.com/en/film-greater-copenhagen-replaces-oresund-film-commission/.

43 For the home site of Germany Land of Ideas, see https://land-der-ideen.de/en.

44 This case follows the argument made by Michael Kunczik, *Images of Nations and International Public Relations*, Mahwah. NJ: Lawrence Erlbaum Associates, 1997, drawing on Joan Campbell, *The German Werkbund: The Politics of Revival in the Applied Arts*, Princeton: Princeton University Press, 1978.

45 The present author heard this from his maternal grandmother, Alice O'Callaghan, but scholarly sources include Frank Reeves, *British Racial Discourse: A Study of British Political Discourse about Race and Race-related Matters*, Cambridge: Cambridge University Press, 1983, p. 50.

46 Herman Muthesius (ed. Dennis Sharp), *The English House* (full translation and facsimile of 1904 edition), London: Frances Lincoln, 2007.

47 For English language sources on the Werkbund since Campbell, see Lucius Burckhardt, *The Werkbund*, London: Hyperion Press, 1987; Frederic J. Schwartz, *The Werkbund: Design Theory and Mass Culture Before the First World War*, New Haven: Yale University Press, 1996.

48 See http://tvtropes.org/pmwiki/pmwiki.php/Main/GodwinsLawOfTimeTravel. The law is named for Godwin's Law of online discussion which holds that the longer any online discussion goes on, the greater the probability of Hitler being mentioned.

49 This Season Two episode of *Star Trek* – "Patterns of Force," written by John Meredyth Lucas – was first transmitted in the United States in February 1968 but because of historical sensitivity was not shown in Germany until 2011.

50 Recent texts exposing this myth include Adam Tooze, *The Wages of Destruction: The Making and Breaking of the Nazi Economy*, New York: Penguin, 2006.

51 For a bilingual treatment in German and English, see Karola Fings (ed.), *Stolpersteine. Gunter Demnig und sein Projekt*, Cologne: Emons Verlag, 2007. The project website is: http://www.stolpersteine.eu/en/home/. At the time of writing, there are 68,000 *Stolpersteine* in 21 European countries and one in Argentina. Demnig was part of the Shanghai display and visited the pavilion but did not speak publicly during the visit. Gunter Demnig to author, April 2, 2018.

52 There are some surprises in contributions to particular categories. Belgium shows up as doing most good in the field of culture. Iceland does most good in the field of climate. Readers should bear in mind that the differences between the GCI and NBI are statistically relatively insignificant; that GCI data are actually collected three to four years before publication, whereas the NBI is "real time," and finally that the GCI is normalized by GDP while the NBI is not. The index may be found at http://goodcountry.org/index/results. Anholt argues that by its very existence, the index provokes new kinds of discussion. Anholt to author.

Chapter 8 Partnership: The Emerging Paradigm

1 Kofi Annan, "Problems without Passports," *Foreign Policy*, February 9, 2009: http://foreignpolicy.com/2009/11/09/problems-without-passports/.

2 For an exploration of this, see Andrew F. Cooper, *Celebrity Diplomacy*, Abingdon: Routledge, 2007.

3 Brian Hocking, "Reconfiguring Public Diplomacy: From Competition to Collaboration," in Jolyon Welsh and Daniel Fearn (eds), *Engagement: Public Diplomacy in a Globalised World*. London: Foreign and Commonwealth Office Books, 2008.

4 Geoffrey Cowan and Amelia Arsenault, "Moving from Monologue to Dialogue to Collaboration: The Three Layers of Public Diplomacy," *Annals of the American Academy of Political and Social Science* 616(1) (2008): 10–30.

5 https://publications.parliament.uk/pa/cm200506/cmselect/cmfaff/903/903.pdf evidence p. 64); https://www.curbed.com/2018/3/26/17165324/expo-milano-pavilion-united-states-unpaid-bills.

6 For cases, see Nicholas J. Cull, "Public Diplomacy and the Private Sector: The United States Information Agency, its Predecessors, and the Private Sector," in Helen Laville and Hugh Wilford (eds), *The US Government, Citizen Groups and the Cold War: The State-Private Network*, London: Frank Cass, 2006, pp. 209–25.

7 http://www.jewishagency.org/partnership2gether-history-overview; and https://www.dfa.ie/media/globalirish/global-irish-irelands-diaspora-policy.pdf, p. 43.

8 http://www.canadainternational.gc.ca/mexico-mexique/cmp-pcm.aspx?lang=eng; http://mea.gov.in/bilateral-documents.htm?dtl/27482/IndiaRussia+Joint+Statement+during+the+Visit+of+President+of+the+Russia+to+India+Partnership+for+Global+Peace+and+Stability.

9 Ringrose to author.

10 https://www.globalpartnership.org.

11 The BBC Monitoring Service was recently the subject of a multi-scholar study by Britain's Imperial War Museum. For a web presentation of findings, see http://www.iwm.org.uk/research/research-projects/listening-to-the-world-bbc-monitoring-collection-ahrc-research-network.

12 For a recently declassified overview, see Joseph E. Roop, *Foreign Broadcast Information Service, History, Part I: 1941–1947*, Langley, VA: Central Intelligence Agency, 1969, esp. chapter 6, pp.164–85.

13 The Russian audience element of the listening project is well documented by Eugene Parta in *Discovering the Hidden Listener: An Empirical Assessment of Radio Liberty and Western Broadcasting to the USSR during the Cold War*, Palo Alto: Hoover Institution Press, 2007. For the memoirs of a participant, see Jaroslaw Martyniuk, *Monte Rosa: Memoir of an Accidental Spy*, Bloomington: Xlibris, 2018.

14 The book was originally published in the United States by HarperCollins and in the United Kingdom by Hamish Hamilton; it was republished in 2001 by Columbia University Press with a helpful scholarly foreword by David C. Engerman. Other contributors were Ignazio Silone (Italy) and Louis Fischer (United States). Engerman's introduction includes details of its promotion by governments. See also Andrew Defty, *Britain, America and Anti-Communist Propaganda 1945–53: The Information Research Department*, Abingdon: Routledge, 2007, p. 160.

15 Benjamin Feyen and Ewa Krzaklewska (eds), *The ERASMUS Phenomenon: Symbol of a New European Generation?* Brussels: Peter Lang Publishing, 2013.

16 https://ec.europa.eu/programmes/erasmus-plus/sites/erasmusplus2/files/erasmus-impact_en.pdf, p. 18.

17 This case is based on conversation with Gregory Pirio of VOA and Elizabeth Fox of VOA and USAID. For context, see Nicholas J. Cull, *The Decline and Fall of the United States Information Agency: American Public Diplomacy, 1989–2001*, New York: Palgrave, 2012, p. 150; on the Bolivian soap, see https://pdf.usaid.gov/pdf_docs/PNACL907.pdf; evidence from the conference is reviewed in attendee Graham Mytton's *Handbook on Radio and Television Audience Research*, UNESCO/UNICEF/BBCWST, London, 1999.

18 For background, see Susan Baker, *Sustainable Development*, Abingdon: Routledge, 2006; and Carl Death, *Governing Sustainable Development: Partnerships, Protests and Power at the World Summit*, Abingdon: Routledge, 2009.

19 For current activity, see http://cleancookstoves.org/. Reports on the evolution of the project may be downloaded from: http://cleancookstoves.org/about/our-mission/index.html.

20 https://www.state.gov/s/partnerships/diaspora/ and http://www.diasporaalliance.org/.

21 https://www.state.gov/s/partnerships/ppp/lionsafrica/ and http://www.lionsafrica.org/.

22 http://fishackathon.hackernest.com/.

23 https://publications.parliament.uk/pa/cm200506/cmselect/cmfaff/903/903. pdf, cited on p. 12.

24 The report is archived at http://webarchive.nationalarchives.gov.uk/2009 0704022438/http://www.fco.gov.uk/en/about-the-fco/publications/publica tions/pd-publication/.

25 See Lord Triesman's speech at the LSE, April 24, 2007, archived at http:// cms.goodwood.co.uk/website-archive/publicEvents/pdf/20070423_LordTries man.pdf. The line is from Shakespeare's poem "Venus and Adonis" and was used to encourage comments from the audience.

26 A version of these objectives appears in House of Commons Foreign Affairs Committee, *Foreign and Commonwealth Office Annual Report 2006–07: First Report of Session 2007–2008*, London: HMSO, 2008, p. 86, item 250.

27 https://www.gov.uk/government/uploads/system/uploads/attachment_data/ file/243287/7099.pdf, pp. 109–12.

28 The present author was part of this process. In 2008, I was commissioned by the FCO to write the booklet which found its final form as Nicholas J. Cull, *Public Diplomacy: Lessons from the Past*, Los Angeles: Figueroa Press/Centre on Public Diplomacy, 2009. https://uscpublicdiplomacy.org/sites/uscpublicdiplo macy.org/files/useruploads/u35361/2009%20Paper%202.pdf .

29 Welsh and Fearn (eds), *Engagement: Public Diplomacy in a Globalised World*. Contributors included Anholt and the present author. The text is archived at http://webarchive.nationalarchives.gov.uk/20090704022438/http://www.fco. gov.uk/en/about-the-fco/publications/publications/pd-publication/.

30 The report is archived at http://webarchive.nationalarchives.gov.uk/2010 0513203926/http://www.fco.gov.uk/resources/en/pdf/pdf9/enabling-state-v3 .

31 The change was highlighted by public diplomacy scholar/blogger Robin Browne on a post of September 10, 2010: https://pdnetworks.wordpress.com/ 2010/09/10/public-diplomacy-the-foreign-office-definition/.

32 William Bratton and Zachary Tumin, *Collaborate or Perish! Reaching Across Boundaries in a Networked World*, New York: Crown Business, 2012.

33 On broken windows policing, see George Kelling and Catherine Coles, *Fixing Broken Windows: Restoring Order and Reducing Crime in Our Communities*, New York: Simon and Schuster, 1997.

34 This paragraph follows the account in Bratton and Tumin, *Collaborate or Perish!*

35 Joel Rubin and Richard Winton, "Crime Continues to Fall in Los Angeles Despite Bad Economy," *Los Angeles Times*, January 1, 2009.

36 On his advice in the United Kingdom, see Vikram Dodd, "Bratton in Britain: Can London Learn Lessons from Former LAPD Chief?" *Guardian*, August 14, 2011. The medal was an honorary CBE (Commander of the Order of the British Empire).

37 On the setup, see Laura M. Calkins, "Patrolling the Ether: US–UK Open

Source Intelligence Cooperation and the BBC's Emergence as an Intelligence Agency, 1939–1948," *Intelligence and National Security* (2011) 26(1): 1–22; Roop, *Foreign Broadcast Information Service, History*, notes that at some points the United States and the United Kingdom looked to create a United Nations listening operation.

38 For a study of more recent years in the partnership, see Kalev Leetaru, "The Scope of FBIS and BBC Open-Source Media Coverage, 1979–2008," *Studies in Intelligence* 54(1) (March 2010): 17–37.

39 Sean McMeekin, *The Red Millionaire: A Political Biography of Willi Münzenberg, Moscow's Secret Propaganda Tsar in the West, 1917–1940*, New Haven: Yale University Press, 2004; Stephen Koch, *Double Lives: Stalin, Willi Munzenberg and the Seduction of the Intellectuals*, New York: Free Press, 1994.

40 This case is based on conversation with Gregory Pirio of VOA and Elizabeth Fox of VOA and USAID. For context, see Nicholas J Cull, *The Decline and Fall of the United States Information Agency*, p. 150; on the Bolivian soap, see: https://pdf. usaid.gov/pdf_docs/PNACL907.pdf. Evidence from the conference is reviewed in attendee Graham Mytton's *Handbook on Radio and Television Audience Research*, London: UNESCO/UNICEF/BBCWST, 1999: https://www.pub licmediaalliance.org/wp-content/uploads/2017/08/audience_research.pdf. The venue was Gallaudet, a university for people who are deaf.

41 The best practices are drawn from the author's own notes of the session rather than any formal volume of proceedings. An outline of the event is preserved at https://business.gwu.edu/sites/g/files/zaxdzs1611/f/downloads/ICR_Unco mmon-Aliances_Bios.pdf.

42 Examples of national collaborative platforms include the UK government's Research Information and Communications Unit (RICU), created in 2007 at the Home Office to try to build a cross-government response to the problem and to develop materials for wider circulation.

43 https://www.thegctf.org/. For a sample of best practice documentation, see https://www.thegctf.org/Portals/1/Documents/Framework%20Documents/ A/GCTF-CE-and-COP-Good-Practices-ENG.pdf.

44 The hub's home page is at http://www.hedayah.ae/.

45 https://obamawhitehouse.archives.gov/the-press-office/2015/02/18/fact-sheet-white-house-summit-countering-violent-extremism.

46 For an overview two years into the project by one its architects, Michael Duffin, see https://blogs.state.gov/stories/2017/05/17/en/role-cities-counter ing-violent-extremism.

47 The Horizon home page notes: "Horizon is a public relations agency that specializes is applying bet-in-class strategic communications to promote, celebrate and strengthen the positive voices and stories of ethnic minority communities here in Britain and abroad," http://horizonpr.agency/. On Moonshot CVE, see http://moonshotcve.com/#g-container-header. Their projects include a spin-off from Google Jigsaw to redirect online searches for radical material, as noted on https://jigsaw.google.com/projects/#redirect-method.

48 Dan Chugg, "Winning the Strategic Communications War with DAESH," *Civil Service Quarterly*, December 20, 2017: https://quarterly.blog.gov.uk/2017/12/20/winning-the-strategic-communications-war-with-daesh/

49 Ibid.

50 For coverage, see https://www.theguardian.com/media/2015/aug/04/anti-isis-youtube-video-notanotherbrother.

51 https://openyoureyes.net/. For especially powerful testimony, see https://openyoureyes.net/the-teachings-of-isis-are-the-opposite-of-islam/ and https://openyoureyes.net/british-ex-jihadi-in-emotional-appeal-not-to-join-isis/.

52 https://www.theguardian.com/politics/2016/may/02/inside-ricu-the-shadowy-propaganda-unit-inspired-by-the-cold-war. The piece claimed that the NGO Help for Syria was created by Breakthrough Media.

53 https://www.opendemocracy.net/ben-hayes-asim-qureshi/going-global-uk-government-s-propaganda-and-censorship-silicon-valley-and-cve. Hayes is a fellow of the Transnational Institute. Qureshi is research director of the NGO CAGE, which has been involved in cataloguing the negative aspects of the UK government's PREVENT initiative: https://www.cage.ngo/. He is the author of *A Virtue of Disobedience: A New Civil Rights Handbook*, London: Byline, 2018.

54 https://quarterly.blog.gov.uk/2017/12/20/winning-the-strategic-communications-war-with-daesh/.

Conclusion: Public Diplomacy and the Crisis of Our Time

1 The term was coined by Hungarian scholar András Rácz in *Russia's Hybrid War in Ukraine Breaking the Enemy's Ability to Resist (FIIA Report 43)*, Helsinki: Finnish Institute for International Affairs, 2015.

2 For early StopFake stories, see http://www.stopfake.org/en/2014/03/. Fedchenko to Cull.

3 On the 2016 training, see http://www.stopfake.org/en/stopfake-trainer-conducted-two-day-anti-propaganda-training-for-young-politicians-in-armenia/ and http://www.stopfake.org/en/stopfake-trainers-told-journalists-in-kazakhstan-politicians-from-georgia-and-azerbaijan-about-fact-checking-combating-propaganda/

4 Christopher Walker and Jessica Ludwig, "The Meaning of Sharp Power: How Authoritarian States Project Influence," *Foreign Affairs*, November 16, 2017: https://www.foreignaffairs.com/articles/china/2017-11-16/meaning-sharp-power?cid=int-fls&pgtype=hpg.

5 These seven lessons were first presented in 2008 in Cull, "Public Diplomacy Seven Lessons for its Future from its Past," in Welsh and Fearn, *Engagement: Public Diplomacy in a Globalised World*, pp. 16–29.

6 https://euvsdisinfo.eu/.

7 The clearest example of this is the way in which the US government successfully pressed the Soviet Union to stop claiming that AIDS was a US-made bio weapon by threatening to suspend all US–Soviet scientific cooperation. See Cull, *The Cold War and the United States Information Agency*, pp. 467, 474.

8 On H. G. Wells's Great War propaganda work, see J. Lee Thompson, *Politicians, Press and Propaganda: Lord Northcliffe and the Great War, 1914–1919*, Kent, OH: Kent State University Press, 1999.

9 https://sustainabledevelopment.un.org/post2015/transformingourworld.

10 https://www.futurelibrary.no.

11 http://genius100visions.com/.

12 See Diogenes Laertius, *The Lives and Opinions of the Eminent Philosophers*, trans. C. D. Yonge, London: Henry G. Bohn, 1853, p. 40.

Selected Bibliography

Aday, Sean and Livingston, Steven (2008) "Taking the State out of State – Media Relations Theory: How Transnational Advocacy Networks are Changing the Press–State Dynamic." *Media, War & Conflict* 1(1): 99–107.

Anholt, Simon (1998) "Nation-Brands of the Twenty-First Century." *Journal of Brand Management* 5(6): 395–406.

Anholt, Simon (2005) *Brand New Justice: How Branding Places and Products Can Help the Developing Works*, 2nd edn. Abingdon: Routledge.

Anholt, Simon (2007) *Competitive Identity: The New Brand Management for Nations, Cities and Regions*. Basingstoke: Palgrave.

Anholt, Simon and Hildreth, Jeremy (2005) *Brand America*. New York: Cyan.

Aronczyk, Melissa (2013) *Branding the Nation: The Global Business of National Identity*. New York: Oxford University Press.

Arsenault, Amelia and Castells, Manuel (2008) "Switching Power: Rupert Murdoch and the Global Business of Media Politics: A Sociological Analysis." *International Sociology* 23(4): 488–513.

Atkinson, Carol (2014) *Military Soft Power: Public Diplomacy through Military Educational Exchanges*. Lanham, MD: Rowman & Littlefield Publishers.

Auerbach, Jonathan and Castronovo, Russ (eds) (2013) *The Oxford Handbook of Propaganda Studies*. Oxford: Oxford University Press.

Bayles, Martha (2014) *Through a Screen Darkly: Popular Culture, Public Diplomacy, and America's Image Abroad*. New Haven: Yale University Press.

Bettie, Molly (2015) "Ambassadors Unaware: The Fulbright Program and American Public Diplomacy." *Journal of Transatlantic Studies* 13(4): 358–72.

Bjola, Corneliu and Holmes, Marcus (eds) (2015) *Digital Diplomacy: Theory and Practice*. Abingdon: Routledge.

Bratton, William and Tumin, Zachary (2012) *Collaborate or Perish! Reaching across Boundaries in a Networked World*. New York: Crown Business.

Castells, Manuel (2010) *Communication Power*. New York: Oxford University Press.

Çevik, Senem (2014) "Turkish Soap Opera Diplomacy: A Western Projection by a Muslim Source." *Exchange: The Journal of Public Diplomacy* 5(1).

Corse, Edward (2013) *A Battle for Neutral Europe: British Cultural Propaganda during the Second World War*. London: Bloomsbury.

Cowan, Geoff and Cull, Nicholas J. (eds) (2008) "Global Public Diplomacy." *ANNALS of the American Academy of Political and Social Science* 616(1) (special issue).

Cross, Maya and Melissen, Jan (eds) (2013) *European Public Diplomacy: Soft Power at Work*. New York: Palgrave.

Cull, Nicholas J. (1994) *Selling War: The British Propaganda Campaign Against American "Neutrality" in World War II*. Oxford: Oxford University Press.

Cull, Nicholas J. (2008) *The Cold War and the United States Information Agency: American Propaganda and Public Diplomacy, 1945–1989*. Cambridge: Cambridge University Press.

Cull, Nicholas J. (2009) *Public Diplomacy: Lessons from the Past*. Los Angeles: Figueroa Press/Centre on Public Diplomacy.

Cull, Nicholas J. (2012) *The Decline and Fall of the United States Information Agency: American Public Diplomacy, 1989–2001*. New York: Palgrave.

Cull, Nicholas J. (2013) "The Long Road to Public Diplomacy 2.0: The Internet in US Public Diplomacy." *International Studies Review* 15(1) (March): 123–39.

Cull, Nicholas J. and Hawes, Michael (eds) (forthcoming) *Canadian Public Diplomacy*. New York: Palgrave.

d'Hooghe, Ingrid (2015) *China's Public Diplomacy*. Leiden, the Netherlands: Brill/Nijhoff.

Dinnie, Keith (2016) *Nation Branding: Concepts, Issues, Practice*, 2nd edn. Abingdon: Routledge.

Dobson, Andrew (2014) *Listening for Democracy: Recognition, Representation, Reconciliation*. Oxford: Oxford University Press.

el-Nawawy, Mohammed and Iskandar, A. (2003) *Al-Jazeera: The Story of the Network That Is Rattling Governments and Redefining Modern Journalism*. Boulder, CO: Westview Press.

English, Robert (2000) *Russia and the Idea of the West: Gorbachev, intellectuals and the End of the Cold War*. New York: Columbia University Press.

Entman, Robert M. (2004) *Projections of Power: Framing News, Public Opinion, and US Foreign Policy*. Chicago: The University of Chicago Press.

Espinosa, J. Manuel (1976) *Inter-American Beginnings of US Cultural Diplomacy, 1936–1948*, Washington, DC: Department of State.

Fisher, Ali (2013) *Collaborative Public Diplomacy: How Transnational Networks Influenced American Studies in Europe*. New York: Palgrave.

Fisher, Ali and Bröckerhoff, Aurélie (2008) *Options for Influence: Global Campaigns of Persuasion in the New Worlds of Public Diplomacy*. London: British Council Counterpoint.

Fletcher, Tom (2016) *Naked Diplomacy: Understanding Power and Statecraft in the Digital Age*. London: HarperCollins,

Gardels, Nathan and Medavoy, Mike (2009) *American Idol after Iraq: Competing for Hearts and Minds in the Global Media Age*. Malden, MA: Wiley-Blackwell.

Geinow-Hecht, Jessica (2006) *Sound Diplomacy: Music and Emotions in Transatlantic Relations, 1850–1920*. Chicago: University of Chicago Press.

Gilboa, Eytan (2006) "Public Diplomacy: The Missing Component in Israel's Foreign Policy." *Israel Affairs* 12(4): 715–47.

Gilboa, Eytan (2007) "The CNN Effect: The Search for a Communication Theory of International Relations." *Political Communication* 22(1): 27–44.

Gilboa, Eytan (2008) "Searching for a Theory of Public Diplomacy." *ANNALS of the American Academy of Political and Social Science* 616(1): 55–77.

Gillespie, Marie and Webb, Alban (eds) (2012) *Diasporas and Diplomacy: Cosmopolitan Contact Zones at the BBC World Service (1932–2012).* Abingdon: Routledge.

Goff, Patricia (2013) "Cultural Diplomacy," in Andrew F. Cooper, Jorge Heine, and Ramesh Thakur (eds), *The Oxford Handbook of Modern Diplomacy.* Oxford: Oxford University Press, pp. 419–35.

Golan, Guy J., Yang, Sung-un, and Kinsey, Dennis F. (2015) *International Public Relations and Public Diplomacy.* New York: Peter Lang.

Govers, Robert (2013) "Why Place Branding is Not about Logos and Slogans." *Place Branding and Public Diplomacy* 9(2): 71–5.

Govers, Robert (2018) *Imaginative Communities: Admired Cities, Countries and Regions.* Antwerp: Reputo Press.

Halverson, Jeffrey, Goodall Jr, H. L., and Corman, Steven R. (2011) *The Master Narratives of Islamic Extremism.* New York: Palgrave.

Hartig, Falk (2016) *Chinese Public Diplomacy: The Rise of the Confucius Institute.* Abingdon: Routledge.

Hayden, Craig (2012) *The Rhetoric of Soft Power: Public Diplomacy in Global Contexts.* Langham, MD: Lexington.

Heath, Chip and Heath, Dan (2007) *Made to Stick: Why Some Ideas Survive and Others Die.* New York: Random House.

Heil, Alan (2003) *Voice of America: A History.* New York: Columbia University Press.

Heil, Alan (ed.) (2008) *US Overseas Networks: Visions for America's Dialogue with the World.* Washington, DC: Public Diplomacy Council.

Fitzpatrick, Kathy. (2007) "Advancing the New Public Diplomacy: A Public Relations Perspective." *The Hague Journal of Diplomacy* 2(3): 187–211.

Kampf, Romit, Manor, Ilan, and Segev, Elad (2015) "Digital Diplomacy 2.0? A Cross-national Comparison of Public Engagement in Facebook and Twitter." *The Hague Journal of Diplomacy* 10(4): 331–62.

Kelley, J. Robert (2010) "The New Diplomacy: Evolution of a Revolution." *Diplomacy & Statecraft* 21(2): 286–305.

Krenn, Michael (2006) *Fall-Out Shelters for the Human Spirit: American Art and the Cold War.* Chapel Hill: University of North Carolina Press.

Krenn, Michael (2017) *The History of United States Cultural Diplomacy: 1770 to the Present Day.* London: Bloomsbury.

Lee, Sook Jong and Melissen, Jan (eds) (2011) *Public Diplomacy and Soft Power in East Asia.* New York: Palgrave.

Luke, Christina and Kersel, Morgan M. (2013) *US Cultural Diplomacy and Archeology: Soft Power, Hard Heritage.* New York: Routledge.

Machcewicz, Pawel (2014) *Poland's War on Radio Free Europe, 1950–1989*. Palo Alto: Stanford University Press.

Melissen, Jan (ed.) (2005) *The New Public Diplomacy: Soft Power in International Relations*. New York: Palgrave.

Metzgar, Emily (2013) *Considering the "Illogical Patchwork": The Broadcasting Board of Governors and US International Broadcasting*. Los Angeles: CPD Perspectives.

Metzgar, Emily (2017) *The JET Program and the US–Japan Relationship: Goodwill Goldmine*. Lanham, MD: Lexington Book.

Miskimmon, Alister, O'Loughlin, Ben, and Roselle, Laura (eds) (2017) *Forging the World: Strategic Narratives and International Relations*. Ann Arbor: University of Michigan Press.

Murray, Stuart (guest ed.) (2013) "Sports Diplomacy." *The Hague Journal of Diplomacy* 8(3–4): 191–5.

Nelson, Michael (1997) *War of the Black Heavens: The Battles of Western Broadcasting in the Cold War*. Syracuse: Syracuse University Press.

Ninkovich, Frank (1981) *The Diplomacy of Ideas: US Foreign Policy and Cultural Relations, 1938–1950*. New York: Cambridge University Press.

Nisbet, Erik C., Nisbet, Matthew C., Scheufele, Dietram A., and Shanahan, James E. (2004) "Public Diplomacy, Television News, and Muslim Opinion." *The International Journal of Press/Politics* 9(2): 11–37.

Nye, Joseph (2004) *Soft Power: The Means to Success in World Politics*. New York: Public Affairs.

Nye, Joseph (2011) *The Future of Power*. New York: PublicAffairs.

Pamment, James (2013) *New Public Diplomacy: A Comparative Study of Policy and Practice*. Abingdon: Routledge.

Pamment, James (2015) *British Public Diplomacy and Soft Power: Diplomatic Influence and the Digital Revolution*. Abingdon: Routledge.

Pamment, James (2015) "Media Influence, Ontological Transformation, and Social Change Conceptual Overlaps between Development Communication and Public Diplomacy." *Communication Theory* 25(2): 188–207.

Parta, Eugene (2007) *Discovering the Hidden Listener: An Empirical Assessment of Radio Liberty and Western Broadcasting to the USSR during the Cold War*. Palo Alto: Hoover Institution Press.

Paschalidis, Gregory (2009) "Exporting National Culture: Histories of Cultural Institutes Abroad." *International Journal of Cultural Policy* 15(3): 275–89.

Pomerantsev, Peter and Weis, Michael (2014) *The Menace of Unreality: How the Kremlin Weaponizes Information, Culture and Money*. New York: Institute of Modern Russia.

Pomerantsev, Peter (2015) *Nothing is True and Everything is Possible: Adventures in the New Russia*. London: Faber and Faber.

Popiolkowski, Joseph L. and Cull, Nicholas J. (eds) (2009) *Public Diplomacy, Cultural Interventions and the Peace Process in Northern Ireland: Track Two to Peace?* Los Angeles: Center on Public Diplomacy.

Powers, Shawn and el-Nawawy, Mohammed (2009) "Al-Jazeera English and

Global News Networks: Clash of Civilizations or Cross-cultural Dialogue?" *Media, War & Conflict* 2(3): 263–84.

Rácz, András (2015) *Russia's Hybrid War in Ukraine Breaking the Enemy's Ability to Resist (FIIA Report 43)*. Helsinki: Finnish Institute for International Affairs.

Richmond, Yale (2003) *Cultural Exchange and the Cold War: Raising the Iron Curtain*. University Park: Penn State University Press.

Sanders, Barry (2011) *American Avatar: The United States in the Global Imagination*. Dulles, VA: Potomac Books.

Scott-Smith, Giles (2008) *Networks of Empire: The US State Department's Foreign Leader Program in the Netherlands, France, and Britain 1950–70*. Brussels: Peter Lang.

Seib, Philip (2008) *The Al Jazeera Effect: How the New Global Media Are Reshaping World Politics,* Washington, DC: Potomac Books.

Seib, Philip (ed.) (2009) *Toward a New Public Diplomacy: Redirecting US Foreign Policy*. New York: Palgrave Macmillan.

Seib, Philip (2012) *Real-Time Diplomacy: Politics and Power in the Social Media Era*. New York: Palgrave.

Seib, Philip (2016) *The Future of Diplomacy*. London: Polity.

Sevin, Efe (2014) "Understanding Cities through City Brands: City Branding as a Social and Semantic Network." *Cities* 38 (June): 47–56.

Sevin, Efe (2017) *Public Diplomacy and the Implementation of Foreign Policy in the US, Sweden and Turkey*. New York: Palgrave.

Shaw, Tony (2012) "Nightmare on Nevsky Prospekt: *The Blue Bird* as a Curious Instance of US–Soviet Film Collaboration during the Cold War." *Journal of Cold War Studies* 14(1) (Winter): 3–33.

Singh, J. P. (2011) *United Nations Educational, Scientific and Cultural Organization (UNESCO): Creating Norms for a Complex World*. New York: Routledge.

Singh, J. P. and MacDonald, Stuart (2017) *Soft Power Today: Influences and Effects*. Edinburgh: British Council/University of Edinburgh Institute for International Cultural Relations.

Snow, Nancy (2011) *Information War: American Propaganda, Free Speech and Opinion Control Since 9–11*. New York: Seven Stories Press.

Snow, Nancy and Cull, Nicholas J. (eds) (forthcoming) *The Routledge Handbook of Public Diplomacy*, 2nd edn. Abingdon: Routledge.

Taylor, Philip M. (1981) *The Projection of Britain: British Overseas Publicity and Propaganda, 1919–1939*. Cambridge: Cambridge University Press.

Taylor, Philip M. (2003) *Munitions of the Mind: A History of Propaganda*, 3rd edn. Manchester: Manchester University Press.

Thussu, Daya Kishan (2013) *Communicating India's Soft Power: Buddha to Bollywood*. New York: Palgrave.

Tomlin, Gregory (2016) *Murrow's Cold War: Public Diplomacy for the Kennedy Administration*. Lincoln: University of Nebraska Press.

Trent, Deborah L. (ed.) (2016) *Nontraditional US Public Diplomacy: Past, Present, and Future*. Washington, DC: Public Diplomacy Council.

Ungar, Sanford (2016) "The Study-Abroad Solution: How to Open the American Mind," *Foreign Affairs* 95(2) (March/April).

Viktorin, Carolin, Gienow-Hecht, Jessica, Estner, Annika and Marcel, Will (2018) *Nation Branding in Modern History*. New York: Berghahn Books.

Villanueva Rivas, César (2007) *Representing Cultural Diplomacy: Soft Power, Cosmopolitan Constructivism and Nation Branding in Mexico and Sweden*. Växjö: Växjö University Press.

Villanueva Rivas, César (2015) "The Use of the Spanish Language as a Cultural Diplomacy Strategy for Extending Mexico's Soft Power in the United States." *Place Branding and Public Diplomacy* 11(2): 139–47.

Villanueva Rivas, César (2017) "Mexico's Public Diplomacy Approach to the Indo-Pacific: A Thin Soft Power?" *Politics and Policy* 45(5): 793–812.

Waller, J. Michael (2007) *The Public Diplomacy Reader*. Washington, DC: IWP Press.

Walsh, Daniel C. (2012) *An Air War with Cuba: The United States Radio Campaign against Castro*. Jefferson, NC: MacFarland.

Wang, Jian (2013) *Shaping China's Global Image: Branding Nations at the World Expo*. New York: Palgrave.

Webb, Alban (2012) *London Calling: Britain, the BBC World Service and the Cold War*. London: Bloomsbury.

Welsh, Jolyon and Fearn, Daniel (eds) (2008) *Engagement: Public Diplomacy in a Globalised World*. London: Foreign and Commonwealth Office Books.

Wiseman, Geoffrey (2015) *Isolate or Engage: Adversarial States, US Foreign Policy, and Public Diplomacy*. Palo Alto: Stanford University Press.

Zaharna, R. S. (2014) *Battles to Bridges: US Strategic Communication and Public Diplomacy after 9/1*, 2nd edn. New York: Palgrave.

Zaharna, R. S. (2016) "Reassessing 'Whose Story Wins': The Trajectory of Identity Resilience in Narrative Contests." *International Journal of Communication* 10: 4407–38.

Zaharna, R. S. (forthcoming) *Globalizing Public Diplomacy: Three Communication Logics for a Digitally Connected and Culturally Diverse World*. New York: Oxford University Press.

Zaharna, R. S., Arsenault, Amelia, and Fisher, Ali (eds) (2014) *Relational, Networked and Collaborative Approaches to Public Diplomacy: The Connective Mindshift*. Abingdon: Routledge.

Index